Overland Echoes

Memories From A Time When Every Journey Was An Adventure

The travel diaries of an overland traveller in the 1980s.

by Adrian Barnes

First published: July 2024
This edition published: July 2024

Text copyright © Adrian Barnes 2024

All rights reserved, including the right to reproduce this book or portions thereof in any form whatsoever.

Published by Cammeraygal Press

ISBN: 978-1-7636362-2-4

Printed in Australia by LuLu

https://www.lulu.com/shop

Unless otherwise noted, all pictures are from the private collection of the author scanned from slides and postcards

Cover Illustration:
Indians: San Christobal de Las Casas - Antonio Turok

Preface

In 1980 I left the comfort of family, friends and a good job in England to embark on a series of overland adventures; adventures that would ultimately take me around the world.

I had the privilege of experiencing international travel before the advent of mass tourism. In a time before Lonely Planet and Google drew the maps, every trip was an exploration. It was an amazing time to travel. It was a time when most Indians rode on bicycles, the Turkish coastline of the Mediterranean wasn't packed cheek-by-jowl with apartment blocks, and backpacking was the only way to reach many exotic destinations. I was lucky to experience a time before mass air travel, before the internet, before the sameness that permeates so many places now.

These early experiences of travelling shaped the rest of my life. What I took away from this time of adventure were my memories, boxes of slides, and a pile of travel diaries. The diaries languished in the bottom of a box for years, unread. But I rediscovered them, in later life, when I turned to sorting through my accumulated possessions. In my diaries, I found a detailed journal of overland travel in the 1980s; a record of adventures that can no longer be experienced.

This book revives those memories of carefree adventure. It describes a journey from London to Australia overland and back through Central America. An account based on the diaries I wrote, the slides I took, and the postcards I collected. It grows out of those faint echoes of overland travel.

My story starts in London……

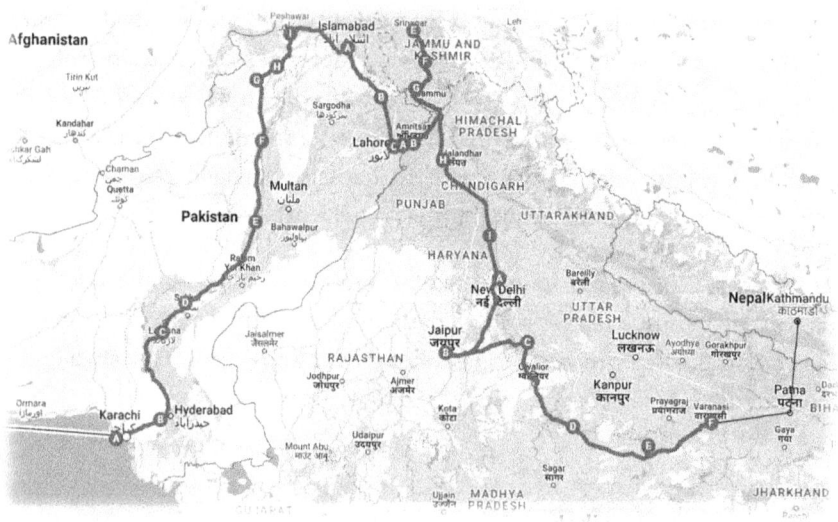

PART 1
Overland to Kathmandu

Across Asia on the Trot

ENCOUNTER OVERLAND

*Remember this is not a holiday
– it's an expedition!

And the passengers are not punters
– they are expedition members*

Tony Jones, Encounter Overland

LONG-RANGE EXPEDITIONS ACROSS SOUTH AMERICA, ASIA & AFRICA

TRAVEL WITH ENCOUNTER OVERLAND

Encounter Overland was a well-organised company and the training of their drivers and the preparation of their vehicles did them great credit. Our first driver, Dave, probably had the most spontaneous humour and mature character of all the drivers I met, it was just unfortunate that he couldn't navigate through towns.

After the first week in Europe, our group was not a particularly lively mob, but we did keep most of the petty irritations under the surface for the rest of the trip. The only major exception was some open alienation between the older Swiss passengers and the rest of us; it turned ugly at times.

Travelling on the truck was great fun; you saw as much as you wanted to, and there was always a great group atmosphere in the back. The adventure just wouldn't have been the same without the dust. But oh, the truck was so slow!

My fellow travellers on this adventure:

AMANDA(UK):
Amanda and her sister Anna were from the Isle of White. On her way to Australia.
ALEX(AUS):
A nurse returning home from the UK. A quiet person – a loner.
ANNA(UK):
Like her sister Amanda, she had been a nurse but was heading out to Australia.
CLAUDINE(CH):
From Switzerland. Older and not comfortable with the flexibility of overlanding.
COLIN(UK):
A chef from Southend with a good sense of humour. Also on his way to Australia.
DAVE(UK):
From Glasgow with a pleasant personality. On his way to Australia to work.
DENIS(AUS):
A solicitor returning home after travelling in the USA and Europe.
FRED(SA):
A South African with stories about his military service. Could understand dutch.
FREDDY & URSULA(CH):
Married from Switzerland. Singularly unpleasant not interested in bonding with the group.
HELEN(CH):
From Switzerland. Got on with everyone. A nurse starting 6 months of training in India.
HELEN(NZ):
A nurse who had been working in Europe, my cooking partner and happy person.
HENK(NL):
Quiet but sensible – a chess player.
JOS(NL):
A social worker and group comedian. A much-needed extrovert.
KARL(NZ):
A plumber who worked in Holand. Happy to get his hands dirty – under the truck.
KEVIN(USA):
The youngest traveller on a world tour. Meeting his Mum in Nepal.
LOTTI(CH):
Swiss. Traveling with, and a good friend of Claudine. Similar inflexible attitude.
MARTIN(UK):
A quiet Cambridge graduate who was uncomfortable travelling overland.
PLONY(NL):
An attractive girl with whom I didn't have much contact.
RON(NL):
Our second Dutch comedian and happy traveller, also an experimental cook!
SANDRA(CA):
A Canadian vegetarian with emotional problems. Was surprised by the rough travel.
THOMAS(CH):
From Switzerland. My best friend, married with a child but his wife had let him travel.
VAL(UK):
A nurse from Oxford. A pleasant companion and a proficient guitar player.
WERNER(CH):
An eccentric Swiss. Spoke little English. Played guitar and read Billy Graham.

LONDON TO ISTANBUL

28th August 1980: Drayton – Bruge

The 28th of August 1980 was a milestone in my life. It was the day I left behind the familiarity of my life in England and traded it for the adventure of exploring the unknown. I had paid £785 for a place on a truck heading for Kathmandu, an adventure that was scheduled to take 11 weeks. It turned out to be the start of a long journey that took me to Australia and back.

I was up early to catch a lift into London with my parents and our pet dog Sheba; it was a fast uneventful journey that early in the morning. We said our farewells; it was a difficult moment as I was leaving a lot behind for an uncertain future.

My fellow expedition members, a diverse group, were gathering on the footpath outside Encounter Overland's offices at 271 Old Brompton Road. Parked outside was our smart Bedford 28-seater truck (GNM592F) towing a trailer for our luggage. We later found out that our truck was a glorious hybrid built in the Encounter Overland workshops, but part of it had a former life as a fruit and veg lorry from Covent Garden. We set out for Dover at 7:30 a.m., but in a coach, as our truck wasn't insured to carry passengers in England!

It didn't take long before we learned about the first variation to the published itinerary. The British passengers, myself included, had been unable to get a visa for Iran. So it was announced when we were on the coach, that we would be overflying Iran to Pakistan.

London – The author preparing for departure

The coach beat the truck to Dover, an early indication that our subsequent progress would be slow; whilst we were waiting for it to arrive I walked along the seafront with two other members of our group, Colin and Dennis. When the truck turned up we had to race through customs and then occupied a corner of the boat lounge, eating pork pies and chatting. It was a hazy day and there were no good views of the cliffs as we all left England behind, for some of us, for a long time. Although the crossing was quick, our disembarking was delayed because of a French dock dispute. We picked up three Dutch members of our group at Ostende, Ron, Joss and Plony, then cruised along the Autobahn to Bruge in a welcoming drizzle!

Our first night was spent in a commercial campsite, something that was to be a rarity as we progressed further east. After a quick guided tour around the truck, we pitched camp. I scored a tent on my own without realising it was harder to put up without someone to help! Preparations for dinner were 'assisted' by two overhelpful group members who wanted to do everything.

Belgium - Camping at Bruge

29th August 1980: Bruge - Koblenz

We were woken before dawn and in just over an hour we were back on the Autobahn heading past Brussels to a morning coffee stop in a small village near Aachen.

Travelling on an Encounter Overland truck was not a passive experience; we were certainly not passengers. Everyone had to take on responsibilities and tasks to help make the trip run smoothly. I volunteered for water duty; it was my task to fill the 45-gallon tank in the truck and dose it with a water purifier. The worst duty was, in my opinion, loading the trailer; the bags had to be packed back in it overnight for security. Denis and Henk volunteered for that job, but as compensation, they didn't have to take a turn at cooking.

Whenever we stopped, someone would stay on the truck as a guard. Whilst on guard duty the first day I tried to find out how to switch on the fluorescent lights in the back of the truck, but it had me stumped. We pressed on to Liege where we had a lunch of salami sandwiches in a service station forecourt. I filled the truck water tank for the first time, using a hose, the easy way!

Further down the Autobahn, we got stuck in a big traffic jam, complete with a chopper flying overhead broadcasting announcements in German we couldn't understand! Whilst we were stationary we entertained the cars behind us by jumping out of the truck, filling a kettle, and brewing up on the stove inside.

The final leg of our journey that day took us to Ahrweiler (northwest of Koblenz) where we had to search to find a campsite. A guy we met in a garage offered to show us where we could camp; but his car broke down and we ended up having to give him a lift. The first campsite we visited was full so we headed up a side valley and looked for a place to pull off for the night. Our truck got entwined in a tree on a corner and a spectator crowd rapidly appeared. Then it started to rain, so we just let things be and put up our tents where we were. We found the light switch in the truck which helped a lot! After dinner, the group headed up the hillside to a 'pub' which served wine and beer.

30th August 1980: Koblenz - Baden

I had to get up early the next morning, again before dawn, as I was sharing my tent with driver Dave. That meant I only had six hours of sleep, but there were plenty of opportunities to catch up in the back of the truck later. A hard day's driving followed; we covered close to 500km. It was quite clear that the focus of our trip was not sightseeing in Europe.

The twenty-four passengers who weren't loading the trailer were paired off into 12 cooking teams. Each team had to manage cooking, shopping and washing up for one day, from the evening meal to lunch the next day. I was paired with New Zealand Helen and this was our first stint, so, to avoid shopping on a Sunday, we went looking for food. We overspent our allowance (nominally about £10) by buying a lot of pork.

After lunch in the warm sunshine on a motorway layby, we resumed driving south at our steady 40 to 50 km/hr! We had to resort to brewing tea on the move; the only time we stopped was at a garage for fuel and water. Confined in the back, we discovered the merits of playing cards in the back of the truck, using the kitchen table on our knees as a table!

As it turned dark we spotted a campsite and turned off to investigate. Unfortunately, it was accessed over a bridge with a weight limit. In the ensuing U-turn one of the rear light clusters on the truck got scrunched; reversing the trailer was difficult because it was narrower than the truck and so not visible from the cab. We returned to the Autobahn but soon found ourselves lost in Baden. Extricating ourselves involved another three U-turns including one in an underground car park!

It was after 9 pm when we eventually found a campsite; the bonus was to find a large swimming pool over a couple of fences. We stripped off and swam in the dark before dinner. Whilst we were getting lost in Baden the cooking team had prepared the vegetables in the back of the truck, with water splashing everywhere as the truck lurched violently. The occasional chorus of 'Always look on the bright side of life' was heard.

I only put up a flysheet that night because it was so late, and of course, it rained; but at least I didn't get wet!

31st August 1980: Baden - Salzburg

Finally, we got a late start, though it was a bit cold when we got up; not a day for a morning swim! After packing up camp we drove the short distance to Zürich station where we picked up the remaining six Swiss passengers.

With a full truck, there was the usual name-learning in the back before we settled in for another long trip. On the way we were stopped by police because lorries were not allowed to drive on a Sunday.

Germany - Lunch between Koblenz and Baden

Our morning coffee stop was so late that we debated whether to make it a lunch stop as well. We were rejected by several restaurants on the grounds of our group size and we had to reject a few more because they were too expensive. Eventually, we found some cheeseburgers which we took back to the truck to eat, just as the heavens opened. We put up one of the tables inside the truck in the dry and ate our meal there, functional but cramped.

I casually asked the driver, Dave, what had happened to one of the Swiss boys (Christian) who was missing from lunch; it transpired that we had forgotten to pick him up! After frantic phone calls back to Zürich station we managed to contact Christian and asked him to take a train to Salzburg. That plan ruled out the option of us spending the night in Innsbruck and also committed us to the long drive over the Arlberg Pass.

With the mountains shrouded in clouds there was little to see. The heavy driving put considerable strain on the newly formed group. It wasn't the type of travel most of us were used to.

We didn't arrive in Salzburg till very late in the evening. which meant there was a mad rush to get some food cooked. I prepared the pork we had bought the previous day with herbs and tomatoes. The verdict was it was quite nice but there wasn't nearly enough of it to go round. Catering for a large group took a lot of learning.

That night we had our first Maloprim malaria tablets though it felt like were a long way from the tropics! After doing the washing-up I lay in bed trying to sleep but was kept awake by Sandra and Val chatting in their tent, and by Werner 'Dylan' strumming away in the back of the truck. I must have finally dropped off in the early hours of the morning after Christian had rolled up at the camp.

1st September 1980: Saltzburg

The prospect of a warm shower and a chance to wash clothes got me up well before breakfast. My cooking partner Swiss Helen[1] made porridge from the Alpen Muesli we carried on board and it set like concrete! I met up with Sandra and Val to take a bus into Salzburg. After wandering around buying stamps and other essentials we had an expensive lunch of fish and chips. Then, when it started raining, we sheltered in the Cathedral. But the bad weather set in, and we resigned ourselves to getting wet. We took the funicular up to the castle, looked around, and ended up soaked to the skin and cold; we dripped back to the camp! In a wet and miserable mood, I worked on installing two speakers in the back of the truck, a job that made me even wetter. This meant that for the rest of the trip, we could all enjoy Dave's taste in music; songs such as Van Morrison Moondance became inextricably linked to memories of long dusty journeys in the back of the truck.

The celebration dinner for Kevin's 18th birthday was held in the campsite restaurant, where we had to wait for tables. The people at my table had a vigorous discussion about foot fetishes and the hazards of hitchhiking in our respective countries. We ate a salad with Wiener Schnitzel; the meat was a bit tough and I couldn't eat it all. Later in the evening, the restaurant cleared a bit and we were able to move our tables together. We had a good time. Val, playing guitar, drank her way under/onto the table, whilst Dave scraped together words that should have laid undisturbed creating terrible postcard odes. Jokes were flying everywhere; in English from Dave and in Dutch from Jos.

---

[1] Helen(S) in this narrative to distinguish her from Helen(NZ) from New Zealand

In the early morning, the party broke up and I led Val back to her tent. Just as I completed that task Alex came up saying two feet were sticking out of her tent! It turned out to be Henk, completely paralytic! With much effort, we got him sitting up and untangled his legs. Others arriving thought the whole thing was a joke and Henk was acting. Eventually, we worked out which was his tent and we managed to steer him there.

I went to sleep but was woken sometime in the night by the sound and smell of Dave being sick. Without waiting to confirm what was going on I packed up my bed and took it into the back of the truck to continue my slumber. So ended the only good party we had on the trip!

2nd September 1980: Salzburg - Bled

I was woken by the cold and by the noise of an unnecessarily enthusiastic cooking team. Everyone was just a bit fragile and suffering from a lack of sleep. It was a misty morning, but at least it had stopped raining.

I sat in the front of the truck for the first time in the warm. We set off going in the wrong direction, back towards Vien, so we had to wait till the next junction to U-turn. The truck then plodded its way up the Tauern Pass giving us plenty of time to observe the scenery as we climbed above the mist and enjoyed blue skies. After going through the long summit tunnel we stopped in the village of Zenderhaus for coffee, shopping and lunch.

We tried unsuccessfully to get back on the main road through a gritting depo, but that was a minor mistake compared to my on-the-spot decision about which road to take after Villach. Instead of taking the direct road to Yugoslavia, I directed Dave down to the Italian border.

The Italian customs at Tarvision let us through in exchange for a cassette tape (we gave them our worst) then we took a winding hairpin road back up to the Yugoslav border. Saying goodbye to Italy involved a 'random' search of the luggage in the trailer; luckily entry into Yugoslavia was quite lax in comparison.

Austria - Zenderhaus coffee stop   Austria - driver Dave with Thomas

The northern part of Yugoslavia was most attractive; it was alpine but without the excessive cleanliness of Austria and Switzerland. We camped for the night in Bled, a holiday resort. I had a quiet evening (some more energetic people went for a run) before tackling dinner which was a spaghetti something-or-other followed by Val's custard. Sandra was a vegetarian and this led to a more experimental form of cuisine when it was her turn to cook. Some of her experiments were outstanding successes but more often they were not. This meal also started our "custard with bits" competition where the diners had to guess what the chefs had put in the custard to make lumps.

It was a brass monkey night; I was woken several times by icicles on my nose!

3rd September 1980: Bled – Slavonski Brod

The camp was woken ½ hour too early by Ron who had forgotten to change his watch at the border. We had our first fine-weather departure in a long time with dry tents but that was followed by a tedious single-carriageway road down to Zagreb. Things were worse in the back of the truck as we didn't have our customary morning stop for coffee and shopping. Eventually, we managed to turn off the main road into a rather sleepy-looking town which yielded a bank and a food shop after some exploration. With just two multi-point turns with an attached trailer, we found our way back onto the main road and had lunch soon afterwards in bright sunshine in a featureless layby. The more energetic amongst us had a game of football.

We were able to wind up the sides of the truck for the first time and set off with a good breeze in the back. But this started a perpetual bone of discontent, whether to have the sides up or down. The climate was such that with the sides down it was stuffy in the back, but with them up, there was an unpleasantly cold breeze.

When it was time to stop for the night. We turned down a side lane to have our first night's rough camping. It wasn't much of an inconvenience except for not being able to have a good wash. Our woodland destruction team got a blazing fire going, and there was a session of the usual pre-dinner writing guild. I had a sneak read of Dave's big black instruction manual and was amused by the description of bad Asian drivers as *Fickwitz*. Dave gave a funny but not very accurate description of the start of the First World War, including the "air had a high lead content" catchphrase. After a meal of soup, we sat around the fire and chatted. The supply of jokes was starting to dry up! I took some flash pictures in the dark but left the polarizing filter on my camera so they didn't come out.

4th September 1980: Slavonski Brod - Nis

There was a heavy mist in the morning. I had pinched the blanket off the truck's front seat and had been quite cosy. Val had tried using a space blanket to keep warm and ended up waking wet and cold underneath. We had left the truck parked on the track, and a local farmer got stuck trying to drive around us on his tractor. We helped dig him out; that was the least we could do. When it came time for us to leave we had no trouble in the mud with our two powered rear axles.

Our route was now down the motorway (Autoput) to Belgrade, and I started to retrace the route of my Balkan Odyssey holiday the year before with Pennworld. The trailer came unhitched going into Belgrade and snaked violently on its safety chain. Luckily we had a button in the back that sounded a buzzer in the cab. Although it was usually used to signal the all-clear when Dave wanted to pull away, we also used it to get Dave to stop in a hurry.

Yugoslavia - Morning at Slavonski Brod

Another back-of-beyond town with just one shop provided a lunch stop. There was even time for some swimming in a rather muddy river and a short time sunbathing before we hit the road again. In the back, the entertainment resumed with games of Mastermind, and Dave battling it out with Henk at chess.

Our second night of natural camping was down a long lane to the sandy shore of a fast-flowing river. Another opportunity for swimming and firewood gathering before dinner. Val was cooking a rice and tuna concoction but unfortunately in the process spilt flour over the back of the truck.

It was a cold night but we built a good campfire. I enjoyed reading a rather flowery poetic guidebook to Kashmir.

Yugoslavia - Camping near Nis

5th September 1980: Nis – Greek Border

The morning that the truck wouldn't start! The two Daves traced the problem to a faulty starter motor and luckily we were carrying a spare. Whilst it was swapped over I washed my hair in the river. Meanwhile, Val and Jos walked into a nearby village and returned with a big plastic bag full of peppers and pears which they had bought from a farmer. After changing the fuel filters as a precaution we were ready for the off, and this time the truck started.

We took a scenic route back to the main road which resulted in the back of the truck getting a good dose of dust, the pleasure of being clean was shortlived. Our usual coffee stop was cancelled because we were running behind time. Instead, we stopped to shop in Skjopi, a city reconstructed after it was devastated by an earthquake in 1963. It had a very busy market.

We still had a long drive ahead of us to reach the Greek border; finally clearing customs and immigration after 6 pm. But we were shocked to find that the time was two hours later in Greece. We raced down the valley but ran out of daylight, so in desperation we turned down a dusty track looking for somewhere to camp. In the end, all we could find was a wide bit of the track to stop on with a small patch of grass for tents nearby. We were all exhausted. I had a good wash then slept till dinner. It was then we discovered that our track was very busy with farmers and there was a noisy railway line next door! The natives didn't seem too worried by our presence and neither was I; I put my earplugs in and had a first-class night's sleep.

6th September 1980: Greek Border – Komotini

When we woke at 6 a.m. we found gravel lorries, farm tractors and even a bulldozer using our track! I continued my sleep-deficit recovery program in the truck until we stopped at a garage for air, fuel, ice cream, and water. In addition to the main water tank that I was responsible for filling, we had six water jerry cans as a reserve for emergencies. The water now had to be chlorinated, with a match head of powder in each jerry can. If I was too generous adding the chlorine the others complained when they tasted their tea!

After Dave had repaired a broken fuel feed pump we drove past Lake Koronia and Lake Volui on our way down to the Mediterranean coast. When we stopped for food shopping I bought a bottle of Ouzo, a rough beverage which I had enjoyed on my earlier trip to Greece.

An outstanding question was answered that day. No one knew how melons grew, and then we saw them in a field.

Lunch was taken by a stony beach; we all swam, then sat about drying off in the sun. We pressed on down the mountainous 'coastal' road, past Kavala and Xanthi, with one long holdup because a truck had overturned on a corner. Our night stop was on a rather polluted beach which gave rise to speculation about whether it was made of sand, mud or dry oil. Since I'd had one swim already I gave the beach a miss. Instead, I finished off my first aerogram letter home ready to be posted when we reached Istanbul.

We were going to have a barbeque that evening but the fire didn't get hot enough so we ended up with disgusting tinned burgers for dinner.

That night I felt I had a cold coming on so went to bed early after taking a dose of medicinal Ouzo.

> *One of the problems with confined group travel was that one person's cold spread around everyone. We all started the trip with a collection of European sniffs, and it was Syria before they had all run their course through the back of the truck.*

Greece – A lunch stop on the coast road

Greece - Camping at Komotini

7th September 1980: Komotini – Kesan

I was woken by Amanda shaking my legs, one hour before sunrise. I found it was easy taking my tent down in the dark when it was put up on the sand; you just gave it a good push. As we drove towards the Turkish border a Contiki coach caught up with us; it was full of Aussies seeing Europe on the cheap. We exchanged rude comments with them by writing on paper and holding it up for them to see. Eventually, we were overtaken, but we were unimpressed by their antipodean sense of humour.

We stopped briefly in Alexandroupolis but it was Sunday and most of the shops were closed. Then before we reached the Turkish border we rolled the sides down and had a tidy-up in the back, removing all the hanging washing. On the Greek side of the border (Ipsala) we were delayed as customs had omitted to stamp all our passports on entry. While we were waiting an Exodus truck rolled up; it was quite empty with only eight passengers on board. Even so, their truck, which was not 4-wheel drive, was much more cramped in the back; they didn't have a trailer to take the luggage. It took some time, but finally, the Yugoslav border post was contacted and all parties were happy that we had legally entered Greece. We then embarrassed ourselves by turning into an army camp on the border rather than going across the bridge into Turkey. Meanwhile, the Exodus truck sailed past us on the right road!

Clearance to enter Turkey also took a long time; it seemed even longer in the back of the truck in the heat with the sides down. The Exodus truck was sent back to Greece as he had something wrong with his paperwork.

We had a quick vote and decided by a small majority not to try and make it to Istanbul that night. We found a wood by a lake to stop for the night, unfortunately, we couldn't swim in the water. We were in a picnic area so our first task was to clear up the rubbish. To help make a quick getaway in the morning we decided not to put up our tents. While a meal was being prepared, a late lunch and early dinner, Jos went and talked to the 'natives' and was given a couple of melons, tomatoes and chillies. In return, we served them coffee after our meal and took the compulsory pictures. My first night sleeping out under the stars wasn't too bad with a shot of Ouzo to warm me first. It was nice lying in bed looking up at the stars, and even nicer when it didn't rain!

Thrace - Open-air camping

TURKEY

Turkey was one of my favourite countries, one that left a memory of friendly people, dönner kebabs and an exciting mountainous southern coast. Perhaps Istanbul wasn't as thrilling as I had found it on my first visit. My trip to North Africa in between had no doubt dampened its 'Asian' surprises.

There was a barely perceptible hardening of attitudes towards us as we journeyed east, and Kayserie was drab in comparison with cities further west.

The mountain ranges stretching down to the coast made progress slow but resulted in spectacular scenery and delightful places to camp like Fethiye.

Of all the 'ruins' to see, Ephesus was undoubtedly the best, but it was too large to take in on such a brief visit. Its memory was soon clouded by more easily assimilated sights such as the Taj Mahal.

And the Turks were so open; they would happily discuss the military coup with us, but that is a story to be told from my diary.

8th September 1980: Kesan - Istanbul

It was not so pleasant to be woken up before dawn and still see stars overhead! Luckily the long road into Istanbul was featureless so we could all catch up on our sleep in the back of the truck. When we got to Londra Camping in Istanbul we had already clocked up 2378 miles from London and were now on the doorstep of Asia.

After putting up our tents, a lunch was served, followed by a race to do our long-awaited clothes washing. The campsite was not as smart as the Mocamp next door where I had stayed with PennWorld; it had a TIR drivers' truck stop and the drivers shared the facilities with us.

I took a group of people into the city as I knew my way around and could show them where the main sights were. My first stop was the Post Office followed by the bank. I searched for information on ferry times to no avail, so I wandered through the bazaar looking for a belt (equally unsuccessfully). After having seen more authentic bazaars in Tunisia the Grand Bazaar in Istanbul now seemed less impressive.

I sat for a while in the quiet of the Blue Mosque where I was mistaken for a German tourist! Then it was time for the obligatory visit by overland travellers to the "Pudding Shop". I enjoyed a Turkish stew followed by pudding, a tasty but not filling meal.

My bus back to the camp got stuck in a traffic jam for ages and it was late in the evening when I eventually got home. I had a few drinks in the camp bar whilst waiting for the others to return in dribs and drabs.

9th September 1980: Istanbul

The next morning I had a rare lie-in because I was on camp guard duty that morning. It was an opportunity to get some more washing done, and the weather was perfect, hot and dry with a cooling breeze. I tried to find out why the indicators on the truck had gone on the blink but it was a wiring bird's nest so I gave up. There wasn't time to go into the city for lunch so I had some tasty but expensive shish kebab in the camp restaurant.

In the afternoon, I returned to the city with a few others. It was another slow bus journey, this time because a lorry had shed its load of plate steel in the middle of the road. We visited the 'carpet salesman' that some others had met the previous day. It turned out that he was the same man who had shown me around the city for free the year before. Together we all visited Hagia Sophia, then we parted company with our 'friend'.

Alex had to get back to cook the evening meal but the rest of us wandered back down the hill as all the shops were closing for the day. I bought two cassette tapes and stocked up with Turkish Delight as a treat. Finally, our wanderings took us to the Galata fish market where we inspected the restaurants underneath on the pontoons. We decided to eat in the Carli Balik restaurant as the owner was particularly helpful in explaining the menu. I chose tekir (striped red mullet), a tomato salad, and a shrimp salad; all washed down with white wine and a Turkish coffee. It was a first-class meal! When we were finished we wandered up to the Galata Tower in an unsuccessful search for night views over the city.

We had to wait a long time for the bus back to the campsite; then we missed the bus stop where we had to get off because the campsite had turned their fairy lights off! I met up with the others, including the trainee driver Mike, in the camp bar. Everyone was just a bit 'Brahms' that evening. I shared my tent with Mike and didn't get to bed till the small hours.

10th September 1980: Istanbul

The weather the next day wasn't so nice with thick clouds and a biting wind; I relaxed at the campsite all morning. At about noon I went to catch a bus into the city but one didn't appear for half an hour. By then Scottish Dave[2] had joined me at the bus stop. The bus we caught had a fuel blockage and struggled to climb the hills half-empty. We decided to switch buses at the Topkapi bus station by the city walls. Our first stop was to grab a fresh fruit juice then I descended into the cool cistern. I took a photo even though I hadn't paid at the entrance for a camera, but I forgot to take the lens cap off! Dave and I then parted company and I went off on my own to select a place for late lunch, another sis kebab and salad.

After lunch, I wandered towards the University where I was accosted by two lads whose main interest seemed to be telling me how I could earn a fast buck with them without breaking the law! Although it was illegal to sell European cigarettes that didn't stop little boys roaming around selling them; the police seemed to turn a blind eye to the activity in return for the occasional packet.

> Most of us welcomed the first chance to escape from the group after nearly two weeks. Our group was settling down socially as we realised how long, and potentially testing, eleven weeks would be with the same group of people.

---

[2] Referred to as Dave(S) for the rest of this narrative to distinguish him from our driver Dave.

Istanbul – The old Galata Bridge and Taksim

Just as I was going to catch the bus back to camp I ran into yet another carpet salesman who offered me a cup of black tea which I accepted, but then was quite unpleasant when I refused to buy anything.

Finding the correct bus stop for the campsite was much easier in the daylight, but crossing the busy dual-carriageway highway was much harder. We had a cold evening meal, followed by a group discussion on the route we would take through Turkey. Before going to bed we had to wash the bird droppings off our flysheets, in preparation for an early morning departure. When I left Jos in the bar to go to bed he was busy speculating which seats people would take in the truck in the morning.

Istanbul - Hagia Sophia Interior   Istanbul - Water seller in the Bazaar

11th September 1980: Istanbul – Bayirköy

The next morning we struck camp, separating the frogs from the tents. It was a slow start as we had to fill up with water and petrol, and also fit purchases such as carpets into the trailer. Jos's seating plan from the night before turned out to be less than 100% accurate.

Our morning coffee stop was Tekirdag where we had fun watching the food sellers descend onto every passing local coach. The coastal road ahead was closed so we had to take a rough and slow inland road south. After a long lunch break near Sarkoy, on a rather polluted beach, we had trouble getting back through the town; Dave was fooled by the one-way system, but eventually, we escaped onto the road to the Dardanelles.

Soon after passing through Bayirköy Dave turned down a narrow lane to the left hoping to set up camp by the sea. Unfortunately, the road ended at a dead-end-looking village. A local 'guide' was enlisted to show us to a potential camping ground, a route that took us up steep sandy tracks putting our 4-wheel drive to good use. Eventually, we reached flat land near the shore, the guide was paid off, and we set up our camp for the night. The area looked a bit mosquito prone so Mike and I elected to put up a tent. It was a beautiful evening to stand on the shore and watch the lights of the shipping going up and down the Bosphorus.

12th September 1980: Bayirköy – Kabatepe

I was plagued in the night by the "Turkish Trots"; I must have been the first person on the truck to get it badly. Trainee Mike took the driver's seat for the first time as we made the short trip from our campsite to the Anzac cemeteries at Lone Pine. Our sightseeing trip was brought to an abrupt stop by a clonking and grating noise below the truck; we stopped, and inspection revealed that the primary drive shaft had broken out of the transfer box. We were left stranded on the hill; the truck drive was useless because the oil had drained out of the broken transfer box.

Diary Extract: Sketch map of Kabatepe

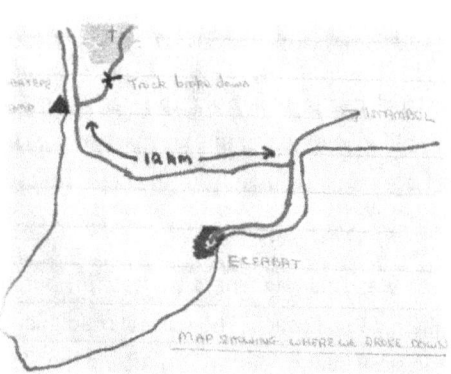

Dave acted excellently as the scale of the disaster became obvious to us all. Tasks were handed out amongst us and the kettle was put on to boil. As 'water man' I was sent out to find water; I found a campsite and water pump about a kilometre down the road by the beach. I reported back to Dave, and the truck and trailer were free-wheeled separately down the hill. Unbeknown to me the camping area I had found was next to a military police post. They spoke no English and we had no Turkish, but they seemed quite agitated. With the help of some patrons leaving a nearby restaurant, we learned that there had been a military coup that morning. The soldiers insisted that we must stay put, which wasn't that difficult with a caput truck and no busses or ferries running.

Meanwhile, my trots were getting a lot worse. One dose hit me far from cover and I amused all by making a mad dash for the sea. Luckily I had my bathers on, but I forgot I had my passport dangling round my neck! Jokes were made about it being the only beach with starting blocks (from Dave of course). We were pestered by the half dozen bored soldiers but a game of football (which we tactfully lost) kept them off our backs for a while.

Whilst Dave, Mike and Karl were busy underneath the truck removing the transfer box, I sat quietly repairing the damage a bolt had done to the seat of my pants whilst I was riding shotgun on the trailer down the hill.

Diary Extract: Sketch of broken transfer box

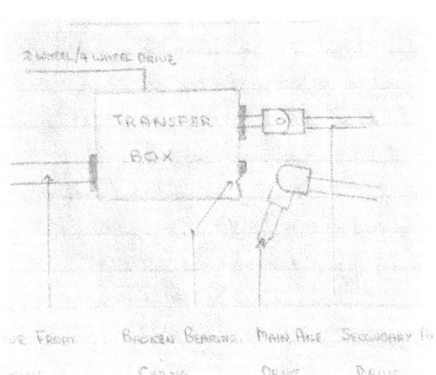

That night I slept in the back of the truck after having dug several strategic holes in the sand. I averaged one hole every two hours and as a consequence didn't get much sleep. I took some Lomotil, but Nurse Helen who was rightly in charge of the first aid box didn't give me enough to have any immediate effect.

13th September 1980: Kabatepe

With the dismantling of the transfer box completed, Mike and Karl set out at an early hour to catch a bus back to Istanbul. Everyone else lazed about getting used to the novelty of a stationary lifestyle. The six-a-side football with the soldiers continued in the blazing heat, and I ran out of anything inside me to put in my trenches. One of the soldiers cut his knee so Helen patched it up using our first-aid kit. He walked around for the rest of the day with a stiff leg, no doubt trying to get out of guard duty.

After the sun cooled down a bit I joined the cherry-red sun worshipers on the beach. Karl and Mike didn't come back that evening so we presumed they had successfully got on a bus to Istanbul. We passed the time playing cards in the truck that night and I had a better night's sleep with only three trips to visit my Gallipoli trenches.

Kabatepe – The author with a spade

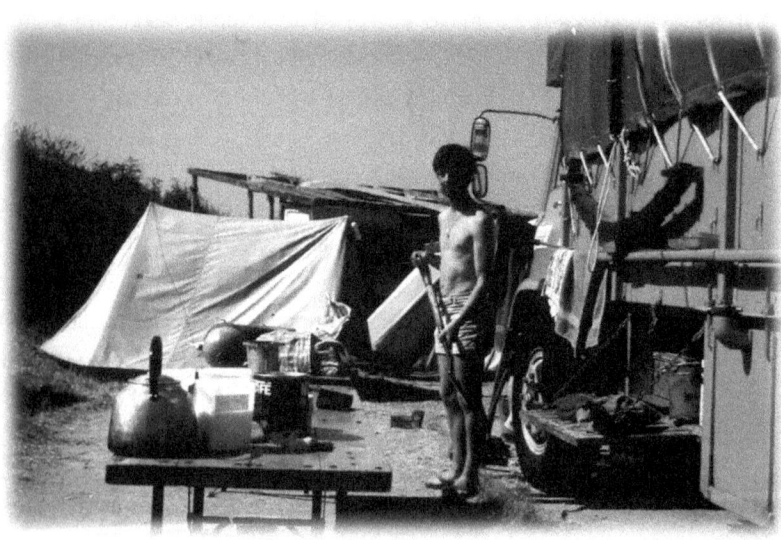

Kabatepe Beach

14th September 1980: Kabatepe

I was woken by the stampede of Ursula cooking breakfast – it not being in her nature to extend much consideration to the sick sleeping bodies in her kitchen. Egged on by hunger I was the first person to speak out to the Swiss ladies, but I wasn't to be the last. I felt quite heroic when the others realised that I had been lugging all the water across from the pump during my illness; Karl wasn't around to help me as usual.

Dave went to the nearest town, Eceabat, and managed to phone through to the Istanbul campsite. The news was bad. Mike didn't get there till late the previous afternoon, and as it was now Sunday, they would have to wait till Monday before going around the Bedford dealers.

Dave reported that he was stopped at three roadblocks on the way to town, and we were warned to carry our passports with us at all times. I finally felt a lot better managing all morning without having to dig a hole. After my afternoon siesta, I went for a swim. I misjudged how unfit I would be after having so little to eat and nearly got into trouble in the water. A nice cool rinse under the pump got rid of the salty feeling. Jos walked into town and had a close call; he hadn't got his passport and the soldiers were reportedly nervous and jumpy.

After the evening meal, we had a bit of a disco. I danced for a while but when Dave put on his Irish music my stomach objected and I had to sit out the rest of the party. Sandra cooked an excellent meal out of eggplant and potatoes. After all that excitement I had my first unbroken night's sleep in four days.

Kabatepe - Disco night on the beach

Dennis reported that he saw quite a lot of wildlife on his rambles, including snakes. But the worst we had to put up with on the beach were flies (which bite) and massive spiders.

Kabatepe - Val gives Henk a trim

After over two weeks together and several days of enforced idleness, you could see social bonds starting to form in the group. Drive Dave was spending a lot of time with Amanda, Val had migrated to the Dutch group with Jos, and Alex & Helen were leading the social group for English speakers.

15th September 1980: Kabatepe

The morning that Sandra made porridge, gallons of it, quite an embarrassment! After filling all six jerrycans I had discharged my water duties for the day, so I set off to visit the Anzac cemeteries. A hazy sun made the walk up the hill past our previous breakdown spot quite pleasant, and a moving experience because the lines of trenches and broken ground were still clearly visible on each side of the road. There were many well-kept memorials to the Allied troops, but none to the Turks, which was a bit strange because they won! That is if losing 85,000 lives can be described as a victory. I wandered along the ridge past Lone Pine, but soon the sun came out and it became oppressively hot. Exhaustion drove me down to the coast from where it was a level walk back on the track to the camp.

Lunch was a fresh fish soup which was very good. It was followed by a siesta and then beach games organised by Dave. The two sides battled it out with ball games and races. The only casualty was a tent pole that got broken in the melee.

Afterwards, a few of us went along the beach for a drink, but in doing so we managed to miss the evening meal. There were a lot of hard feelings because we were within earshot when the meal was served but the Swiss didn't bother to shout out to us.

The evening was spent sitting on the beach singing, but it wasn't much of a party. The truck's battery was now flat; that meant we had no audio and no lights. The former was a blessing, but the latter was quite inconvenient.

> Sandra was quite concerned about the two scavenging puppies that plagued our campsite. She even bought them some meat, quite a strange move for a vegetarian!

16th September 1980: Kabatepe

A morning with scrambled egg for breakfast and NO porridge, as our catering lurched from one extreme to another. That day we saw the Exodus truck driving around the cemeteries; they had presumably been held up in Istanbul by the coup; apparently, there was still a curfew in place.

Dave set off to the town to phone for news whilst Val and Freddy went in to do food shopping. I had a do-nothing day, not difficult because there wasn't a lot to do! Dave returned after lunch with good and bad news. The bad news was that the parts we needed had to be flown out from England and would arrive that evening. The good news was that an empty Encounter truck had arrived in Istanbul which could come and help us.

Before dinner, I walked south along the beach and around the headland. I didn't find the sandstone coastal scenery particularly inspiring but on the way I met Sandra who was sitting on the rocks painting.

Dinner was delicious! I enjoyed eating food again! We had spaghetti with sauce and then another 'guess-the-lumps' custard from Val, with apple this time. After the meal, we had another 'party'; it was something to do with welcoming Karl back, even though he hadn't returned yet! Whatever the excuse we all consumed our 100TL of wine and then sat about talking. I must have had a bit too much to drink and vaguely remember wandering around with my own wine bottle.

> Anna bought one of the soldiers a Turkish/English dictionary and he was as pleased as punch. She also had an irresistible urge to buy everything she saw; I wondered how she would get it all back home!

17th September 1980: Kabatepe

I was up bright and early because Val chose the wrong tent to sing outside to summon her breakfast helper! I had filled all the jerry cans the night before so I was ready to leave camp early on my first trip to the nearest town, Eceabat. The accepted mode of transport was to hitch a lift on a passing tractor, and so it was that Dennis, Anna and I soon found ourselves bouncing along in a trailer full of wet sand. We were joined in the trailer by one of the soldiers from our army post.

Our stately progress down to the sea was halted by an armed roadblock at the entrance to the town. There were soldiers on guard every few yards down the main street, and I had to show my passport to get into the Post Office. We did some shopping but there was little to detain us in the town, so we decided to take the ferry across the Dardanelles and visit Canakkale on the other side. Our trip to Asia took 15 minutes and only cost 10 Turkish Lira. Jos and Henk were on the same ferry; they had set out before us and were hoping to hitch to Troy, but there had not been an earlier ferry they could catch.

Eceabat viewed from the ferry

In Canakkale we first looked for the museum, following signs to Müse but it turned out to be closed (and somewhat uninteresting). So we wandered round the back streets up to the castle. After having our cameras removed (because it was a military base) we were offered a guided tour of a very un-English fort. They were particularly proud of a shell from a British warship that was embedded in the thick wall. We paid off our castle guide, retrieved our cameras, and then went in search of lunch. Incredibly, we ran into the guy who ran the restaurant near our camp, and on his recommendation, ate at a restaurant that had excellent Dönner Kebab.

I left the others and walked out onto a jetty where I dozed and watched the activity on the harbour. The first ferry back was not expected till late in the afternoon. I had arranged to meet up with Dennis on the ferry back, but he wasn't on board. It was getting late when I got to Eceabat; there was a distinct lack of lifts as the farmers had already headed home. So I walked all the way back to camp, about 5 ½ miles. At first, I thought I could make it back to camp before dinner, but it soon became obvious that I couldn't make it in time. I completed the walk in a creditable 75 minutes but arrived just in time to see the washing up being done. I headed over to our local restaurant to have a soft drink and watch TV (we drank the place out of beer on the second night).

It turned out that Dennis and Anna caught an earlier ferry whilst I was asleep and got a lift back, just my luck!

18th September 1980: Kabatepe

Understandably I had stiff legs the next morning from my exercise the previous afternoon. I was able to get some washing done at the pump using some local cold-water detergent I had bought; it was nice to see some clothes clean again. Colin came back from town with some specially cut chopping boards about 1" thick to replace the ones that had slipped off the back of the truck.

In the afternoon a group was taken on a free trip to see the nearby official campsite; this was perhaps a somewhat academic exercise as we couldn't move the truck. The group came back with bags of apples that were free for the picking. Even the fish we had for the evening meal was gifted to us by a Turk who had been out fishing.

There was a minor panic when Colin was not back in time to cook dinner; it turned out that his lift had broken down. Then the gas ran out whilst the meal was being cooked and as a result, the food wasn't ready till well past 8 o'clock. By then it was pitch dark, and the sight of everyone trying to pick bones out of the fish by torchlight was quite amusing. Sadly there was no sight of a second rescue truck, no light, and no alcohol, so we went early to bed.

19th September 1980: Kabatepe

A nice late start because the English were cooking a 'proper' breakfast. Encouraged by those who went the previous day, another group walked along the shore to look at the campsite. Those remaining helped the soldiers to beach their leaking boat that had sunk.

And then the rescue truck appeared unannounced. Almost a week to the hour after we had broken down and become stranded the end was finally in sight. Alan, the second driver, had a brand new small truck. He had been heading back to London after taking an earlier group to Damascus. Karl and Mike had a tough time getting the parts through customs but were helped in the end by the 'carpet salesman' who had befriended us in Istanbul.

Unfortunately one of the supplied parts was not correct, the replacement for a broken oil seal. The idea of finding all the bits of the old seal and sticking them together was rejected in favour of drilling holes in the replacement seal in the correct place. It was a big relief when the modified part fitted and the box could be reassembled. With fingers crossed we gave our dead truck a tow start, and it burst back into life.

We had electric light again that evening meal, and with Karl back, the task of filling up the jerry cans was much easier. Karl now had to come to terms with the social changes in the group that had happened over the week he was away.

It was becoming difficult to find a good camp bed. After a week of being used for seating on the soft sand, many of the new camp stretchers had broken.

Kabatepe - Help arrives

Kabatepe - Fixing the transfer box

20th September 1980: Kabatepe - Altinov

After eight nights on the beach, we were finally on the move again. A new rule was enforced that tents had to be packed before breakfast. It wasn't such a good change of routine; the first to finish got the first take of breakfast and they didn't leave much food for the others. We needed another tow to start as the battery was still flat, and then the two trucks drove in convoy as a precaution. We got to Eceabat at 8 am. but our haste was to no avail as the first ferry didn't leave till 10!

Kabatepe - Starting the truck

We said our farewells to Alan who was going to resume his trip back to the UK, then we crossed on the ferry over to Asia. Our disembarkation was delayed because a lorry ahead of us had to be towed off, but our truck started OK. We headed directly for Troy without stopping in Canakkale, and a steep climb out of the town tested out the truck repairs. The transfer box behaved itself without even a hint of a leak.

Our visit to Troy was a bit of a non-event. Apart from the ludicrous wooden horse gracing the entrance to the site (which Anna was convinced was the 'real thing'), the site was hard to interpret due to the many stages of occupation. The entrance was only 7½ Lira (4p) but as 2½ Lira coins were just about out of circulation we had to go in in pairs. After lunch in the car park, we headed south again.

Turkey - Alan following us to Eceabat

It would have been a non-stop journey but for Plony being ill and us having to pick up some wine for Colin's birthday. We turned down a dirt track for the night but didn't quite make it to the sea, stopping instead on a flat field with a water trough. On closer inspection, the field turned out to be rather well used by sheep so it was necessary to carry a torch everywhere!

Dinner was late – a sausage rice mixture followed by muesli for dessert, both rather filling. After the meal, we started on the cheap wine/paint stripper/brake fluid we bought earlier and gave Colin his presents; a cake with candles, sweets, and a few other things. A disco followed; we had music once more; but the dance floor was a bit rustic and had to be damped down! The party was broken up by a shepherd bringing his flock to the water and to graze.

21st September 1980: Altinov – Bafa Lake

I was woken by the sheep in the night and also by the cold; there was quite a mess by the truck where we had been dancing the previous night. After flushing the trough clean we set out for Izmir. As was usual in large towns, Dave got lost, and we exited on the wrong road. On the second attempt he found the right road and shortly afterwards had to stop for a loo stop in a cemetery; it was an unusual experience as the urinal was full of fruit and vegetables!

Turkey - Ephesus

We reached Ephesus (on the outskirts of Selçuk) on a stinking hot day and there was little shade. With the help of a guidebook I bought, I attempted to take in the massive area of ruins in the allotted two hours. It was undoubtedly a first-class site; the best places to explore were the narrow alleyways between houses where it was easy to imagine oneself in a different age.

Back at the truck we had a meeting and decided to press on to Fethiye rather than breaking the trip with a night nearby. Unfortunately, that plan didn't take into account Sandra. She hadn't returned to the truck; she didn't have a watch. So Dave(S) and a few others stayed behind to look for her, whilst the rest of us were transported into Selçuk to look at the museum. The museum wasn't very interesting, but by the time we had looked around long enough to justify the 12½ Lira entrance and had had a drink, we were all reunited again.

Our route now headed southeast climbing up a pass. For a while, we raced a train; it must have been a slow train! Then we had to stop to fill up with water; it was a long water stop because the tap was very slow. So it was now getting late. We pressed on in the dark, even though that was against Encounter Overland's rules; I guess there were extenuating circumstances as we were running way behind schedule. We were looking for Bafa Lake, but when it didn't materialise we just pulled off down the usual dirt road. There was no grass for tents so I slept in the open between some shrubs.

Turkey - Ephesus

Turkey - Scenery near Bafa Lake

22nd September 1980: Bafa Lake - Ölüdeniz

I slept in my parka and, as a result, was quite cosy sleeping in the open; it wasn't really cold. Breakfast was served with an iron fist by Dave(S) who was the first to implement another new rule that stated that all packing had to be finished before breakfast. He also implemented the second rule that food should only be served for 15 minutes. Poor Werner, always hard to wake in the morning, nearly missed his breakfast.

A local came up whilst we were eating and filled up a tank on his horse-driven cart from a nearby well.

The scenery along the road to Fethiye was similar to Greece, with high passes between each town; a feature that made it slow going in our truck. We had our shopping break in Muğla, a lovely town with an interesting bazaar. After the previous day's fiasco, everyone managed to get back to the truck at the nominated time.

Near Bafa Lake - A local collecting water

Lunch was in a layby by a dried-up river. There were plenty of jokes about going for a swim and comparison with the 'lake' at our campsite the previous night. The sun was so hot we huddled up on the shady side of the truck to eat.

Fethiye was another 12 km further on, over a very steep pass, and from there on to Ölüdeniz, an isolated paradise with no development and a campsite with hot water. The beach was lovely with gravel shelving steeply into crystal clear water, and excellent swimming, but as I found out it was also easy for a weak swimmer to find themselves out of their depth.

One advertised feature of our stay at Fethiye was to be a boat trip around the islands. When we arrived we found out that the boat was away and wasn't expected back for two days. In another democratic meeting, we decided to stay longer and wait for the boat.

The evening meal was a bit of a disaster cooked by Jos and Anna. There was no meat or fish, just vegetables, and not enough to go around. The corn on the cob we were served was so tough it must have been animal feed!

The camp was well organised. We could buy drink cards at reception which could be exchanged for a fixed amount of drink in the bar. This avoided all the need for small change which was in short supply.

23rd September 1980: Ölüdeniz

After a few drinks the previous night I had agreed to be adventurous and join Dave on a tramp up the local mountain, Babadag (1969m). When I unpacked my cagoole ready for the walk I found it was mouldy, having been packed away wet after Salzberg's rain. I had to soak it in vinegar overnight!

We packed a lunch and set off at about 9 a.m. Our route first took us south on a track that led to the next bay. We had a 'guide' with us from the camp, but he was only a lad, and it turned out he had only ever been up the mountain by the easy route (a forestry track up the far side).

Turning inland, we headed up a valley following a small stream to the base of a series of waterfalls. The climb then rapidly degenerated into a very difficult ascent up a scree slope which was made worse by the route chosen by our 'guide'. Those climbers who were following chose a different path with the result that half of us ended up high on one bank, and the rest high on the other. By shouting, we agreed to meet again in the centre, at the top of the scree slope. However, when we got to the top we found that there was a mass of large boulders which prevented us from seeing more than a few yards ahead. After jumping from boulder to boulder for a while and getting nowhere, Dave(S) found that it was much easier to make progress away from the edge and closer to the mountain. We came across a melon field and after much blowing of my whistle and shouting we rendezvoused for lunch.

Climbing Babadag – A drink stop

Climbing Babadag – The melon field

Just up the hillside, there was a small village sheltering under the main ridge of the mountain. A local farmer there gave us some grapes and enlisted a boy to show us how to get up onto the ridge.

During the subsequent climb out of the village in the full mid-day sun I had a bad attack of heat stroke and could only manage to walk a few steps at a time. Confusion set in between those who thought the goal was to reach the ridge, and those who wanted to go over the ridge and find the easier forest road. When the path ran out at about 1400m Colin, Christian and the 'guide' set out separately over the ridge looking for paths. They were away for a long time without any contact, so we left a message and headed back down to the village. After retracing our steps down the slope a view of Ölüdeniz bay appeared and a few members of the group took a shortcut in that direction. It looked too rough and overgrown for my liking and I was quite exhausted, so I returned to the village with Fredy, Denis and Ursula. We found our friendly farmer and in sign language asked him where we could find a road down. He wanted us to stay the night but it was too complicated to try and explain that we weren't planning to go back to Fethiye that day.

The farmer showed us a gently sloping mule track that led to the top of the cliffs above our bay. Freddy and Ursula elected to follow the track contouring round the bay till it met the metaled road from Fethiye, whilst Denis and I took a steep path down the cliff pointed out by a local.

Included in the Encounter trip price was a group meal in each country. This was a break from camp cooking, and a chance to sample the local cuisine. The Turkish group meal was held in the campsite restaurant that night. Denis and I got back in time for a shower before the meal, Dave's party arrived about an hour later. The three who ascended the ridge finally got in after we had finished our meal. They had come back down to the village where the friendly farmer had given them a lift down to the bay. The three-course group 'Meal of the Country' was excellent Turkish food but I was too exhausted to properly enjoy it and had to crash out soon afterwards.

24th September 1980: Ölüdeniz

We needed a quiet day after the previous day's exertions. Washing, writing, and watching the driver fix an oil leak, were the order of the day. I was on cooking detail but missed all the morning lifts into Fethiye so had to order what we needed from the camp shop. The camp was providing a lamb or goat that we could have as a meal on the boat; our contribution was to make a salad and collect wood to pre-cook the meat in an open oven. I set off collecting dry driftwood in the hot sun with Helen and Colin. When we had accumulated a big pile I returned to the camp to get a rope so we could drag the logs, but when I returned Helen and Colin had disappeared. So I ended up starting the fire using wood that others had collected.

To relax I took a swim in the lagoon at the end of the beach using borrowed goggles and my flippers. I resolved to leave the flippers with the truck when we had to overfly, they would be of little use in India and beyond.

Ölüdeniz bay

Meanwhile, Helen had arranged for a lorry to collect the wood and as a consequence, we ended up with far too much, so much that the fire wouldn't die down enough to cook on. The meat finally went in late in the afternoon; we prepared a delicious rice salad to have with it, and also another inferior salad using cooked rice sludge provided by the campsite.

The boat was expected to return early in the evening, but when it passed 10 o'clock and the boat hadn't appeared, we ate our meal at the camp. There wasn't much meat on the animal.

Our cooking duty wasn't finished for the night as Helen and I had to pack all the food for the following day. When the lights of the boat were seen at the entrance to the bay we walked round to the pier in the lagoon. Whilst we waited for the boat to dock we sang rounds led by Helen(S).

It was gone midnight when we boarded the 50-year-old yacht, but then we still had to wait whilst clearance was obtained from the police to break the curfew. We then sailed along the bay and put down anchor in a cove surrounded by Byzantine ruins. Some people took a dinghy so they could sleep on dry land, whilst others found a bit of spare space on the deck to lie down. A few lucky ones got a stuffy bunk down below. I drank raki and coke and turned in at about three in the morning!

> In the first big split in the group, the Swiss passengers didn't come on the boat trip as a 'protest'. Unfortunately, Dave wasn't sure exactly what the protest was about but we guessed it was triggered by the boat not turning up as announced in the afternoon! Understandably there wasn't a lot of sympathy going around for them in the rest of the group.

Fethiye Cruise - Anchored by ruins

Fethiye Cruise - Our boat

25th September 1980: Ölüdeniz (boat trip)

The bright sunshine and the sound of people having an early morning dip woke me up. When I had cleared a space in the cramped galley and got the 'fresh water' pump going we were someway towards preparing breakfast. Working in such a small space took a lot of organisation. It transpired that we had forgotten to bring washing-up liquid, and there was only a small saucepan to boil water on the boat. Hot drinks tasted a bit strange because the water in the tank was a bit suspect.

Fethiye Cruise – Sun worship

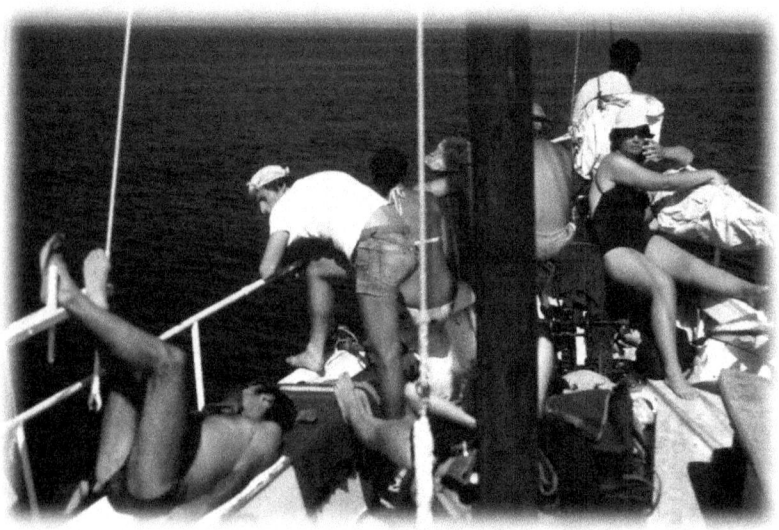

There was no problem with the water around the boat which was crystal clear and you could watch fish swimming past. Our yacht sailed and motored around the headland and then across the wide bay of Fethiye. There were several small islands on the north side of the bay which we wound our way through.

For lunch, we anchored by a gravel spit in an area of shallow water. It was a great place for swimming, diving off the boat, and looking at the abundant marine life in the shallows. The crew rigged an awning so those who wanted could stay out of the hot sun.

All too soon it was time to make our way back to Ölüdeniz with a diversion to take a close look at eroded cliffs and ruins on the way. When we got back to the beach the dinghy was loaded up with our bags and then we all swam to the shore. After giving the plates and crockery a good hot wash Helen and I completed our cooking duties.

26th September 1980: Ölüdeniz – Near Kemer

After the excitement of the boat trip, I woke with a stuffed-up nose and the symptoms of a developing cold. Our stock of Alpen Muesli had run out and I was shocked to find how addicted I'd become to it, a very expensive habit. I slept for most of the journey down the coast towards Finike until we hit the dirt roads. The big drama of the morning was when, on the rough coast road cut on a ledge into the cliffs, we met a bulldozer and transporter coming the other way. They were stuck trying to negotiate a sharp bend ahead of us and had completely blocked the road. We resigned ourselves to an extended delay and served lunch on the roadside where we were stopped. The agile members of the group scrambled down the cliff so they could swim off the rocks.

The road left the coast and turned inland over a pass before dropping down to the quiet town of Finke. We stopped for food shopping; I stocked up on Turkish Cornflakes and some better-quality wine. After another even higher pass, we skirted the Lycian Mt Olympus (Tahtalı Dağı) and stopped for the night just before reaching Kemer. Only Lotti and Claudine now insisted on putting up a tent, the rest of us set up our beds on a patch of flat ground between the road and an irrigation canal. By damming the canal we were able to make a passable washing place.

I chatted with a local who wandered up from the nearby village; he was studying English, a common occupation for those who aspired to be guides. We sat about in our camp for a long while because the cooks had overcooked the rice and had to start over again; in the end, dinner wasn't worth waiting for. I quickly demolished my bottle of wine with assistance from others and then headed for bed. The local I was talking with had said there were lots of mosquitos and snakes in the woods, but neither troubled us.

Finiki - Road blocked by a transporter

27th September 1980: Kemer – Anamur

It was a relatively fast run on the flat coast road for about 50km to Antalya. The regional capital presented a good opportunity for an early food shop and a brief chance for the others to look at the historic sights. It may have been the circumstances of our visit but I didn't think it was a very nice city, or at least it didn't live up to the poetic description in the guidebook. The harbour was spoilt by decrepit old buildings and tasteless modern ones. We were a bit early for the bazaar which wasn't awake yet and I looked in vain for an English-language newspaper to catch up on the news.

On the road to Antalya

Antalya Harbour

We pressed on to Aspendos where we had just half an hour to look round the perfectly preserved amphitheatre. It was all too soon time to press on to our lunch stop on a bleak building site by the sea; a place whose only redeeming feature was the building blocks that made good seats. Just when I thought I might have shaken off the trots that had been with me since Kabatepe I had to engage in some rapid spade work. By now everyone on the truck had had a dose except for Ron. He was now the honorary chairman and secretary of the anti-diarrhoea club.

Aspendos - Amphitheatre

After Aspendos, there was a dramatic change in scenery as we passed through groves of banana trees crisscrossed with complex irrigation schemes. We were able to stock up on bananas from a roadside stall. When we didn't go and look at Side due to the pressure of time the back of the truck was full of 'side-stepping' jokes.

Alanya was supposed to have a Roman harbour but I couldn't make it out from the headland where we stopped. Unfortunately, the road then deteriorated and there were few level or straight sections; it was the sort of road that slowed the truck's progress down to a crawl.

It was already getting dark when we dropped down into Anamur and took a side turning to the Roman ruins at Anamuryum. Unfortunately, Dave's information that we could park at the ruins overnight was suspect. Halfway down the lane, there was a gate across the road and a NO CAMPING sign. We tried to turn the truck around on the narrow lane without success. When the gate was opened to let a farm cart out, we managed to convince the warden to leave it open so we could chuck a uey. A local boy pointed out to us a turning off the lane which led to a bit of beach we could use for camping. It was a bleak and desolate spot.

Anamur - Mamure Kalesi

I kept accounts for the trip and was relieved to find that I was spending just £6 a week; life on the truck was very cheap!

28th September 1980: Anamur - Mut

This time my trots came on worse with fever and horrible stomach cramps. I lost count of the number of times I had to get up in the night. Breakfast was late to give people time to go and look at the extensive ruins nearby; I had to give them a miss. Helen[S], a trainee doctor, came to my rescue by giving me more Imodium and a course of Mexaform from her personal first-aid kit. I wasn't up to looking around Mamure Castle, but it was an impressive Crusader castle from the outside.

The road heading inland from Anamur to Ermenek wasn't clearly signposted. We missed it and so ended up going a bit further along the coast before heading inland. We ended up on a scenic road that climbed from Aydincik to Gülnar.

Mut - Campsite high in the Taurus Mountains

Val and Fredy did a quick food shop in Gülnar before we hit the steep climb up into the Taurus mountains. As afternoon turned into evening we ground our way up the unrelenting grade, and we broke the tedium in the back by having a vicious nut fight.

We stopped for the night somewhere near Mut high up on the side of a wide rocky valley. I set up my camp bed, had sick rations of rice, and then crashed out, splitting my sleeping bag by trying to get in with my parka on. It was a very cold night; the camp must have been up at about 3,500 ft. I was happy though; Helen's medicines worked well and I had an unbroken night.

29th September 1980: Mut – Goreme

It was Ron's 21st birthday! I wrote in my diary that I was feeling much better! This could be because the scenery was wonderful, or perhaps because digging holes in the scenery was near impossible, but probably because Helen had given me an antibiotic. The final few kilometres up to the summit weren't very scenic as the pass had a very rounded top. The north side of the Taurus Mountains was completely different with smooth hills and only a slight drop to the central plateau at 3,000 ft.

When we stopped for food shopping in the rural town of Karaman I stayed with the truck, but Ron bought a jug full of curd in the local market which we eagerly consumed.

The central plateau had flat fast roads, a welcome change after the mountain passes along the coast, but the scenery was uninteresting. Lunch was only memorable for the light tuff stone boulders by the side of the road. We picked up a hitchhiker who wanted a lift to the next village; it was good to repay the favour that others had given us when we were stranded at Kabatepe.

Karaman – A peasant cart

Confused by a badly signposted diversion, we ended up approaching Goreme on a dirt track; we even drove past the camp because of the unfamiliar route we took. That night we enjoyed a pleasant organised campsite, pitching tents because both rain and mosquitos were forecast. I beat the queues by doing my washing first and then having a shower. A visit to the camp bar (for fruit juice) was interrupted by the arrival of an Exodus truck which we went out to greet. They had a pleasant English driver with a gearbox that was falling apart on him, but the truck had been subcontracted to Topas. His passengers were a load of unfriendly Danish tourists and their long-suffering courier. They were returning to Greece before flying on to Pakistan.

We had our evening meal in the camp dining room sitting at tables and chairs but we ate the food we had prepared. Then Ron had his birthday presents which included his watch which he had lost but which had been found and saved up for this occasion by Henk.

30th September 1980: Goreme - Develi

Rain caused panic amongst the 'freelancers' who hadn't put up a tent! It rained quite a lot in the night and the washing strung out between the tents got an extra rinse. A serving of my stale Turkish cornflakes for breakfast brought back memories of how much better Kellogg's was in the U.K. After breakfast we visited the Goreme Valley but unfortunately we were too early, the museum on the site didn't open for another hour. The valley was full of cave dwellings and chapels carved out of the soft volcanic rock by persecuted Christians in the 10th and 11th centuries. We had a good three hours to look around the site. The chapel paintings were unfortunately mostly vandalised so instead I found time to walk up the valley side to the top from where there were spectacular views.

Goreme – Waiting for the museum to open

Goreme

In the truck, on our way to Kayserie, I performed a post-mortem on my torch which had become impossibly intermittent; I decided to ditch it! In the city, my first stop was to collect my mail from the Post Office. The mail wasn't filed and sorted in alphabetical order, so finding letters was difficult and confusing, but I eventually recovered the two letters I was expecting.

Round the corner was a nice restaurant where I met up with Helen(S) and Werner for a solid meal of meat and two vegetables. Helen then accompanied me to buy a stock of medicines in case my trots got worse again.

Finding a bank that would change travellers' cheques was difficult; I tried about five, the last three with Dave. Finally, Dave was recognised by a bank because he had tried to pick up $200 there in July. They didn't think the order had been cancelled so they paid him, after deducting a hefty fee for telexing. After that I was small fry; I just changed $10!

Goreme - Chapels carved in the rock

Wandering around the large bazaar I found a tiny shop selling torches; I was able to buy a nice plastic one with three cells for a bargain price. After completing the purchase I sat in the shop for a while drinking tea and having the usual one-way conversation with the shopkeeper talking to me in Turkish!

I stocked up on some more Turkish Delight before returning to the truck. Dave took longer to return after trying, and ultimately not succeeding, to contact London by telephone or telex.

By the time we had extricated ourselves from the town centre, it was dusk and we drove on in the dark through Incesu and down the road to Develi. We pulled into a road works site intending to camp but were re-directed to somewhere more suitable, a patch of flat land close to the road. We pitched tents because it was spotting with rain.

Whilst waiting for dinner I repaired the splits in my sleeping bag with Ursula showing me how to sew.

Develi – Remote campsite

1st October 1980: Develi – Kahramanmaraş

A sharp wind got up in the night and the wind chill made it feel very cold in our exposed campsite. I had to dig my gloves out for the first time. We gave a local a lift into Develi and on the way passed Eroiyes Dagi (3916m), Turkey's third-highest mountain.

As we passed through Develi we were given a thorough search by the local police. Shortly afterwards Denis found an unusual object in his bag so we tossed it out the back without investigating further. Then the tarmac road ran out and we had big dust problems in the back. It was far too cold to have the sides up. We were soon completely saturated with dust, a situation that we were unfortunately now accustomed to. From what we could see out the back, it wasn't a particularly scenic road over the hills to join up with the main road south to Kahramanmaraş, though we did stop at the top of one pass for a toilet stop and to admire the views.

Our back road joined the main road at a small town where we were able to buy some fresh bread for lunch, and we pulled off the road soon afterwards to eat it. Val and Jos climbed the local hill and made it back down again just in time to grab some food. The hills appeared to be made of granite and they reminded me of Scotland. The geology must be a volcanic mess with the rock type and scenery changing every few miles.

As we drove down the valley to Kahramanmaraş we saw many bridges that had been washed away by the river and there were frequent detours onto dirt roads to bypass washouts.

Lunch stop south of Kahramanmaras

Viewpoint from pass after Develi

In Kahramanmaraş Dave and Mike went off once again to try again to phone London, whilst Karl and I went in search of a card and presents for Dave(S)'s upcoming birthday. Unfortunately, all the shops were either closing or closed and we were unable to purchase anything. Instead, we went to a café and waited for the drivers to get back. At 7:30 p.m. they gave up trying to phone and we drove just outside town to set up camp by the river. There was a good pump nearby so I was able to have a much-needed wash.

2nd October 1980: Kahramanmaraş - Yayladağı

It rained in the night which caused a bit of a panic as most of the group were sleeping in the open. I got my space blanket and spread it over me then went back to sleep; luckily the rain wasn't that persistent. I decided to get used to sleeping without a pillow as my parka which I had been rolling up as a pillow was now so dust-impregnated it made me sneeze in the night.

The journey to Antakya (Antioch of old) was uneventful and accompanied by heavy rain. We arrived before midday just as the rain seemed to be easing. Antakya was Dave's last chance to contact the Head Office in London; he wanted confirmation that it was still OK to enter Syria and over-fly to Pakistan. The Gulf War between Iran and Iraq made the situation in Syria volatile and uncertain.

I did a stint of truck-watching and diary writing (someone was always left on the truck in remote towns to deter theft). Then I wandered around the town and was successful in buying Dave(S) some presents including sweets. I found a synthetic blanket which I bought to supplement my thin sleeping bag as the nights were getting cold. I had to pay in US$ as I had run down my holding of Turkish Lira in preparation for crossing the border and leaving Turkey. After another stint on guard duty, I went to a nearby restaurant and had the usual kebab for lunch.

Kahramanmaras – The approach from the north

Good News! Dave got through to London and confirmed that everything was set up for us to fly from Damascus to Karachi. So, in the late afternoon, we set out for Syria. Well, that was the plan, but we missed the road and stayed in Turkey heading unexpectedly south to Yayladagi. After filling up all our jerry cans at a roadside spring we stopped just before the border.

Dave parked the truck off the road in a wooded area. What looked like gravel turned out to be mud and soon the truck was well and truly stuck. It took nearly an hour of shovelling, placing 'sand' mats and pushing before we got the truck back on the road. By then it was quite dark, so we moved to the opposite side of the road where the ground looked firmer.

SYRIA

Entering Syria did nothing to contradict my prejudices against Arabs; it came as an unpleasant surprise after an enjoyable month in Turkey. I suppose our chance decision to go down the West Coast, the worst bit of the country, was partly to blame.

The contrast between the historic site of Palmyra and the rest of the country made it worth the desert excursion to get there; the only helpful Syrians we met were in Palmyra.

Damascus summed up the country. It had a dirty and uncared-for air without any redeeming colour.

Neither did Syria appear to have any culinary treats. Our group meal of roast chicken was nice but it could have been cooked anywhere. It reinforced an observation that the local fare in a country is rarely the exciting dishes one finds on offer in restaurants back home.

3rd October 1980: Yayladağı - Baniyas

There was heavy rain in the night but we had put up tents in the woods with everyone abandoning the convenience of sleeping in the open. It was still tipping it down when we were woken early by a cock crowing. After a cramped breakfast in the back of the truck, the rain eased. We cleaned the mud off the sand mats in a big puddle and then we were ready once again to leave Turkey.

But once again Turkey didn't want to say "Goodbye". The verge we had parked on had also become slippery overnight and the truck preferred to slide down into the ditch rather than go where the front wheels were pointing. So we had to do some more pushing before we got back on the tarmac again.

As we passed the last Turkish houses before the border we were stopped by three rather bored soldiers. They looked at our passports, lined us up outside the truck, frisked us, and searched our hand luggage. Getting across the border took three hours but was uneventful apart from a moment of drama when the Turks asked all the men to get out of the truck. However, they just wanted us to help lift their barrier and put it back across the road!

We celebrated with a coffee break in a café on the Syrian side before driving down to the coastal town of Latakia. Helen and I had to do the food shopping because we had volunteered to do Dave's turn on his birthday. We overran the allotted 45 minutes because we weren't familiar with shopping in Syria, and it was hard to find shops on the outskirts of town. It was also made difficult because it was Friday, prayer day, in a strict Muslim country. We were also the first shopping team who had to grapple with Arabic numbers on prices and coins (challenging even though I had done my homework). It seemed that we had paid over the odds for a big bag of potatoes till I rechecked and found we had counted the change wrong. I tried again, without success, to find any bread when the truck relocated to the town centre. The group officially had to register with the police, but the police weren't interested!

We stopped to fill up with water before sunset, which was an hour earlier now we were in Syria. Then stopped for the night in a building site between the road and the sea just past Baniyas.

The birthday dinner Helen and I cooked was OK but the dehydrated Chicken Supreme from the truck supplies came out as a soup. The candles were lost so we used matches on Dave's cake but they kept blowing out.

That night, some people slept in pipes on the building site. But it didn't rain!

4th October 1980: Baniyas - Homs

As I was on breakfast duty I had to get up early and was surprised to find that it was already broad daylight because of the time change entering Syria. We hadn't managed to buy any bread the day before so we served porridge and scrambled eggs instead.

Our shopping stop was Tartus, a town Jos's guidebook raved about. Jos wanted time to look around, but even he admitted afterwards that it wasn't all that spectacular. We were aiming for the fine Crusader castle at Krak des Chevaliers, but we got distracted by the cheap booze on sale from roadside stalls as we passed briefly through the northern tip of Lebanon and missed the turning to the castle. There was a vote to decide if we wanted to turn back or to press on, a vote which the driveaholics won. When we stopped for lunch by a desert waterhole there was discontent amongst those who had wanted to see the castle (myself included).

With all the dusty roads my hair was now unpleasantly saturated; my hands would get dirty just combing it; that is if you could even get the comb through it at all. When we reached Homs I gave wandering around the town a miss and sat in the truck; I'd already had enough of dirty Syrian towns.

As we headed south we missed yet another turn-off, this time the road to Palmyra; the signs were all in Arabic script so there was an excuse. When we realised our mistake we did a U-turn and pulled off the road onto desert scrub for the night. I had a good wash then tidied up my luggage trying to make room for my new blanket.

5th October 1980: Homs - Palmyra

We had an early start to make good use of the daylight hours. I rode in the front of the truck as we backtracked to Homs looking for the road into the desert that we had missed the previous day. We found it the second time and sped across the barren landscape past military installations on our way to Palmyra. The only drama was one wrong turn that we took; sitting in the front I saw how insignificant the signposts were and how they didn't distinguish between major and minor roads.

In Palmyra, we were met by the English-speaking guide with the grand title of "Director of Antiquities". He showed us around the extensive ruins including the grand Temple of Baal/Bel (Zeus). It was strange to see lorries speeding through the ruins on the road to Iran. At lunchtime, we moved the truck on to the hotel, where the only place to camp was in the car park. It was a shady place but the showers and toilets were dirty.

After washing my hair with the water hose we set off in the truck to have a sulphur bath. Unfortunately, the guy in charge of the baths wouldn't let us in during the day and said we had to go back at night and hire the baths as a group. Back at the hotel, the hose pipe was pressed into service again for us all to have showers instead.

Palmyra - Starting our tour of the ruins

Palmyra - Entertainment in the amphitheatre

Palmyra - Temple of Bel

We sat about drinking wine, talking and writing, till it was time to walk into town for our Syrian group meal. The meal was unspectacular, but we were served a large portion of chicken each. The wine and the early start proved too much for me so I left early, got a lift back to the hotel, and put up my camp bed under a palm tree.

6th October 1980: Palmyra - Damascus

I wasn't disturbed by those who got up before dawn to climb up to the castle and watch the sunrise. Instead, I got up at a much more civilised time and had a cup of coffee and cereal (there was no official breakfast service).

I set out with Mike to climb up the hill and visit the ruined 17th century Arab castle. It was already getting hot and the climb up was exhausting; we even had to do a bit of rock climbing to get in as the bridge over the moat had collapsed. Though the Director of Antiquities had described the castle as 'of no particular interest' it was fun to wander around its maze of rooms and look at the desert views. The ruins had plenty of good barrel-vaulted roofs, but there was no central courtyard as the hill continued up behind the curtain walls.

I sat on the highest tower to rest before taking a short route back down a scree slope without twisting my ankle. Lunch was early so we could be back on the road to Damascus soon after midday. We took a new metalled road southwest that wasn't shown on the maps, stopping on the way to look at a camel train passing us in the distance.

After we had joined the road to Baghdad the camel trains were replaced by coaches; we saw some of the desert buses that ran overland to Iraq. Because there were no border posts in the desert we had to pass through an Iraq customs post even though we had not left Syria. This triggered a lot of searching for passports but we had the right stamps and passed through.

Palmyra - The author in the castle (check out the sun tan!)

Palmyra - Funeral towers viewed from the castle

Palmyra - Temple of Bel   Palmyra – View from the castle

After stopping in a village to get supplies, we pressed on, arriving in Damascus after dark. The city roads were busy (we hadn't seen so much traffic since Istanbul) and the Syrians were terrible drivers. As usual, we couldn't find the campsite because we had entered the city on the 'wrong' road. We picked up a local to help us navigate, but he didn't know the way either! When we did locate the campsite, it was on the opposite side of the expressway and we had to do a U-turn on the busy road.

The campsite was a pleasant oasis from the city noise. It had lots of cold water and clean facilities, but there was no water in the swimming pool. I washed my dusty sleeping bag liner and jeans in a bowl pounding them with my feet, and in the process got my feet particularly clean. I felt better with clean hair, but the air was very dry.

Palmyra - Encounter Truck

Syria - A passing camel train in the desert

7th October 1980: Damascus

I was woken by mistake by Denis trying to rouse Dave(S) who was meant to be cooking; I found I had a cat sleeping on my feet! Apart from the cats and a horse grazing the grass, the camp was pretty empty; the only other campers were two Germans and an empty Hann Overland coach. I had time to get some more washing done before we all left in the truck for the centre of the city.

The truck parked near the Tourist Office so we could all collect city maps. Alex had lost a filling so she set off in search of a dentist, whilst I joined Ron, Henk and Helen(S) on a quest to find an optometrist as Ros had broken his spectacles.

I tried to get a new quartz face for my watch with no success. Then, after the obligatory stop at the Post Office, we wandered around the impressive souk. I left the others when they got sucked into a carpet shop. I had plenty of Syrian money but couldn't find anything I wanted to buy with it. Instead, after a long search, I found somewhere decent to eat. I ordered kebab, a minced meat 'scotch egg' and two types of curd, one thick and soupy and the other thin with mint and cucumber. It was probably my only real Syrian food. I liked the way they served the meal between two flatbreads; one kept the plate clean and soaked up juices, whilst the other stopped the food from getting cold.

Having exhausted the more obvious things to see in the old town, I walked to the National Museum; unfortunately, it was closed so I relaxed in the nearby gardens for a while. On my way back to the truck I bought some handcream and stocked up on Lomotil. The camp was very quiet that night so I went to bed early.

Damascus – Archway near the museum

Damascus - Campsite

8th October 1980: Damascus

It was a disturbed night with sleep frequently interrupted by the unwanted affection of cats. Nevertheless, I was up nice and early, ready to embark on an expedition with Denis and Karl. We planned to visit the village of Maaloula on the edge of the mountains north of Damascus. Outside the camp, a taxi picked us up and took us to the bus station for the princely sum of £20. It was quite a waste of money as the bus we caught retraced our route and passed the campsite on its way out of the city on the Homs road.

It was nearly an hour's ride to Maaloula, mostly along the expressway; and it was much cheaper than a taxi. We bought a drink in the village and then climbed up the hill to the Mar Sarkis convent high above the village. It was a Christian community that still spoke Aramaic, the language of Christ. The convent appeared to only have one monk who showed visitors around. The church dated from the 4th century with an original dome. The altar (287 – 385) had three niches for sacrifices (later banned). The interior was decorated with paintings, some over 400 years old. In all, it was well worth the visit.

Back down in the village, we boarded a bus back into the city, after first confirming if it could drop me at the campsite. It did, even though Denis and Keven continued on the bus to the depo. I did very little for the rest of the afternoon; it was entertaining to watch Dave and Mike trying to reconcile the books.

In the evening we had a small party to say farewell to Mike who was going to take an incoming group back to London. Sandra cooked a nice meal, a nutty salad wrapped up in a flatbread. Most of those who had bought Arab clothes in the bazaar dressed up for dinner. Dave's costume was by far the best. Amidst much joking we handed Mike a poster with all our pictures on it. I flaked out soon afterwards; I was exhausted by the dry desert heat.

Maaloula Village

9th October 1980: Damascus – Dubai

It was time now to tidy up the truck ready for the next group. Everything had to be taken out, the inside cleaned, and then things put back again in the correct place. We couldn't take bags of supplies with us to Pakistan, so we all secreted medical items and dried food in amongst our clothes. I had a last cold shower before we left for the airport mid-afternoon. We checked in our luggage as a group to avoid problems with the weight of our bags, many of which were way over the allowed 20kg. Our plane was a Syrian Airlines jumbo which took off just before 8 p.m. A standard hot chicken meal was served before we landed an hour later in Dubai. The plane had poor cabin pressurisation and each takeoff and landing were agony, leaving me temporarily deaf.

Damascus
– Our drivers doing the accounts

Maaloula
- The altar of Mar Sarkis Convent

PAKISTAN

It was a big surprise to me to find out that most of Pakistan was desert. I hadn't planned to visit the country and had done no reading in advance.

I also expected the country to be full of people like the Pakistani immigrants I had met at home. Instead, I found people who were neither 'Indian' nor 'European', a proud race, inquisitive, and above all helpful. Our first encounter with their curiosity in Sehwan was quite terrifying because we weren't aware we were objects of such interest. Subsequently, their fascination with us became part of our lives, and on many occasions could be turned to our advantage.

In the north of the country Pakistan had retained the atmosphere of the long-gone British Raj. This was partly due to the well-kept army buildings, but equally because of their pride in keeping things up. The cantonments of the major towns had survived virtually unaltered.

We had an excellent group meal in Pakistan, undoubtedly the best 'Indian' food that I had tasted.

10th October 1980: Dubai - Karachi

After a couple of hours layover, the plane took off for a 90-minute hop to Karachi. We were served the same meal as we had on the first leg, but it was now cold! I dozed till the landing which triggered pain in my ear again; I found out that others were suffering in the same way. As we exited the aircraft we felt the sticky heat of Pakistan, and it was the coldest part of the night!

Only one man was taking the fingerprints of foreigners from our flight, and a slow-moving queue soon formed. After I picked up my luggage I headed towards the 'green' channel, but an official sent me back. That confused me, so when Fred wandered along I tagged on to him and both went through the 'red' channel together. This time I was stopped by an official who said the two bottles of duty-free whisky I had couldn't be brought into the country. I was too tired to argue, so I opened both bottles, drank a bit, and then handed them over. In return, I got a handwritten receipt and resigned myself to a $12 loss. No one else got picked on in the same way so it was just my bad luck.

I changed some money and then pushed through the crowds of welcoming relatives swarming by the arrival gates. Outside the terminal building, it was bright daylight and early morning. It was easy to spot our new home, a blue 24-seater truck (SVC 339H) parked outside. We also had two new drivers, Tim and Pete; they had driven the truck down from Nepal.

Karachi - Camping on the beach

Our first campsite was just a local beach. The sun was getting hot, so I rigged up a flysheet as shade. The fine sand stuck to everything; I had to go for a swim, my first and only dip in the Arabian Sea. The water was warm, but it was also very sandy! By the time I was ready to use my shade, the wind had got up, turning the dunes into a mini-sandstorm. I took the flysheet down and put it up in a more sheltered spot further inland.

There was time for a bit of sleep catch-up before dinner, but then the drivers took the truck back to the airport so Tim could fly out. That took away our light so there was little to do other than go back to sleep again

11th October 1980: Karachi - Hyderabad

The heat and sun woke me in the morning even though my watch was running two hours slow. Breakfast was a lot more basic now we had low stocks of food in the truck. There was some friction with the Head Office; Dave had received a telex telling him to drive our truck back to Karachi from Delhi. He wasn't too pleased about this as he wanted to lead a rafting holiday and sent them a rude telex back! Another logistical challenge was that driver Pete had to stay with us to get the truck out of Pakistan as its entry was entered in his passport.

As we drove back into Karachi the temperature reached a humid 39°C; this was the first time I had experienced 100°F. We walked to the market area where a group of us decided to buy the local shirt and baggy trousers (shalwar). The light cotton fabric was much more suitable than jeans in the sticky heat. We bargained the price down to 125 rupees each for a bulk order.

On the way back to the truck I looked for a bank where I could change a travellers cheque; after buying the shalwar, I was now short on cash. A local pointed out the bank to us, but they wouldn't change cheques without a receipt. So I decided instead to change a precious $US 20 note. After a mound of paperwork had been filled in, and 30 minutes later, I walked out with my money. Back at the truck, I tried on my new local garb. It suited me and the trousers were indeed nice and cool.

The truck drove hard across the desert towards Hyderabad. The new sights on the road were decorated Pakistani trucks and camel carts. On the journey, Fredy's shirt, stuffed between the seats, caught fire; the result of a poorly disposed cigarette butt.

Karachi – The author in a shalwar

Karachi Market

When it was time to stop and set up camp we realised we had no water, and none was to be found despite being close to the Indus River. We stopped by an irrigation canal whose water was a health hazard, a breeding ground for mosquitos, and quite unsuitable for washing, let alone drinking. We put our beds out and then sat around waiting for Karl to conjure up a fresh meat curry. Werner helped out by making some water using a pump/filter unit he had in his 28kg rucksack.

12th October 1980: Hyderabad – Mohenjo Daro

The night was hot and sticky, so I slept in the open with just my sheet sleeping bag liner. Breakfast was served early, ostensibly to make good use of the cooler part of the day, but as we always stopped at dusk the reality was we ended up spending longer in the back of the truck.

Finding water was our number one priority having drunk the truck dry. We found a high-pressure hose on the outskirts of Sehwan which filled the tank in seconds. We then drove into the centre of the town to buy food, an expedition that took us down a dead-end street. It didn't take long before the truck was swarming with little kids having fun, it is fair to assume they had never seen a truckload of Europeans before. We had to launch a major counter-offensive directed at maintaining truck security; in other words, we had to chase them away. It was all good-natured (thank heavens) but the numbers were a bit frightening. As we turned the truck around and headed out we had to maintain a watch to stop the boys from turning on our water tap and wasting the precious water.

Lunch was enjoyed in a shady, if a bit muddy, layby near an irrigation canal. All the ditches had muddy Indus water and weren't attractive for us to swim in. But that didn't stop some local boys from turning up to watch us and have a splash in the canal. A passing car burst a tyre and pulled in next to us; we lent them our heavy-duty lorry jack.

Sehwan - Lunch by an irrigation canal

Mohenjo Daro - Water Buffalo

The view from the back of the truck was of flat flooded plains with rice being grown, water buffalo cooling in the ditches, and villages built on patches of higher ground. We got a bit lost in Badah and had to ask the way; when we stopped, a small boy jumped onto our trailer and wouldn't get off, so we took him for a ride and frightened him!

Mohenjo Daro - Paddy fields

The tourist office at Mohenjo Daro was closed and we couldn't camp in their compound as planned, instead, we took two rooms in the 'hotel' and slept on their lawns. After dark, a lot of wildlife started to fly around and there was fierce competition to sleep in the rooms. I found a quiet corner of the building and slept under the verandah. We used the shower so much that it flooded the corridor outside!

13th October 1980: Mohenjo Daro – Shikapur

After a good night's sleep, I was surprised to find that I had no new insect bites. Before breakfast, we had to unload everything off the truck so it could be deep cleaned. Then in the cool of the early morning, I set out to look around the ruins.

Mohenjo Daro is a city dating back to the Indus civilisation in about 1900 B.C. Built in red brick it pre-dates Roman urban design but has good streets, drains, and a residential area with high-walled buildings. It was a memorable place to visit, one of the few bonuses of the change of route to overfly Iran.

Mohenjo-Daro - View from Citadel towards main baths

It was getting hot by the time I returned to the truck for a late breakfast. One of the reasons the truck had to be cleaned was to evict some mice who had hopped on board back in Delhi. Dave chased Horace and three of his followers out the back. Then everything had to be put back in the truck.

I had a cold shower, changed into my local clothes, and then sat under the fan in one of the rooms writing letters.

Mohenjo Daro Private Bath Room

Mohenjo Daro - Main Baths

Meanwhile, the truck was infested not by mice, but by a party of schoolchildren on a visit to the ruins. The Topaz tour we had met in Goreme turned up as well, though with a different truck of course. I filled the truck tank, with plenty of help, from the mosque pump; it was a slow job as we only had saucepans; the 'new' truck had lost its hose en route. I put my kit bag padlock on the tank tap to discourage curious fingers until Dave had a chance to buy one.

Mohenjo Daro – Filling the tank using saucepans

With everything packed back in the truck, we headed into Larkana to do some shopping. The Topas crew followed us and parked nearby. Once again our presence attracted a large crowd, but we succeeded in diverting them to pester the Danish tourists instead. Also, as usual, we had trouble finding the correct road out of town due to the near-total lack of signposts.

As we passed through each village there was a very distinctive sweet-scented smell. Eventually, I traced it to the local brickworks burning water buffalo dung.

Our overnight camp that night was on a flat sandy pasture just after passing through Shikappur. There was a hut close by complete with a pump. We were soon found by the locals, one of whom could play two 'recorders' at once, with one as a drone. We all slept near the truck as natives were lurking in the shadows.

14th October 1980: Shikapur – Jampur

A heavy dew in the night settled on our open-air beds, and our bedding was quite wet by the morning. I put my towel over me to absorb the worst but still woke cold and damp. The damp sand stuck to our shoes making a mess as we packed up camp and leaving a mini-beach in the back of the truck. I had a unique combination breakfast, Porridge + Alpen + Milk + Honey + Jam; it didn't taste too bad! We didn't have any sugar on board as it was rationed in Pakistan and we had been unable to buy any, so we had to substitute honey or jam. Luckily shopping in Rajanpur that morning we managed to stock up on many other basics, and we had an abundance of bread because two people thought they had been tasked to buy some; no big matter because bread was cheap. We stopped outside the town for lunch to eat all the bread, and to hang out the sleeping bags to dry.

I had a long afternoon nap but woke in time to catch us passing through Jampur. Shortly afterwards we turned down a track into a dry paddy field for our overnight camp. We were able to save our tank water by finding a pump nearby. And once again, soon after finding the pump, the locals found us!

I was getting fed up with the dew and mosquitos so I put up a tent and fumigated it. After an unusually early dinner, we discussed the possibility of driving up to the top of the Khyber Pass. Then I headed off to bed, hopefully in the dry.

> *Along the way, we became wary of buying Pakistani Coke because the bottles were rusty around the neck, an outcome of being reused many times and being kept in iced water.*

15th October 1980: Jampur – Dera Ismail Khan

To save time we drove the truck to the pump in the morning to fill up the tank. Unfortunately, the cooking oil bottle tipped over in the truck whilst we were relocating which left a mess to be cleaned up before we could depart. Although our route continued to take us up the Indus Valley the topography was increasingly affected by runoff from the Sulaiman Mountains that were closing in on our left. The main road had degenerated to a single rack of asphalt with dirt verges on each side; overloaded trucks would approach us in the middle of the road unwilling to pull over for fear of toppling. There were also occasional missing bridges; they presumably had been swept away in the monsoon floods earlier in the year.

The Sulaiman Mountains at dusk

Dera Ghazi Kahn - Karl guarding the truck

Dera Ghazi Kahn - Old men

Dera Ghazi Kahn - Street scene

Shopping in Dera Ghazi Khan was relatively uneventful as most of the population was at school or work; the presence of a policeman near our truck probably discouraged a crowd from forming. Again we bought too much bread, as we adjusted to how cheap it was.

After an unmemorable lunch stop and featureless afternoon drive, we pulled into an area of baked mud, that might once have been a field, to set up camp. We soon found a pump within walking distance.

Our campsite was teeming with wildlife. After dinner, I saw a mouse in the truck confirming that we still had a castaway rodent on board; the ground was swarming with ants, and a snake was spotted nearby.

After dinner, Thomas and Ron had a long argument in German with Werner, apparently about religion. They asserted that Werner was quite a religious fanatic, believing that the Bible says that man's place is to be close to God whilst women do earthly things.

16th October 1980: Dera Ismail Khan – Bunda

A centipede joined the wildlife collection, at 4 a.m., inside my sleeping bag. The good news was that the ants didn't get up as early as we did; on the other hand, we were plagued with flies at breakfast!

Dera Ismail Khan was a large town, but the main streets were too narrow for the truck. We parked in the bus depo and walked into the old town to do our food shopping. The shops were very primitive; we had left supermarkets far behind. In town, we saw our first Afghan refugees. When I got back to the truck I found it inundated with locals; I got quite angry with Colin who was supposed to be on guard duty. He was using the opportunity to try and sell a bottle of whisky. Karl got lost in the town, walked out on the wrong road, and then took nearly an hour to get back to the truck. As a result, we didn't bother getting water before lunch and pressed on towards Bannu.

The search for a lunch spot took us down a track that wound precariously between flooded paddy fields. When the track ended at a village we stopped by a palm plantation and set the tables for lunch. We were soon surrounded by two-thirds of the village population (the males and children); we were certainly the first tourist coach to come their way.

We were now in Pathan country, a fairer race and visibly proud. I had an interesting conversation with a man from the village who worked in Peshawar and who had a fair grasp of English. Our water ran out during the meal so afterwards we drove into the village and filled up at their pump.

> *Dave(S) had a close shave when he walked out onto a rear flap on the trailer that had been left unfastened after removing tent poles. He fell and it wasn't exactly a soft landing on the hard ground. Without access to a hospital, this could easily have turned serious.*

Bannu - Lunch in a palm plantation

In Bannu, a boy pushed his friend, who was on a bike, into the truck. We had to stop whilst our nurses patched up the graze on his face. He looked pretty shocked; I'm not sure if that was because of the accident or the first aid he received from two white women. Thankfully the crowd knew it wasn't our fault, we were very lucky things didn't turn nasty.

As usual, we got lost leaving town but found the right road by trial and error; with all the practice we got, we were becoming proficient at getting "un-lost". We left the fertile valley and started climbing into the mountains with impressive red and grey sandstone cliffs. Our camp for the night was on a dry river bed and was possibly the most scenic stop on the entire trip.

During the night we were visited by two Pathans with guns who seemed to be guarding the nearby road. They left early in the evening and we somehow got the impression they were working with or were the police.

Bannu - The wrong road to Kohat

Bunda – Our campsite in the morning

Bunda – Our campsite

17th October 1980: Bunda – Peshawar

A late breakfast was organised to give people a chance to go for an early morning walk and admire the stunning scenery. I packed my flysheet and then started to climb up the side of the valley. I got high enough to take aerial shots of the truck. Cornflakes and copious quantities of white bread were on offer for breakfast.

The two highlights of the short trip to Peshawar were the ascent to the Kohat Pass and the village of Darra Adam Khel where almost every house and shop was a gun factory.

Peshawar - Dean's Hotel

Our base in Peshawar was the Dean's Hotel. Among its distinguished guests in the past were Rudyard Kipling, Sir Winston Churchill, Quaid-e-Azam, and King Nadir Shah of Afghanistan (in 1929). But in 1980 it was a shadow of its former colonial glory. We pitched our tents on the hotel lawns and then thought about lunch. Those who thought of their stomachs fastest (myself included) got into the dining room first and ordered mutton curry (everything else on the menu was not available). We were served promptly; those who wandered in later got appalling service.

After the meal, I walked from the British Cantonment (where the hotel was located) into the Old City and met up with Henk and Christian on the way. I had some curry powder mixed for my next cooking turn and bought some oven-fresh nan to eat on the way back.

Peshawar – The old city

After dinner, I felt quite bloated, possibly because I wasn't used to eating so much food! The drivers had gone off with the truck keys so I wasn't able to do my duty and fill up the tank. Instead, I chatted to a British student who had come out to do some research on the Pathans. In a strange coincidence, he had arrived in Karachi on the same flight as we had been on.

The Dean's Hotel had been quite smart in its day, and the rooms had aircon and running water. Staying there gave one a flashback to the days of the Raj, with the old architecture and the staff wearing their traditional uniforms. I handed a bundle of washing in; it came back minus one belt and two key holders, but on the other hand, it only cost 25 rupees to get things thoroughly clean for once.

18th October 1980: Peshawar

I had bad cramps in the night but they eased after I took the long walk in the dark from my tent to the room we had rented for a shared bathroom. In the morning I filled some jerry cans; a frail old hotel servant insisted on carrying them for me.

We set off on an expedition to the Khyber Pass leaving the trailer and a few of our group behind. As we were leaving Peshawar we sped past an informal checkpoint but decided to turn around and go back to pay the 'protection money' being charged by the Pathans. No one wanted to find out what happened to those who didn't pay. There were sprawling Afghan refugee camps on each side of the road.

Khyber Pass - Pathan checkpoint

We travelled for the first time with half of the truck roof rolled back; this gave us an excellent view of the mountains. The Khyber Pass consisted of an initial twisting ascent, then a flatter run through Landi Kotal, followed by a steep descent to the Afghanistan border controls at Torkham. The steep sections were made more interesting by a railway line that zig-zagged its way up beside us. The actual pass and land border was littered with fortifications, from small forts to large army barracks.

On the trip out my cramps returned; by the time we reached Torkham the bad runs had restarted; I was very ill again. Painkillers helped me survive the journey back and then I crashed out on a bed in our hotel room. I was feverish all afternoon and evening and slept in the room overnight to be close to the toilet.

Peshawar - Afghan Refugee Camp

Khyber Pass - Climbing to Landi Kotal

Khyber Pass – The descent to Torkam and Afghanistan

19th October 1980: Peshawar - Islamabad

Helped by the right medicines I was feeling better in the morning though still weak and groggy. I struck my unused tent which was wet with dew, then relaxed till we set off.

We left the mountains behind and now followed the Grand Trunk Road through the fertile plains of the upper Indus valley. There was an interesting crossing over the Indus at Attock on a long single-track girder bridge shared with the railway.

We had an unscheduled stop near Islamabad for Werner who had an urgent appointment in the bushes, but unfortunately for Werner, we stopped a few seconds too late. We extended the stop to make it our lunch break and give him time to clean up.

In Islamabad, the capital of Pakistan, we drove to the central Tourism Campsite without getting lost! The camp appeared to be the home of groupies and other persons *non-gratia* waiting for paperwork to come through. The facilities were disgusting with the toilets blocked and people going in the bushes instead. Across the road was the 'city centre' but it had more of the appearance of a suburban shopping centre. For a new architect-designed city Islamabad was depressing and made Milton Keynes feel like a buzzing metropolis in comparison.

Our diversion to Islamabad was not to enjoy the tourist sites but rather to call in at the Indian Embassy to get Karl, Christian and Jos Indian visas. But the day after we arrived was the major Muslim festival of Eid al-Adha; all businesses would be closed. Eid al-Adha was when sacrifices of decorated sheep or goats were made, and the devout would make their pilgrimage to Mecca.

Attock – The Grand Trunk Road

Attock Fort and the Indus River

Islamabad – An unscheduled lunch stop outside the city

We found the Islamabad Hotel a couple of blocks from the camp, but it had no bar. Then a few of us hired a taxi and headed across town to the Holiday Inn. Imagine our surprise when we entered the posh foyer and found our drivers there, dressed in vests and scruffy jeans. The Holiday Inn couldn't serve alcohol to non-residents so we settled for a smart meal (sitting at a table with chairs) and then lounged around writing postcards.

20th October 1980: Islamabad – Lalamusa

There was no peace in the morning with the mosques calling the faithful to prayer at dawn. The campsite was so unhealthy we decided that we couldn't wait there till the Embassy re-opened. So we invoked Plan B which was to leave the visa-less behind and to all meet up again in Lahore.

After lunch, we set out leaving the lads in Rawalpindi. At first, the roadside scenery was familiar but then as we neared Jhlem there was a dramatic change to deeply eroded valleys. We stopped for fuel and drinks on the outskirts of the town, and then for water a bit further on near the cantonment. The water in Islamabad had been heavily chlorinated so it was good to go back to tea with my lighter dosing. For those who didn't like the water the choice for bottled drinks was generally Coke, Fanta (orange) or Tops (mango).

Jhelum - Scenery

We turned off the road as usual at the end of the day but in such a heavily cultivated area it was hard to find a patch of flat land we could use. We were lucky to find a small wooded area which was also close to a good concrete pump.

Our incendiary squad built a bonfire but the locals came and told us to put it out. Diner was curry which I should have skipped, but I didn't. I had a long talk with Werner (in English) before going to bed; I felt I was more than a match for his half-baked ideas.

21st October 1980: Lalamusa – Lahore

I was woken at dawn by the sound of heavy lorries; our camp was being invaded by a regiment of soldiers who seemed to have a prior claim to the area. They wanted to set camp on top of us so we decided that a quick getaway would be diplomatic. Their presence explained the trackmarks we had noticed the night before. Surrounded by vehicles, armed soldiers and military police we missed out on breakfast, which was just as well because we had no milk or bread.

The next major town on our way was Gujat; we bought supplies there and stopped shortly afterwards to have brunch by the side of the road. Then it was a quick trip down the Grand Trunk Road to Lahore, arriving early in the afternoon. Lahore was a big city, so of course we got lost trying to find the campsite.

The Zenobis Hotel in the Gulberg district had long since closed down (my guidebook advised travellers to avoid it), but Encounter still camped in the little garden at the rear. It was oppressively hot and humid so putting the tents up was a slow chore. Once again we were to be disappointed; the promised hot showers turned out to be just a warm dribble. Another blitz on the truck with conscripted 'volunteers' resulted in the last(?) mouse being evicted. As a bonus, my metal comb which I had given up as lost turned up between the seats in the truck tidyout.

I took a walk into the small circle of shops that made up Gulberg Market. Many businesses were still closed but the wide selection of goods potentially available was impressive. I stocked up on cakes, biscuits, soap and washing powder.

The evening meal was the third chilli-hot dish in a row; the curry powder I bought was being put to good use. This was good because I had missed out on using my spices when I was taken ill in Peshawar.

Anna shared my tent because there was heavy dew and she didn't have a flysheet. Karl and the others arrived quietly in the night complete with their Indian visas.

22nd October 1980: Lahore

Breakfast at 7:15 was a compromise, between having it at 7 or 7:30. I couldn't find anyone who wanted to share a taxi with me, and as I found looking around towns with others annoyingly slow, I took a scooter taxi on my own to the city centre. Gulberg was some way out and the metered journey cost me 10 rupees. There was some confusion telling the driver where I wanted to go, but I ended up, just where I wanted to be, at the entrance to the bazaar. The shops were opening for the day as I navigated to the old walled town. From there it was still a long walk to reach the Fort and the Badshahi Mosque.

Lahore - Courtyard of Badshahi Mosque

I had a cold drink and then tackled the mosque. It was billed as the biggest in the world but I was unimpressed as it achieved this status by having a massive courtyard that made the buildings seem insignificant. One entire wall was modern after the British Army made some modifications to the original. The highlight for me was being able to climb to the top of one of the minarets for just two rupees; there was a good view over the city from the top.

Retracing my steps back to the Mall I searched without success for a restaurant recommended in my guidebook. I wandered past the impressive British-built courthouse and had to stand to one side as someone important drove past in an escorted cavalcade. In the end, I settled for a tasty lamb dish (not too spicey) washed down with tea in a restaurant near the museum. As I was paying the bill two locals sat down at my table and we had a chat (in English) exploring the problems faced by both Pakistan and England.

Despite assurances to the contrary the museum wasn't going to open in the afternoon. The Jinnah Gardens were also closed, either because of the 'Festival of Islamic Art', or perhaps because the prime minister was due to hold a press conference there, or both. Admitting defeat I grabbed a taxi and headed back to camp.

Lahore – Boys outside the Badshahi Mosque

Lahore - View over castle and city looking east from the minaret

That evening we had our Pakistan group meal. Pete had found a good restaurant about ½ mile away on a previous visit he had made to the city. It was within walking distance, but I took a taxi there as I had done plenty of walking earlier in the day. It was an open-air restaurant; we had a large table illuminated by candles. The food was excellent, tasting as good if not better than Indian food in England. We had meat and fish curries in a Punjabi/Mogul style together with curd followed by lassi. I walked back to camp very satisfied, particularly as many of our party weren't into curry and left all the more food for me!

INDIA

The India that I saw split into three distinct areas, Kashmir, the Punjab, and Delhi.

Kashmir, a picturesque valley with a character of its own was spoilt for me on three counts. Firstly, there was open exploitation of tourists and unceasing pressure to buy. Secondly, the weather was past its best as it headed into winter. Finally, the physical discomfort caused by the houseboat's primitive hygiene tarnished its reputation.

The Punjab by contrast was characterless; apart from the tourist highlights, it was best described as a rural sprawl. The villages were drab and the people would gaze and beg but rarely make contact. Driving through a Punjabi town was like swimming through a human and animal sea. Whereas the Pakistanis would react to our presence, the Indians seemed to be too preoccupied with what they were doing to notice us.

After Kashmir and the Punjab, Delhi was refreshing for its lack of a true Indian atmosphere. The European influence and different attitudes of the educated city inhabitants allowed one to relax and enjoy sightseeing.

If one wanted a contrast then seeing Varanasi after Delhi was as good as they come in India. I would describe Varanasi as an experience; a term which I suppose could be applied to all of India apart from Delhi. The squalor of the old town, the poverty and overcrowding, combined with the religious fervour of the pilgrims was as uncomfortable as the Western values and standards of Delhi were reassuring.
To visit just the Taj and Delhi would have been to miss the complexity and contradictions that define what India is truly like.

23rd October 1980: Lahore - Amritsar

To get a good start crossing the contentious land border between India and Pakistan we started early. As usual, we got lost trying to leave the city; no credit to me as I was in the front trying to map read! Fuel in India was more expensive than in Pakistan but we were unable to fill up before reaching the border which was only just outside the town.

On the Pakistani side, there was a hassle with immigration who spotted that Dave's passenger list had Jos's passport number wrong. Then there was quite a wide no man's land between the two border controls. Lorries were not allowed to cross the border and all their cargo had to be carried across by hand. The porters were colour-coded to indicate which side they came from, and presumably where they had to return to at the end of the day.

Getting into India was slow, it took four hours in all, but there were smiles from the officials all the way. The India Tourist Board had a café where we were able to drink excellent coffee whilst we waited.

Amritsar is very close to the border, so it didn't take long to reach our campsite located within the grounds of the Youth Hostel. The hostel advertised hot showers, but once again they didn't materialise. We celebrated the end of Pakistani prohibition with a beer!

It was an easy rickshaw ride into the centre of town and my first stop was the Post Office to post two letters home. 'Rick', my driver, found the change I needed to buy stamps and then told a man behind the counter to frank them (to avoid them being on-sold). The next stop was the market where I wanted to stock up on spices. I relied too much on my driver/interpreter to get a good bargain and ended up paying way too much; though I did get a cup of tea and an incense stick thrown in!

After the evening meal, we all set off to see the Golden Temple by moon/flood light. We all took bicycle rickshaws, three to each one, and once again I was pedalled by 'Rick'. The rickshaws were goaded into a hair-rasing race on the way to the temple which left the drivers exhausted. There was a full moon that night, and we spent nearly two hours in the temple precincts; it lived up to expectations. The view of the central shrine across the lake was particularly memorable, as were the fine inlaid marble floors.

I didn't bring my camera with me which was frustrating because Rick had put a turban on me that he said suited me. Regardless of whether that was a sales pitch or not, I did find it easy the blend in with the worshipers. I was able to watch the end-of-day service; which consisted of unwrapping the book, reading the book, wrapping the book, and then carrying it away from the temple.

> The rickshaw was a poor transport bargain in Amritsar because all passengers had to get out and walk across the bridge to get into town.

'Rick' then took us to an ice cream shop where we ordered cones, including one for Rick, but unfortunately, the waiter gave it to the wrong guy! On our way back to camp we spotted an EO truck in another hotel so we went to investigate. It turned out to be Tim, whom we had last seen in Karachi, now driving an empty truck up to Kashmir. We had a chat with him and helped him to unhitch his trailer. It was close to midnight when we got back to camp, with Colin pedalling to give Rick a break!

24th October 1980: Amritsar – Domel

Although Tim had mentioned that he might drop in for breakfast (and we had not told Dave to keep it a surprise) in the end he didn't appear. We had a fast exit from the city through the morning mists heading towards Jammu. On the state border, there was a Tourist Commission milk bar that served delicious safe chocolate milk. While we were at the border Amanda and I did some food shopping in the village; I was standing in for Colin who had taken over my cooking detail when I was sick in Peshawar.

After Jammu, where we stopped briefly to raid an alcohol shop, we turned into the hills heading for a long-established Encounter Overland camping spot; a rare patch of flat land by the side of the river. Before needing to cook dinner I had a quick dip; the river was not cold but flowing too fast to swim in. With Amanda's help, we put together a spiced egg and tomato dish with an aubergine curry, and banana fritters as a dessert; it was a good meal!

Amritsar - Early morning street scene

Domel – Our riverside camp

25th October 1980: Domel – Banihal

I was on cooking duty, so that meant no lie-in for me in the morning. It was the cook's duty to wake everyone else; I did it with a saucepan and wooden spoon! Having put the porridge to soak the previous night there wasn't too much cooking to do.

Soon after setting out, we stopped Dave to tell him about a warm smell in the back; but we forgot to tell him about the regular knocking noise. After a few more miles a rim fell completely off a rear flat tyre (there were double tyres at the back). As we had to pull over to change the wheel, we brewed our morning tea and coffee.

Udhampur - Competition for the main road to Kashmir

In Chenini, a town clinging to a steep hillside around the road, we ordered sixty chapatis from a very happy roadside vendor; we had to sit and wait while they were freshly cooked. Then it was a slow grind up to Patnitop and the first pass at over 9,000ft.

Chenini

Chenini - Cooking chapatis for lunch

After a leisurely high-altitude lunch the truck briefly made good progress on the down-hill run until we joined a traffic jam trying to enter Batole; this was the first of many delays on the busy narrow mountain road. All the way our progress was hindered by the number of domestic animals being herded along the road. When a sacred cow decided to have a rest in the middle of the road it couldn't be disturbed and a protective barrier of stones was erected around it!

The road had dropped to 2,300ft when we crossed the Chenab River and started a more gentle climb up a side valley. It was well after dark when we wound our way into the tourist bungalow at Banihal. A decision was made to have our meal in the bungalow's dining room later in the evening giving us time first for a quick visit to the town. The main attraction was the 'Roxy' bar which even had English pint beer glasses! After weeks off alcohol in Syria and Pakistan, we were suitably plastered by the time we staggered back to the bungalow for our vegetarian meal.

One feature of the roads in Kashmir was the roadside quotes that some officials with a shocking sense of humour had placed on each corner.

BETTER BE LATE THAN THE LATE!
NO HURRY – NO WORRY!
DO NOT BE RASH AND END IN A CRASH!
KEEP YOUR NERVES ON THE SHARP CURVES!
BETTER BE LATE THAN DEAD ON TIME!
DRIVE WITH YOUR NERVES CALM – AND SEE THE VALLEYS CHARM.
SLEEPING WHILE DRIVING PROHIBITED!

Patnitop – Lunch stop

Banihal – A cafe and grocer

Banihal – The author and truck on approach to the tunnel

Banihal - Climbing up to the tunnel

26th October 1980: Banihal - Srinagar

It was only a short, but steep, climb up to the second pass and the tunnel through to Kashmir. Christian and Jos had set out early to walk straight up the hill and had even managed to hitch a lift through the tunnel before we caught up with them.

We stopped to admire the view over the broad Kashmir valley; it was much cooler on the north side of the mountains and the scenery was very different with wooden houses, saffron fields and lower mountain peaks.

An easy run took us down to Srinagar. The truck parked by the lake whilst the group was divided up and allocated to houseboats. I was allocated to the three-bedroom 'Chicago' with six others. A houseboat boy paddled us out across the lake in a shikara. We were somewhat stunned by the deluxe accommodation; we were also somewhat isolated from the group of interconnected Montreal houseboats where everyone else was staying.

Srinagar - Houseboats on Lake Dal

Chicago was a new boat built in the traditional style moored on an artificial island in the shallow lake; it didn't need a separate kitchen boat (to manage the risk of fire) as its kitchen was on dry land. We had our own shikara with all its trips paid for by Encounter.

Diary Extract: Sketch plan of Houseboat Chicago

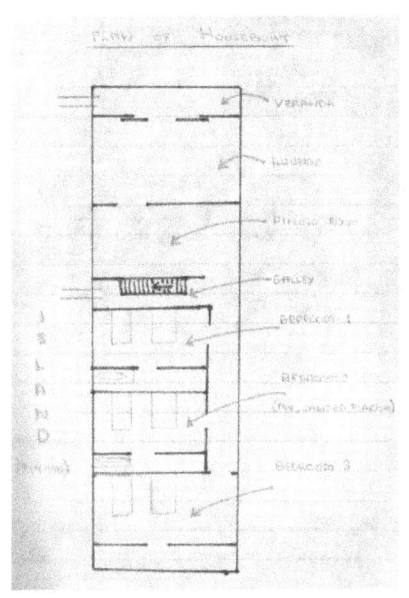

We soon discovered that the Montreal houseboats weren't up to the same standard as ours, and we rejected an offer to move in with the others halfway through our stay.

The first and obvious drawback to living in luxury on the lake was the quality of the water; water for washing and cooking was drawn from the lake and eventually returned by the houseboat guests through the toilet back into the lake. Our houseboy cooked fried egg and toast for lunch, and then we took our shikarra over to the Montreal group of boats to have a planning meeting and to pick up our mail; I had four letters from home, all of them somewhat dated in their news because we were running behind schedule.

Srinagar - Houseboat Chicago

Srinagar - Inside our houseboat

Srinagar - Our shikara man

The evening meal cooked on our houseboat was ever-so British; lamb chops, cabbage and mashed potatoes. The lighting in the living room was too weak for reading or writing so we played cards, a Swiss game which I didn't know.

27th October 1980: Srinagar (tour)

We had requested breakfast at 8 but our sleepy-eyed houseboy told us that it would not be ready till 9, The Swiss were annoyed as we were now accustomed to getting up at the crack of dawn; it appeared that you could choose whatever time you wanted breakfast on a houseboat as long as it was 9 o'clock!

We took a whistle-stop tour of Srinagar which had the virtue of being free. On the tour, we visited the main Friday Mosque which was in an unusual Persian style with pagodas. Then the tour ended in the inevitable carpet showroom. The workers in the carpet-wearing shops that we passed all appeared to be children; apparently, the youngest earned just 6 rupees a day and it took two of them a year to make a 6 ft x 4 ft rug. One manager proudly told us that his carpets were very cheap because he employed local orphans!

Diary Extract: Sketch map of houseboat location

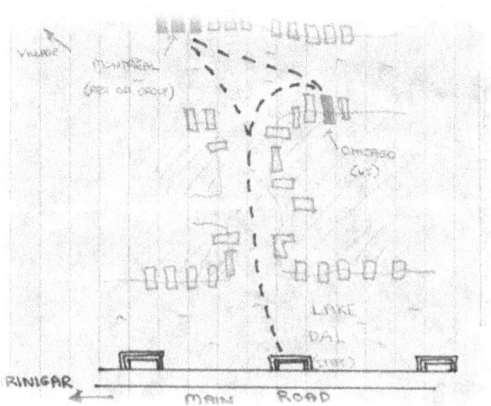

I had seen quite enough carpets and didn't want to buy one, so Martin and I wandered off outside. It wasn't a hot day like those we had become accustomed to in the Punjab and the sun was hazy; it was a much more pleasant temperature to go for a walk. Our wandering took us in search of a branch of the State Bank of India. The directions we received from passers-by resulted in our getting completely lost. It was only after we gave up and started walking back that we found the bank hidden up a side alley. I changed a twenty-pound note but had to wait whilst the teller went off in search of change. A taxi took us back to the lake, and as our shikara wasn't waiting at the steps we paid a boy to row us home.

Lunch on the houseboat was Indian-style, a mild vegetable curry, much more to my taste

In the afternoon the houseboy organised a trip around the village (as opposed to the town of Srinagar which is on dry land). Only Werner and I went; we saw water gardens and the old buildings fronting the canals. It soon became obvious that the houseboy's main interest was taking us to showrooms. I bought a walnut bowl in one shop (to be shipped back to England) and thus did what was expected of 'rich' European tourists.

After dinner, Martin, Werner and I were enticed to the shore by a promise of some Tibetan music. I was annoyed to find that this was just another way to get us into a shop. Werner broke the ice by breaking into one of his absurd modern dance routines. I learned in just one day that 'Kashmiri' was synonymous with 'Salesman'. Even boating on the lake was a sales opportunity; floating shops in shikaras chased after the tourists plying goods like painted paper-mache pots. The only vendor that I encouraged was the 'macaroon man', a floating sweet salesman. Other than that I resolved not to buy anything more in Kashmir.

Lake Dal was not the wide-open expanse of water that I was expecting but rather more like a swamp with shallow waters and reclaimed islands. Because there was little current small boats had no problems with mooring or paddling. The water was not crystal clear but at least it didn't smell.

Our houseboy showing us around the village

Srinagar –River houseboats

28th October 1980: Srinagar (Lake Dal)

We chose to have our breakfast at the diplomatically correct time of 9 a.m. We also elected to have fresh bread rather than toast as the latter had to be cooked laboriously one slice at a time over embers, and would inevitably arrive at the table stone cold.

Mid-morning the group set out on an organised tour of the lake by shikara. When we set out it was chaotic with sales boats nudging up to both sides of our shikara. But when we rendezvoused with boats from the other houseboats things improved.

Srinagar - Paddling across Lake Dal

One evening we hosted afternoon tea for Christian and Anna on our boat. They were surprised to find out how much cheaper beer was on Chicago compared to the Montreal boats.

We passed under a low bridge into the northern part of the lake and headed at speed to the Nishat Garden with three people rowing. The 17th century Moghal Shalimar gardens were pleasant but not at their best without the roses flowering. After a very uninspiring picnic lunch, it clouded over and we wound our way back to the houseboats through the floating gardens.

It was a bit chilly in the evening but some of the Swiss grumbled to Dave and that resulted in a stove appearing in the boat to warm up the living room.

I tried to tune into the BBC World Service news at 5:30 p.m. but that was the time when all the houseboats turned their lights on and the supply voltage dropped so much that the valve radio stopped working.

There was a bath in our bathroom and so I was able to enjoy the luxury of soaking in about an inch of warm water. Dinner was duck, and once again I lost playing cards with the Swiss to their rules. Dave came round in the evening to brief us on plans for the next day.

29th October 1980: Srinagar (Gulmarg)

I was sick during the night and I had little tolerance for the constant talking between Martin and Sandra in my room. How I got myself trapped on a boat with four grumpy Swiss and two cranky lovers escaped logic. Four of us got up for an early breakfast (it happened because Dave requested it) but only Werner and I made it to dry land to join the truck for an excursion to Gulmarg (8600 ft); a town with the world's highest 18-hole green golf course.

Srinagar - On the road up to Gulmarg

When we arrived the group went pony trekking, but I was too sick for that. I found a quiet viewpoint and rested in the warm sunshine. I was so ill I just fell asleep wrapped up in a scarf and parka. Two soldiers who were patrolling nearby came and woke me up and hung around until I took their pictures. I returned to the truck mid-afternoon but had to wait another 1½ hours for the last of the mountain walkers to return.

Gulmarg - Two soldiers I met on the golf course

By now I was not the only person sick in the back of the truck. The poor hygiene in the houseboats affected most of the group; even Dave had succumbed. We drove straight back stopping only to look at a family of baboons in the woods.

·····

Our houseboy was quite open about expecting a tip at the end of our stay. His mantra of 'If you're happy then I'm happy' became quite tiresome.

·····

Srinagar - Drying saffron on a houseboat

30th October 1980: Srinagar

The colonial houseboats were complemented by a day of dismal English weather. Breakfast was at the 'normal' time despite a request from the Swiss to have it earlier! After the abuse the Swiss had given the houseboy the previous night about the quality of food and meal times I wasn't surprised he ignored their request.

When we arrived in Srinagar I had employed a tailor to make me a shirt out of blue silk fabric. Two days later he returned the shirt I had lent him as a pattern; I also received back the small change from the postage for my woodcarving. Whilst the salesmen might be persistent they also appeared to be honest.

With rain showers all day and low clouds there wasn't much to do but sit inside in the warm catching up on letter writing and my diary. Later in the afternoon, I went on a social visit to the Montreal houseboats then returned in a power cut to have an Indian dinner of spiced meat, vegetables, rice and dahl. I didn't think the meal was very exciting but they were presumably toning down their cuisine to suit the Swiss.

I relented and bought some Indian brandy from a floating salesman. It cost 35 rupees for a half bottle and was surprisingly good, particularly when mixed with coke.

31st October 1980: Srinagar (Halloween)

The rain blew over in the night and we woke to a much better day though it was still overcast. After breakfast, my tailor returned with the silk shirt completed but we sent him back to fix up some poor fitting on the shoulders. Then the man I had bought the wooden bowl from visited the houseboat and I accompanied him to the Foreign Post Office. There, in an upstairs room, I had to post the parcel thus apparently avoiding some Indian red tape about exports. There was an elaborate ritual involving the filling in of triplicate forms and sewing up the parcel in cloth. In the end, the postage cost more than the shop had calculated so I had to pay the difference.

Srinagar - Lake and village viewed from Shankaracharya Hill

When I left the Post Office I found the path up to the Shankaracharya Temple which overlooked the town. I raced to the top for a panoramic view of the city and lake; then found a path down on the lake side of the hill which took me to where the shikara was waiting.

Srinagar - Halloween costumes

A Halloween party was planned for the evening and there was some confusion as to where we would be having dinner. Since the phone on our boat had "broken down" and coincidently the shikara man was off duty, I had to row myself over to Montreal to find out what was going on. With one paddle at the rear, my course was somewhat zig-zaged. Dave decreed that all should eat on Montreal, news that I relayed back to the Swiss faction after paddling back in a less drunkard style. I read my guidebook and listened to the BBC for the rest of the afternoon.

At seven, all the fit and healthy members from our boat set out to Montreal to eat, but when the Swiss found out that the food wasn't ready as promised they stormed back in a huff. It was a fancy dress party but the best I could do was to wear my Pakistani togs with my sleeping bag liner as a turban. We had a fireworks display that broke all the safety rules, followed by punch served with a cold buffet. Someone had carved a nice pumpkin lamp, and directed by Dave(S), we played a particularly messy game that involved eating honey-coated cookies off a string, blindfolded.

Alex was made up as a particularly sick-looking old lady and Jos was a really good punk. The punch was potent and it was nearly midnight when we realised we ought to go back to our houseboat. By then, understandably, the shikara man had gone to sleep so Martin took the oar and propelled us back in a classic beginner's zigzag. It appeared that the clue to linear progress was to remove the paddle with a twist that corrected the course.

Srinagar - Halloween firework display

1st November 1980: Srinagar – Banihal

Back to the old routine of getting up and packing so we could hit the road early; there was no time to nurse a hangover! The whining of the houseboy about needing warm socks reached such an intensity that I was direct in reply and told him just what I thought of his continuous pestering. I gave the boss, Nabbi, a small tip which appeared to upset him; I guess he had us lined up for a big payout. The houseboy I liked was ill in bed so I couldn't place the tips where they rightly belonged, and I had no trust that Nabbi would distribute tips fairly. I gave the shikara man a small tip in a separate transaction.

Srinagar - Saffron fields

Back on dry land, it was nice to sit in the sunshine whilst the truck was sorted out; I still wasn't feeling well. When we stopped for lunch at a popular viewpoint I had trouble finding a secluded toilet spot. Then a short climb to the tunnel (a secret installation that one couldn't take pictures of) and down a short way brought us back to the tourist bungalow at Bandihal.

I put up a camp bed in the room we had hired, close to the bathroom and let the sickness pass. Werner was also on the sick list with me in the room.

Srinagar - Kashmir valley from the north end of the tunnel

2nd November 1980: Banihal - Domel

It was a wet cold mountain night but that didn't worry those of us who were sleeping inside. I felt a lot better, helped no doubt by the Lomitil. Our onward journey was punctuated by frequent toilet stops so progress was slow. We made it over the pass at Patnitop but the truck developed problems so we abandoned plans to get past Jammu that night. Instead, we returned to the campsite we had used on the way into Kashmir, by the river near Domel.

I had the difficult job of filling the water tank with river water in my weakened state; I enlisted some reluctant assistants. Meanwhile, Karl and Dave were busy underneath the truck replacing an oil seal on the main drive shaft.

3rd November 1980: Domel - Jullundur

Retracing our route took us back through Jammu; the mountain scenery was now improved by the dusting of snow that had fallen on the peaks in the past few days.

Jammu – Monkey spotting

We stopped to photograph some Rhesus monkeys but then someone jumped off the back of the truck and frightened them all away. Another stop was to take pictures of vultures by the roadside that we had noticed when passing through Jammu on our way up to Kasmir.

We gave a lift to two schoolboys on their way to school; their arithmetic homework was done on wooden slabs. We gave them each a biscuit which they clasped as if it was their last meal. Our trip into and out of Kashmir was completed with another visit to the Pathanker Milk Bar.

Running short of time, lunch had to be prepared and eaten in the back of the truck on the move, a messy business. But even with a good run on flat roads we only just got past Jullunder by dusk. Our camp for the night was by a ruined Hindu shrine.

Jos cooked beans for the evening meal, but far too many. Whilst we were sitting around eating, a tree snake was spotted on a branch over our heads. I zipped up my tent well that night and slept nurturing a still tender stomach.

Jullunder - Camp by a shrine

4th November 1980: Jullundur - Kamal

That night I fell asleep to the sound of trains passing by hawled by smart black steam engines. And in another first, we spotted an Indian elephant on the outskirts of Ludhiana. All the villages in the Punjab seemed the same, a kind of rural suburbia; it didn't do much to stop us from dozing –off in the back.

Navigating in Ludhiana was a challenge, but after getting lost in the centre and then working back out we found the hospital where Helen(S) was going to do six months of training. We took our group photo in the hospital car park; then it took over an hour to say "goodbye". As a result, we ditched whatever slim chance we previously had of reaching Delhi that evening.

Khanna - Street scene

Punjab - Steam train

Ludhiana - group picture (taken by the author)

With stops on the way for shopping, water and lunch and with hard driving in between we got just past Karnal before sunset. We had a terrible campsite there; it was on a small farm, perched up on a track. The locals were initially helpful but later in the evening, their curiosity became a provocation as they started looking into our tents. We went to bed early and so narrowly avoided war breaking out! I spent the night in the back of the truck and, surprisingly, had a good night's sleep.

5th November 1980: Karnal – Delhi

I woke feeling 100% for the first time in weeks so was able to enjoy a fairly typical truck breakfast; porridge, cornflakes, tomatoes, bread, jams, tea and coffee. We had parked in the dark with the truck straddling a small irrigation canal. Even by daylight, people forgot it was there, putting their feet in the mud, or in Ursula's case, her bottom.

The drive into Delhi took a very uneventful three hours. The view from the back was of a few factories, then a few houses, then a few fields, the visual monotony of the Punjab. In Delhi, we quickly got lost (perhaps I should have just recorded when we didn't get lost in towns) and we had to hire a motor scooter to show us the way to the central tourist camp. We collected our mail from the campsite office, though some had been badly tampered with because of being put in a public collecting box.

The cheapest way to get from the campsite to Connaught Place was by a shared motorcycle rickshaw which seated six people. I wandered around looking unsuccessfully for a food shop where I could buy supplies for the evening meal. But I did find the Tourist Office which gave me a map, a post office where I could post letters, and the Thai Airlines office where I could change the date of my flight out of Nepal.

Looking for food I headed towards New Delhi railway station where I found a local market; I wandered through collecting bits and pieces. I had agreed to meet up again with Helen at the Tourist Office late in the afternoon and we completed our food shopping together. Shopping locally near the campsite we were able to buy yoghurt and 3.5kg of best buffalo shoulder. I was expecting the meat to be tough but it wasn't. I spent the rest of the evening enjoying cooking a meal of Buffalo Biriyani, Onion Raita, and Tomato and Onion Salad. The biryani was dressed with pineapple and cashew nuts and looked impressive; it was voted as one of the best truck meals.

After a cold shower, I wrote letters in the camp bar then finished the day off by breaking my torch bulb whilst trying to change the battery.

Delhi - Connaught Place

6th November 1980: Delhi

The day started with a big shock. After breakfast, there was a group meeting where we were advised that our arrival date in Kathmandu had been pushed back to the 19th of November. This would give us time to visit Jaipur. But it also meant that I wouldn't arrive in Nepal in time to get a trekking permit before the trek I was booked on. Together with Jos and Karl who had fixed dates to fly back home, we discussed ways of getting to Nepal earlier. Talking with the campsite travel agency we settled on a plan to leave the group in Varanasi, take a train ride to Patna and then a cheap flight to Kathmandu.

> *Delhi was warming up to Diwali which was in a couple of days; Nuts, colourful decorations, and fireworks were on sale everywhere.*

After a quiet morning washing and writing ten postcards, the agency gave us our unconfirmed tickets for the flight from Patna. After a vegetarian meal in the camp restaurant, I set off into town to visit the Tourist Office for more information. Because of the difficulties driving the truck in a city, we were left to make our own sightseeing arrangements. At the Tourist Office, I booked the morning tour of New Delhi the following day; I was impressed by how many Indian tourists there were on holiday in their own country.

> *I was standing waiting to cross a road at traffic lights. When they turned red I started to walk across and was mown down by a police car!*

A cheap cycle-rickshaw ride took me up into Old Delhi where I started my sightseeing at the Red Fort. This was an impressively sized complex but ultimately not of such interest as the palace in Istanbul. I visited the Diwan-i-Aam (Hall of Private Audience), the Rang Mahal pavilion, the emperor's apartments (Khas

Mahal), and the Diwan-i-Khas (Hall of Public Audience). In the latter, I was disappointed to not be able to find the much-quoted Persian couplet:

If heaven can be on the face of the earth,
It is this, it is this, it is this.

Anyway, I was tempted to disagree with the sentiment!

The museum didn't detain me long. As I left the fort the setting sun was painting the red fort walls a photogenic deep red.

My next stop was the Jama Masjid, India's largest mosque built by Shah Jahan in 1656. The vast courtyard was far smaller than the mosque in Lahore but as a result, was much more attractive.

Delhi – The Red Fort at sunset

I chatted with a man who was waiting for prayers and ventured the 'safe' statement that I preferred Pakistan. But no, it turned out that the Indian Muslims view themselves as being better educated and more progressive than their Pakistani neighbours. Then I had to take a picture of another shabby man; what a waste of precious slide film!

Looking for an evening meal I headed for the Tandor restaurant in the Presidential Hotel near the campsite, but I found Dave there making arrangements for our group meal. Deciding not to eat there twice I returned to the Moti Mahal on Netaji Subhash Marg where I enjoyed a chicken tikka with rice, raitha and naan.

Tired of cold showers I took some warm water to my tent, sat in my washing bucket, and flooded the place! I went to bed to the sound of fireworks being let off in the streets. I decided that I liked Delhi!

7th November 1980: Delhi (Diwali)

With my clothes washed and hung up to dry before breakfast I was ready to head off early to Connaught Place and get a seat allocation on what turned out to be an overbooked tour coach. It was a bit of a rushed tour but at least it allowed me to see many places would otherwise not have reached. The first stop on the tour was the modern Shri Laxminarayan Temple built in the 1930s in the Nagara style, then down Parliament Street to see the Jantar Mantar. This fascinating observatory built in 1724 was set in a garden of palms. I climbed to the top of the Samrat Yantra sundial to get a good view.

> *Delhi was a strange town. Cattle roamed the streets, there were beggars everywhere, but there were 21-variety ice cream parlours and plenty of other very Western shops.*

Moving on, the coach went past India Gate and to the Old Fort (Purana Qila) which had a rather plain mosque inside. The drive out to see the Qutb Minor made the tour worthwhile. The 13th-century tower looks over several buildings including India's oldest mosque containing a famous iron pillar. After visiting the pretty Safdarjung Tomb on the way back to Delhi the tour ended where it had started, in Connaught Place.

Delhi - Qutb Minor

Our group Indian meal was held that evening in the Presidential Hotel. The service of the meal was slow but the food was good. We gave our driver Dave a bird book, a pen, and some food for his trip back.

The alcohol served with our meal had to be disguised because Diwali was a dry day, so beer was served in a teapot!

The menu for our group meal was:
Chinese-style chicken sweetcorn soup
Barbequed chicken
Chicken Curry
Rice & Two Veg Curries
And the sweet was cheesy Rasgullas.

Group meal in Delhi

Delhi - Jantar Mantar

8th November 1980: Delhi – Jaipur

Dave was going to drive the large truck we had picked up in Karachi back to Pakistan, so we now had to squeeze into a smaller truck (NRB 956J) with the extra passengers shoehorned into a VW Kombi Van affectionately known as Van Ordinaire.

After a final farewell to Dave, we made an early departure from the campsite, driving in convoy with the truck ahead of the Kombi. I sat in the front of the truck with Thomas and chatted with our new driver, Tim. We had to get used to his style; he was a more aggressive driver than Dave, using the 'constipated cow' horn a lot. His mantra was:

If you aren't keeping the passengers awake in the back, then you're not using the horn enough!

On the road, we initially had trouble with the VW's engine but that was soon fixed. The highlights of yet another featureless Punjabi road were seeing mongooses crossing the road ahead of us and a recent accident where a truck had shed its load of onions.

After a late-morning chai stop, we entered an area with more interesting scenery; the agricultural plains gave way to rocky outcrops, dry valleys and palm trees. Shortly before reaching Jaipur, we stopped for lunch enjoying a delicious fruit salad and fresh cheese.

Most of us skipped the expensive elephant rides up to the Amber Fort, opting instead to climb the 500 or so steps. The fort which was dismissed in some guidebooks as 'a shell' turned out to have beautiful 17th century rooms and a maze of passages to explore.

Amber - A lorry with onions overturns

Amber: - View from the fort

On to the nearby city of Jaipur to look at the City Palace. This charged an admission fee because the palace included a museum, but I found it a bit of a disappointment after the Fort.

We camped for the night in the cramped grounds of the Jaipur Inn. When we came to put up our tents we discovered that we had packed some beds in the wrong truck and now we were short. After dinner, which featured pineapple again, we listened to an excellent sitar recital[3] in the hotel lounge.

---

[3] I have subsequently been told that it was probably the young and unknown Ravi Shankar who performed for us that evening.

Sitar Recital in the Jaipur Inn

9th November 1980: Jaipur - Agra

With two new vehicles, the morning start was somewhat chaotic as we had to discover where everything had to be packed. Although we had two hours to look around the Red City it was Sunday and the streets were pretty dead. They were cleaning rubbish out of the open drains/sewers; I guess it was nice to know they did that sometimes! The back streets I wandered through were the worst smelling I had encountered yet.

The main Post Office was close by where we parked the truck; I asked an old man which letter box to put my aerogram in, I posted it and then another man told me it was put in the wrong box! Then off to have two glasses of chai, a warm sweet liquid with lots of milk. I would never have entered places like a chai shop two months before; how one's standards changed on the road!

Jaipur - Street scene

For variety, I travelled in the VW on the next leg of our journey; the ride was much smoother than the truck but the ventilation in the back was poor.

On the way to Agra, we met a bus coming the other way on a single-track road. Tim pulled the truck slightly to one side but then refused to move. A shouting match ensued between the two drivers, but eventually, the Indian gave in and drove through the narrow gap. He didn't drive straight through though and made a big show about how difficult it was. I quite enjoyed telling the frustrated bus passengers that I was in no hurry and we were thinking of stopping there for lunch!

Drama on the road to Agra

We left Rajasthan and late in the afternoon, as we neared Fatehpur Sikri, the VW got a flat on a rear tyre. The truck went on ahead whilst we jacked the Kombi up enough to get the spare tyre on. Then we went on a few miles, past the impressive ruined city in the red setting sun, and stopped at a village tyre repair shop to get a good spare. It turned out there was an inch-long chunk of metal in the tyre which punctured the inner tube in multiple places. While we were waiting for the tyre to be repaired we had chai and cokes. The man in the chai shop sensing a business opportunity wanted to charge me 2 rupees for a glass of chai. I told him I would pay 60 Re and when he wouldn't give change from 1 rupee I gave him 50 Re, bargaining hard like a local!

Agra - Puncture Repair

We rolled into the Highway Inn in Agra well after dark, but in time to put up tents and have a cold shower before dinner. It was Freddie's birthday and we had an 'Italian' meal cooked by Werner and Val. It was not exactly to my taste, but that could have been due to the difficulty of buying the correct ingredients so far from Europe. I had a very squeaky bed that night and every time I got up I woke Thomas who was sleeping in the same tent.

My reputation from the Buffalo Biriyani lived on, and the cooks kept asking me what the spices I used were.

10th November 1980: Agra

We all got up well before dawn to walk the kilometre from our camp to the Taj Mahal. I walked so fast with Thomas that we even beat those who took bicycle rickshaws for the short trip. The Taj, built in 1653, lived up to expectations; it was a beautiful building greatly enhanced by the absence of crowds. I spent over an hour walking around it, watching the changing colours and shadows as the sun rose.

When the coach trips arrived I finally went inside the mausoleum but I was disappointed, it was dark and dismal. The inlaid marble floors were fine but there was not enough light to see them well. I left the Taj and wandered around looking for some breakfast, ending up in a smart chai shop well off the tourist track; tea and buttered bread stoked me up for the walk back to the camp.

Agra - Taj Mahal from the east

Agra - Taj Mahal at sunrise

It turned out to be a very hot day; frustratingly there was no water in the campsite because a power cut had stopped the water pumps. Peter and Tom were doing routine maintenance on the truck and trying to find out why the battery was always flat.

When everyone was back from the Taj we had brunch and then set out without the trailer to look at Fatehpur Sikri. This deserted city was built by Emperor Akbar in 1571 and abandoned in 1584, just 13 years later. It was an impressive collection of red sandstone palaces. It didn't have the ornamentation that featured in the Amber palace but was still fascinating to wander around and explore. The highlights for me were the Diwan-i-Aam, the pyramidical Panch Mahal, and the carving on Birbal's Palace. I found out that I had to be very firm, verging on being rude with the persistent roaming salesmen and guides.

On the trip back to camp Tim regaled us with stories about his life on a Kibbutz. It was a memorable day already but then we had green custard for dinner!

The 'new' truck had less headroom in the back and was quite cramped so we took to cooking outside with the stove top hung between the two tables.

11th November 1980: Agra – Mauranipur

The scenery as we headed south from Agra was interesting. The cultivated fields of the Punjab soon gave way to rounded sandy hills. The road then climbed onto a barren plateau with rocky outcrops. On top of the hills were temples that we assumed were Jain. On the flat ground, Mogul-styled palaces dominated the landscape. The morning chai stop was in Gwalior where I had a delicious vegetarian samosa with my tea. Despite frequent toilet stops, we made good progress, getting to Datia for lunch. After an extended lunch break, we had to race to get within 100 km of Khajuraho before sunset. A long dusty day finished with rough camping beyond Mauranipur.

Fatehpur Sikri - Dwan-i-Aam

12th November 1980: Mauranipur – Khajuraho

Reveille was Amanda calling out "Breakfast in 10 minutes; tents down before breakfast". Then Pete tried to get Tim out of bed by telling him the truck had a flat tyre. I went easy on the marmalade at breakfast as I'd been out with the spade on 'night business'.

After a short shopping stop in Chhatarpur, we arrived in Khajuraho, just before the President was scheduled to turn up on an official visit. We were unceremoniously kicked out of the Dak Bungalow where Encounter normally camped, and the terms of a nearby hotel were outside our budget. So it was the usual piece of open land on the outskirts of town for our lunch spot.

In the main temple complex, everything was closed and locked down for the President. We switched plans and jumped in the truck to visit other temples in the Southern and Eastern groups. Our first stop was the Chaturbhuj Temple dedicated to Vishnu, then back in the truck through the village to the Jain Parshwanath and

Adinath temples, both dating from the 11th century. Unfortunately, I was back spending more time crouched over a toilet than actually sightseeing, and I had run out of toilet paper!

While we were sightseeing Tim had found a third hotel where we could camp for the night. The drinks in the bar were expensive due to higher taxes in Madhya Pradesh state. A dew developed before we went to bed so I slept with my space blanket over me and a towel underneath to absorb most of the condensation.

Khajuraho - Camping in a hotel grounds

13th November 1980: Khajuraho – Chachai Falls

The plan was to get up early so we could visit the main temple group before leaving. Unfortunately, the cooks overslept so that didn't happen. Instead, the truck came to pick us up later from the temples to save time. However, we then got stuck in the car park for half an hour whilst we waited for the presidential convoy to drive past.

Khajuraho Temple

When we eventually got clear of Khajuraho there was an uneventful drive to a shopping stop in Satna. This was a busy small town with plenty of small shops and a large railway marshalling yard. I found a nice chai shop with fresh dahi (curd) and passed an hour quite pleasantly.

Just outside the town, we met a Sundowners coach travelling in the opposite direction. They warned us that the next town, Rewa, was swarming with the President and his entourage. We managed to get our lunch stop back down to an hour but, even so, by the time we got to Rewa, the President had moved on. Late that afternoon, we reached the Chachai Falls, down a narrow road that was only surfaced in the middle. The falls were unfortunately in the shade when we arrived, and the post-monsoon rush of water had subsided; nevertheless, it was worth the visit.

That night we slept on the verandah of a small government rest house by the falls and enjoyed pancakes for dinner.

Chachai Falls

14th November 1980: Chachai Falls – Varanasi

It appeared to be raining in our campsite the next morning, but it was only the spray being blown up from the falls. After retracing our route back to Rewa we then continued our journey east. The generally featureless trip was punctuated by the VW having to go on a search for petrol and an unpleasant incident where children threw rocks at the truck.

Lunch was not very substantial, but as a result, it had the virtue of being quick. Another search for petrol was successful as we passed through Mirzapur, but then the road deteriorated badly. The VW picked up two flat tyres; the second one stranded it on the outskirts of Varanasi. Luckily Vin Ordinare wouldn't be carrying so many people on the final leg up into Nepal.

We camped fairly centrally in Varanasi on the grounds of the Dak Bungalow. This was convenient as we could pop into the tourist office next door to ask about the train we were catching. They advised us that we could not reserve seats on the

'Express' which would leave at 1:30 taking 5½ hours to reach Patna. We elected to travel second class; I sold my now unwanted sleeping bag to a guy in the Dak Bungalow for half the price of a first-class ticket and a fraction of what it had cost me in England.

Whilst I was in the tourist office I booked onto the official city coach tour for the following day.

15th November 1980: Varanasi - Patna

I had a rough night sleeping in the back of the truck; the campsite was very noisy. To catch the tourist coach around the city I had to skip breakfast. Driving down empty streets we parked close to Dashashwamedh Ghat for a boat trip up and down the Ganges. There was a good view of ritual bathing at dawn, and also the city washing men hard at work. We also passed the burning Ghats but thankfully, that early in the morning, nobody was being cremated.

After the boat trip, the group wandered through the narrow Chowk laneways passing the main Hindu temple (the Vishwanath Temple); I thought it was unprepossessing for such an important religious place.

Back at camp after the first half of the tour, I revived my flagging energy with a delicious 'last' breakfast including curd, cereal and toast. Then we (Jos, Karl and myself) finished packing, loaded our bags onto the coach, and set out on the second half of our sightseeing tour; which visited a few more temples and the expansive university precinct.

Varanasi - Flood-damaged temples

Varanasi - Early morning on the Ganges

The streets were now much more congested so progress was slow. The best temple we saw was the 18th century Monkey, or Durga, temple. The coach dropped us off at the station where we bought our tickets and had our luggage weighed, mine was 20.5 kg. The station restaurant served a passable lunch which we ate whilst listening carefully to all the platform change announcements. When we heard that our train had been diverted to Platform 4 we raced there, found seats in the train standing by the platform and settled in.

Then the train left the station in the wrong direction!

We were confused until the ticket collector told us that we had boarded a train to Delhi that started from Platform 5. There was no alternative but to carry on to the first stop, Zafarabad Junction, and wait for a train back. Our arrival in a rural backwater station was clearly quite a surprise; the station manager invited us into his office to sit in the shade and have tea. An hour later we jumped on a near-empty train back to Varanasi, a train that terminated there.

Back where we had started, we retreated to the station restaurant whilst we waited for the next train to Patna. When the time was right we fought our way onto a crowded platform that had a likely-looking train, but it turned out to be going to Bombay. As we were sitting on the platform trying to work out what to do next we were approached by an old man who offered to get us seats on the obviously full train to Patna for a small commission. We agreed! He took us over to a siding where a coach that was going to be attached to the train was waiting. We all got seats and then had an anxious time waiting till the coach was moved and attached to the train; there were a few other passengers in the know who were in the coach with us which gave us more confidence.

At 6:30 we finally left Varanasi, in the right direction! The wooden seats were rock hard but there was English-speaking company in our carriage, and seeing the crowds and activities going on at stations on the way was a great experience.

It was late at night when we got to Patna railway station so we hired a couple of rickshaws to set off on a search for a hotel. After trying two places that were full, we ended up at the Hotel Jaysarmin; it was a basic hotel but at least the room had a cold shower and there was a bed to sleep on.

16th November 1980: Patna - Kathmandu

There was no chance of sleeping in as I was up several times in the night to go to the bathroom; probably induced by a surfeit of railway food the previous day. After a suitably light breakfast, we took a taxi to the airport arriving well before the check-in opened. When the airport coach from Patna arrived everything burst into life, we were found in the restaurant and whisked through baggage check and emigration in an efficient way. Our twin-engine aircraft was ready for boarding at noon and it took off soon afterwards. The high spot of the 30-minute hop into Nepal was seeing the snow-covered mountain peaks appear like clouds above the haze of the Punjab plain. On landing, we sped through non-existent immigration; they didn't even check my health card or my passport picture. All we had to do was sit and wait for our luggage to appear.

I was impressed by the beauty of the Kathmandu Valley; wherever I went in the town I would see white-topped mountains poking up from behind the buildings. To a traveller arriving from Varanasi, Nepal was pleasantly clean and appeared prosperous, but I could imagine that had I come directly from England I wouldn't get quite the same impressions.

I took a taxi from the airport to the Kathmandu Guest House in Thamel; the hotel had a booking for me because I was travelling with Encounter. They gave me a single room in the hotel annex where I could stay for four days till I set off trekking. Unfortunately, they couldn't give me a firm room booking for when I was scheduled to come back.

I spent the rest of the day getting my bearings and finding my way around, firstly to the Post Office to collect two more letters, then back to Thamel to buy a few supplies. Before returning to my hotel for a lovely hot shower I sampled one of the Kathmandu delicacies, a pie from a cake shop.

For dinner, I went to the restaurant downstairs in the hotel, the Astha Mangalam, where I had a great sweet-sour pork. I then sat around chatting with two oil workers from Scotland till we were chucked out at 11 o'clock. I wasn't used to sleeping in a proper bed; I slept well but got a bit cold in the morning.

Kathmandu - My room in the Kathmandu Guest House

17th November 1980: Kathmandu

I was used to getting up early, so I was downstairs in the Astha Mangalam having breakfast before it got busy. It was a joy to order from a menu, and the porridge, omelette and coffee were all perfect! Whilst the sun warmed up the chill morning air I tackled the mountain of washing in my kit bag.

My first task of the day was to find a hotel that would give me a confirmed booking for when I returned from trekking, but I was initially unsuccessful. Desperately seeking news I found the British Council reading room in an impressive modern building, and from there on down Indra Chowk to change money in the Nepal Bank. For lunch, I found the 1st-floor Aunt Jane's Place and demolished a cheeseburger and chocolate cake; all washed down with a hot lemon juice to assuage a sore throat I had developed.

In the afternoon I started my tour of the essential sights around the central Durbar Square, first the Jaganath Mandir with its erotic carvings and then the three-storey golden pagoda Taleju Temple. The view from the UNESCO-restored towers in the palace was excellent and the history of Nepal's democracy described in the museum was interesting. Finally, I retired, as all travellers did, to sit on the steps of the Maju Deval in the sun watching all the passing life in the square below.

Kathmandu - Durbar Square

My day's purchases were a pair of long warm cotton socks and two trekking maps.

An Encounter Overland rafting group arrived just as I got back to the hotel so I was unable to arrange my trekking visa application with the office. Instead, I went next door to the Star Hotel where I was able to make an advance reservation for a double room with a bathroom.

I felt a bit under the weather so took my temperature; it was over 100°! I decided I better take things easy; however, I still managed to eat chicken chop suey for dinner.

Kathmandu -Swayambhunath Temple

18th November 1980: Kathmandu

Whatever ailment I had the previous day it didn't stop me from ordering another tasty breakfast with curd muesli, honey toast, coffee and a lassi. Feeling fragile but substantially better I visited the Encounter Overland office on the ground floor of the Guest House where they opened and filled out trekking visa forms for me. Then I shared a taxi to the Central Immigration Office with some other fellow trekkers to pay for the visa; this was later refunded by Encounter. On the way back I hired a down sleeping bag from a shop recommended by Encounter.

Kathmandu viewed from the Swayambhunath Temple

After lunch in Astha, I walked over the river and then up the hill on the other side, up to the Swayambhunath Temple with its 13th-century stupa. The tramp up the stairs was good training for trekking! From the top, there was a fine panorama of the mountains but it was too misty for good photography. I returned over the footbridge which led to Pig Alley (where most of the pie shops were).

Before dinner, there was a meeting in the Encounter Overland office for those of us going on the Brief Encounters trek. Afterwards, it was much clearer what we needed to take with us and what we could leave behind. The evening meal that night was excellent value and I had pleasant company at my table.

19th November 1980: Kathmandu

The down sleeping bag was lovely and warm but it didn't fix my cold, and the cold didn't affect my appetite; I sampled honey pancakes for breakfast.

After a quiet morning, I walked into town by a new route hoping to find a decent restaurant, but ended up eating in a pie shop in Freak Street. By the time I had posted some expensive aerograms and picked up my trekking permit, the Encounter truck and Vin Ordinare had arrived in Kathmandu and were parked in front of the hotel. The group meal was scheduled for that evening.

I started packing my bags ready to go trekking the next day, but felt peckish at the thought of waiting till 8 pm for the group meal, so I popped out for a quick cake and tea. The Tibetan meal was delicious, but there was so much food I couldn't eat it all; the main course had seven dishes!

The next morning I would be going trekking, which is the start of my next story.

Cost of 83 days from London to Kathmandu
Encounter Overland £785
Overflight to Karachi £80
Overflight Patna to Kathmandu £16
Spending Money £162

Kathmandu – The Encounter Truck arrives

Encounter Overland farewell meal in Kathmandu

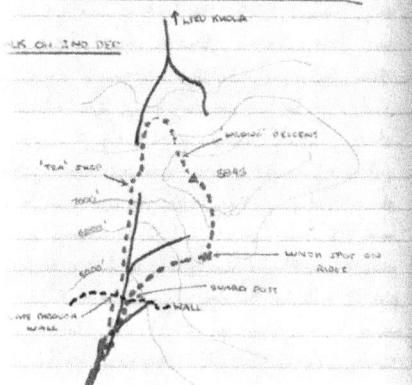

PART 2
Kathmandu to Sydney

South East Asia on my stomach

NEPAL

Nepal was two countries in one. The cosmopolitan Kathmandu city and the mountain people. Although Nepal was poor there was little obvious poverty. Kathmandu was notable for its old timber buildings and its excellent restaurants. After the rigours of overland travel, I could have eaten there forever, though I did get a bit tired of the budget Chinese food towards the end of my stay. The other towns in the Kathmandu Valley had similar architecture but without the prosperity granted by a resident foreign population. The Nepalese in the city were quite Westernised in their attitudes and so it was good to see that more traditional values and lifestyles were entrenched in the hill villages.

The life of porters, Sherpas, and the mountain people was simple but effective; they were a race that always seemed to be either singing or telling jokes. On my short trek, I was able to observe the mountain life in villages along the busy Jonsom trail and also on the back paths. On the former, there was quite a bit of begging by children, and Western food could be bought in the many tea houses along the way. On the back trails, there were no such compromises.

Taking a trek into the Himalayas was full of unforgettable experiences. The first memorable feature was that the route descended valleys and climbed back up again, maybe up 1000 ft, and there were still higher mountains towering overhead. My second treasured memory was seeing the snow-covered mountains in the clear morning air; it was almost spiritual.

20th November 1980: Kathmandu – Pokhara

The sound of barking outside the Kathmandu Guest House woke me in the night; apparently, they were upset by a minor earthquake that went unnoticed by me. So many guests were leaving that morning that the serving of breakfast was a shambles, and so distracted was I, that I forgot to pay my bill as I left! I left most of my luggage with the hotel taking only a stuff sack with personal possessions; I was probably travelling lighter than anyone on our trek.

The short trek I had booked was organised by Encounter Overland and paid for before leaving the U.K. It was a relatively easy assisted trek with all the supplies and luggage being carried by Sherpas. There were sixteen other trekkers from the USA, England, Europe, South Africa and down under. It started in Pokhara which was a day's drive from Kathmandu down a mountainous dirt road with great views. We followed the Trisuli River to a lunch stop at Mugling; eating an omelette and a bowl of dal bhat in the 'Mugling Sheraton'. Then our route turned up another white water rafting river, the Maryangdi. We later learned that the reason our trip was so slow was that the Encounter truck we were in didn't have very good brakes!

A camp was set up for us in Pokhara by our Sherpas. The tents were erected within the grounds of the Himalaya Inn opposite the airfield. From there we were treated to a clear sunset view of the peak of Lamjung Himal, the most southwestern mountain in the Annapurna range. While the Sherpas were cooking dinner we had a warm-up walk to the nearby Green Lake, getting as far as the Tal Barahi temple. Before the lake level dropped this had been on an island. The lakeside was far more 'hippy' than Kathmandu and we had tea in a dope-joint on the way back to the camp.

The evening meal that was prepared for us was simple but well-cooked. We then sat chatting on the groundsheet that doubled as a table till it was time to go to bed. That night my torch died, yet again.

The Trisuli River west of Kathmandu

Pokhara – Our campsite

21st November 1980: Pokhara - Naudanda

I had a surprisingly good night's sleep considering we were lying on hard ground on foam mats and not camp stretchers. As the sun rose the view of the Annapurna range was breathtaking with the sharp peak of Machapuchare predominant. A morning mug of tea was served in bed, and a breakfast of fried egg and porridge whilst we stood around packing. It took two truckloads to ferry us, the luggage, and the porters to the trailhead in North Pokhara. I tried once again to get a bulb for my torch but they only stocked one type that matched the one brand of torch that they sold.

Pokhara - Assigning loads to the porters

The trek started with a gentle enough walk up the broad Mardi Khola river valley to the Tibetan refugee camp. There was a near-continuous row of houses alongside the trail with plenty of tea shops and the ever-present cries of hawkers. It was an easy walk and we got beyond the village of Hyengia before stopping for lunch. The porters had gone on ahead and there was a mug of lemon tea waiting for us when we arrived. We sat on the groundsheet in a dry paddy field close to the rushing Yamdi Khola River. It was a hot clear day in the valley but the peaks, when they were visible, were draped in cloud.

Hyengia – Stopping for lunch

Resting on the ascent to Naudanda

At the end of the day, we had an introduction to the steep climbing that would characterise the rest of the trek. We left the valley floor at Suikhet and climbed over 1000 ft to the ridge-top village of Naudanda. It wasn't too tiring for us as we weren't carrying a pack, but it certainly made the porters sweat. At the top, there was a welcome cup of chai. I had to give up drinking Coke as the price now included a porterage charge.

The Sherpas set up camp on the grounds of the local primary school. From the ridge, there were fantastic views, one way down the valley to Pokhara and the Green Lake, and the other way over to the peaks of the Himalayas. Our evening meal was soup, some unusual-tasting noodles, and fruit. Once again the group sat around on the groundsheet after dinner, sharing stories of the most embarrassing moments in our lives. As the sun set, the clouds lifted and we had a view of the mountains by moonlight. A view that could not be photographed or adequately described.

Naudanda - Fishtail at sunrise

22nd November 1980: Naudanda - Hille

What better way could there be to wake up? With a cup of tea from the tea boy, and a fantastic view of the mountains at dawn. Our camp was broken by the porters before we had finished breakfast and we were soon back on the trail. First, we climbed gently up the ridge to Khare, then we descended down a pleasant valley towards the Modi Khola river. At Lumle we stopped following the stream and contoured on the valley side to the village of Chandrakot. There were now a lot of pony trains going both ways, loaded with cargo and unfortunately damaging the path. And the children became a bit more insistent in their demands for pens, sweets, or simply just money. There was no shortage of tea shops (bhatti) and with so many excuses to stop, our progress was leisurely.

Lumle – The descent to the Modi Khola

From Chandrakot one could look up the Modi Khola to see Annapurna South shrouded in cloud. There was also a bird's eye view of the path we were going to take down to the river some 1800 ft below us, a tricky descent on a path that the pony trains had damaged. We crossed the river on our first suspension bridge at Birethanti Bazaar then followed the Bhuranda Khola valley up to our lunch camp.

Birethanti - Lunch by the Bhuranda Khola

I was one of the first to arrive so there was time for an ice-cold swim/wash before we were served a meal of chapatis and jam. The climb in the afternoon was easygoing, past waterfalls and small farms, with only small diversions where the stream had washed the path away. As a result, we got to Hille in good time and had to sit around in the spotting rain waiting for the tents to arrive. After a vegetable curry for dinner, there was a dance display by the local school for which we each chipped in 2 rupees. I broke my rum bottle so had to finish it off before heading to bed early.

Hille camp in the morning

23rd November 1980: Hille - Ghorapani

The clouds lifted overnight and with all the exercise the previous day we all had a good night's sleep. The day started easily enough with a gentle walk to the small mountain village of Tirkhedhunge, followed by two river crossings, but then we encountered a stiff climb up to Ulleri. It was steps all the way up, climbing 1900 ft; I paced myself and got to the top in about 90 minutes. One feature of the trails was the provision of stone benches so porters could rest and take the weight off their backs. We were now so far from the main road that even tea was more expensive, but we had time to enjoy a cup in the sun as our lunch stop was only an hour away.

After Ulleri the track levelled out; there was even a depressing descent to our lunch spot by a small stream. After another ice-cold wash, we warmed up in the sun sipping lemon tea. But the sun disappeared during lunch and it became overcast.

Climbing up to Ulleri

Lunch had to be abandoned because it started to rain. Then the rain got heavier and heavier, and all I had to keep me dry was a towel. Walking turned into a dash between the shelter of trees or rocky overhangs. Our miserable situation was made worse by a local who shattered the peace with a blaring radio.

Ulleri – A refreshment stop

Ulleri - A little boy

Wet and cold we reached Ghorapani at 9,300 ft; there were even traces of snow beside the path. Ghorapani was a small hamlet sheltering on the south side of the pass over the Thak Khola watershed. We huddled around a fire in the 'hotel' drinking hot chocolate and eating delicious lemon pancakes.

When the porters arrived they lit a fire in the lodge hut and we retired there. It was so cold my pen stopped working!

24th November 1980: Ghorapani - Ghandrung

Even with 18 sleeping bodies in one room and a fire, it got very cold overnight. We were woken before dawn so we could be out walking soon after 6 a.m. There was a hard frost and the icy path uphill through the woods was very slippery. Turning off the busy Jonson trail the route was at times ill-defined; quite early on we lost contact with a couple of members of our group. After a quarter of an hour climbing the views from the path opened out, and after a further hour, we reached a mini-summit with excellent views at about 11,000 ft.

The Annapurnas - Our porters arrive at the viewpoint

The sun was now out, triggering a quick thaw, and converting the paths into muddy slopes. One of our group was a professional photographer writing an article for a travel magazine. I copied a few of his shots and used a polarising filter to advantage on the clear blue sky.

Mountain view

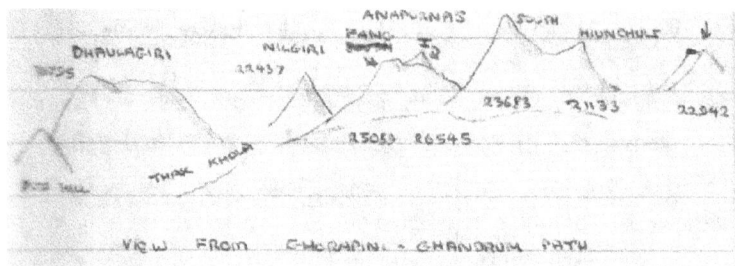

Annapurna 1, South and Miunchuli

Going over the actual pass, from where the views were not as impressive, we followed a fast-flowing stream, descending on steps down the side of waterfalls in a deep gorge. Lunch included a nice cake the Sherpas had baked in an improvised Dutch oven the night before.

As we skirted around the headwaters of the Bhuranda Khola we were treated to views down to Ulleri where we had rested the day before. There were now so many competing paths we walked in convoy with a Sherpa picking out the correct route. It was nice to be able to walk freely without being on the lookout for pony dung that littered the main Jonson trail.

Descending through a rhododendron forest to Ghandrung

When we dropped out of the rainforest we found ourselves walking on an attractive woodland path with plenty of autumnal colours. It took 3 ½ hours to reach Ghandrung; a pleasant large village spread out on a steep hillside dropping down to the Modi Khola river. Our camp for the night was in the grounds of the secondary school right on the edge of a ledge; it had excellent views down the valley, and up to the Annapurna South range.

Some of the more energetic members of our party played Frisbee till poor light stopped the game. After a meal of curried vegetables with spaghetti, we sat about chatting. The hard-core insomniacs who didn't believe in going to bed at 8 p.m. had a sing-song to keep everyone awake!

25th November 1980: Ghandrung - Dhumpus

It was nice to be woken again with a cup of tea, but it came with the usual problem; you ask for white tea then the Sherpa asks if you want milk in it! I had to get used to asking for 'milk tea'.

From Ghandrung the track dropped steeply down to the Modi Khola. As usual, the porters raced down, passing us on our staggering descent. It took us 90 minutes to get to the rickety wooden bridge, and a further 30 minutes to climb back up the other side to Landrung village.

Ghandrung - Sunrise on Annapurna South and Hiunchule

Landrung - Crossing the Modi Khola

As we were getting close to Pokhara I splashed out on a Coke which turned out to be a good idea as others reported that the local tea tasted bad. Compared to the past couple of days it was an easy walk down the valley to Bhichuk where we were served thick stodgy pancakes for lunch; the sort of meal it was hard to walk off afterwards. We had success in getting the Sherpas to break out the jar of Branston Pickle they had been carrying which made lunch marginally more edible.

The author in front of Annapurna South

The supposedly gentle walk uphill that followed lunch turned out to be a stiff climb over the ridge between the villages of Landrung and Dhumpus. By now my kneecaps were starting to complain about all the ups and downs. We crossed the pass in the cloud and on the way down the other side the porters were fired up, like horses returning to the stable. They were whistling, singing and shouting to each other in the distance. You always knew when a porter was behind you; they didn't need to ring a bell!

The slope down to Dhumpus was on a well-maintained path and we reached the campsite well before dusk. A campfire was lit and we sat around it eating dinner; a meal which included the potato salad we had been eyeing all trip. The party was broken up by the weather; it started to rain quite heavily so we retired to our tents.

26th November 1980: Dhumpus – Pokhara

Dhumpus – A view down to the valley

We woke to a misty morning with an easy day's walk ahead of us back down to the Tibetan Refugee Camp where we were served a delicious lunch. I had a chat with a local spelling bee who came up behind me; she introduced herself by chanting 'T-O-U-R-I-S-T'. We reached the trailhead early in the afternoon and killed time playing football till the Encounter Overland truck arrived a couple of hours later.

On our way through town, the two Nepalese women sang, a combination of piercing voices and smooth Nepali words. We returned with a rousing rendition of Waltzing Matilda!

Back at the Himalaya Inn our evening meal took a long time coming, but was quite nice (a description that sums up most of the Sherpa's cooking with a few notable exceptions). We gave the porters their tip and we sat around on the ground singing for the last time.

Our Sherpas and porters

The Encounter Overland Trek group

Nepal trekking permit

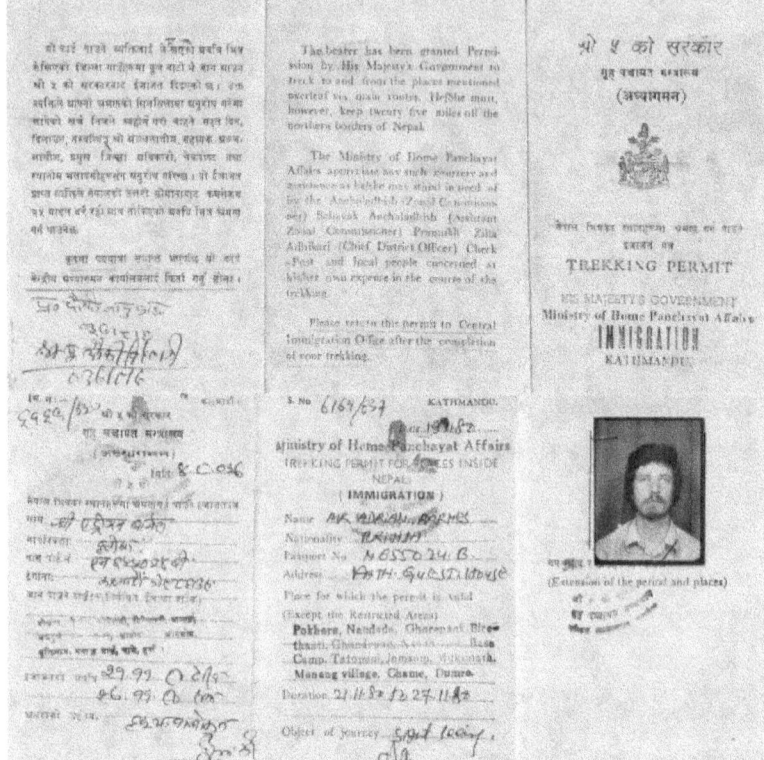

The Encounter Overland publicity was somewhat coy about the distances to be covered in the 'short' trek. Although the tracks used have long since been replaced by roads it appears that we covered close to 100km with a total elevation gain of 4,800m.

27th November 1980: Pokhara - Kathmandu

The Sherpas had a heavy night so breakfast was late, but that was forgiven because they had baked another cake for us. The journey back to Kathmandu retraced our route out, though the weather wasn't as nice and the road was in the cloud as we set out from Pokhara.

Back in Kathmandu, I checked in to the Star Hotel next to the Kathmandu Guest House. Although I had made a reservation they didn't have the room I had asked for, but upgraded me to a double for the agreed price. The shower was warm which was significantly better than washing in mountain streams.

That evening the trekking group had a farewell meal in the Astha Mangalam restaurant at the Kathmandu Guest House. We had to pay for our meal which was the restaurant's standard Tibetan feast. Most of us retired to the Roxy Bar across the road where I drank Rum and Coke till after midnight.

Cost of 8 days trekking
Encounter Overland £105
Equipment hire £3
Spending Money £4

A trekking map bought in Kathmandu

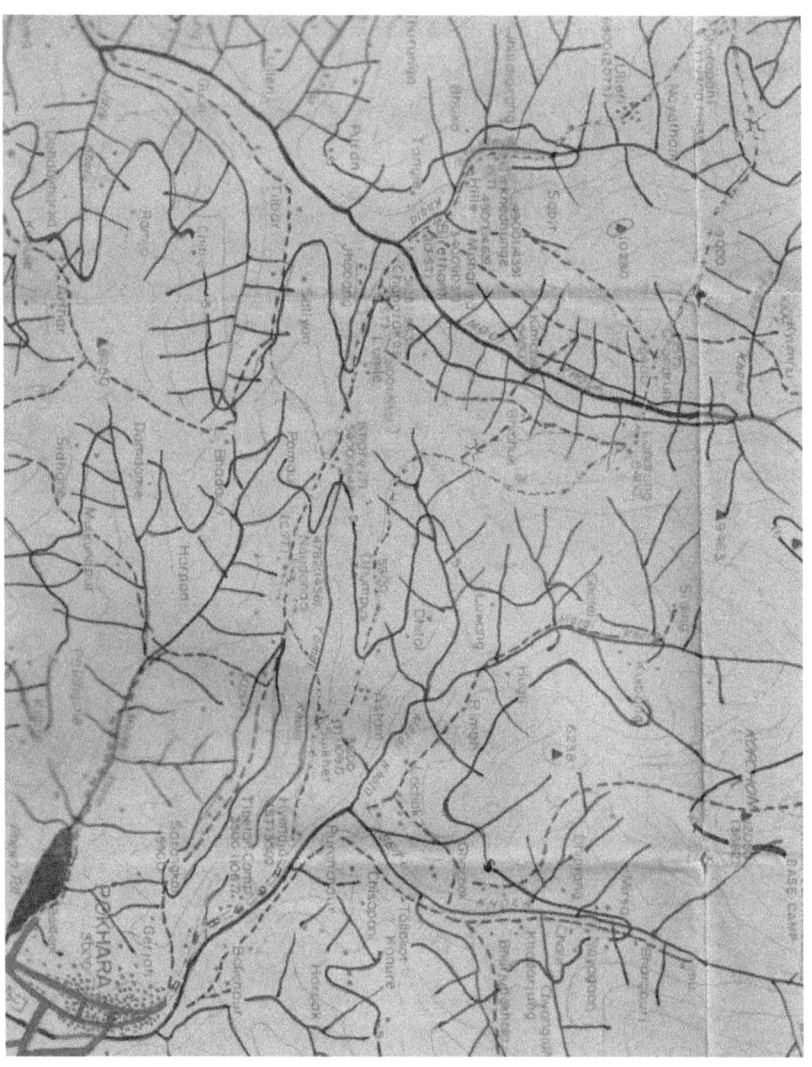

28th November 1980: Kathmandu (Rest Day)

A good night's rest in yet another strange bed, but significantly a bed with a comfortable mattress. As always, I met up with people I knew in Astha's when I went to breakfast and arranged to join a group for an evening meal that night.

Kathmandu - Thamel

The morning was dedicated to writing letters and doing washing. Then I grabbed a pie and tea in the Melody Fruit Bar and headed to the Post Office to collect letters, to the bank to change money, and to the Thai Embassy to find out how to get a visa. On my way back up Freak Street I purchased a bucket for washing, candles for the next power cut, and a bulb for my torch. Finally, I called into the British Council to read newspapers.

The sizzling steak at KC's that evening was expensive but delicious. There were about 25 Encounter Overland passengers and crew at the meal.

Patan - Durbar Square

29th November 1980: Kathmandu (Patan)

I tried out my new washing bucket overnight; its dimensions were such that it would fit at the bottom of my kit bag. After a quick breakfast, I hired a bike from the hotel and set off towards Patan, the second-largest town in the valley. On the outskirts, I stopped to check out the Christian School but they didn't advertise any Sunday services.

Like Kathmandu, the centre of Patan was marked by a Durbar or Palace Square. Of all the temples around the Square, the Krishna Mandis was the most interesting, built in an Indian style and made of wood. There was a lot less bustle than in Kathmandu's Durbar Square, presumably because there were fewer tourists.

Patan - Garuda statue

On the bike again I pedalled out to the golden temple, Hiranya Varna Mahbar. It didn't live up to the guidebook's hype, but the 14th-century temple of a thousand Buddhas, Mahabouddha, was more interesting as each brick contained an image of Buddha. It was also possible to climb onto an adjacent roof for a better view of the temple and also over Patan.

After a nutritional lunch of Coke and biscuits, I set off on a devious and at times rough route to the Chobar Gorge. All the water from the Kathmandu valley drains through this narrow opening. When the road started to climb steeply I had to resort to pushing the bike but was soon plagued by lots of boys who made my life unbearable.

I retreated past the Swayambhunath temple to take a quick look at the suburb of Balaju. There was a park there but it didn't seem worth investigating further so I headed back. I was just in time; the left pedal fell off just as I got to the hotel!

My accounts clearly showed that enjoying the food in Kathmandu was breaking my budget. So I stocked up with bread and peanut butter for lunches, and a piece of chocolate cake for immediate consumption.

Patan - Durbar Square

Kathmandu had the most incredible bypass, presumably built by the Indians or Chinese. It was deserted because no one wanted to bypass the town!

30th November 1980: Kathmandu (Sundarijal)

After making peanut butter sandwiches for my expedition to Sundarijal, I hired another bike for the day and my first stop was the temple of Boudhanath. This is one of the largest stupas in the world and could possibly date from the 4th century. I walked round it; what else can one do at a stupa? Then I followed a valley up through Gokarda heading to Sundarijal. It turned out to be the most perfect day, without the usual gathering of clouds on the mountains.

> The children on the way to Sundarijal, instead of learning the usual 'hallo' had concentrated on saying 'bye bye'. It was disconcerting when they started their usual begging with a cry of 'bye-bye'.

I ate my lunch sitting by the river as it tumbled down into the Kathmandu valley. To vary the route on the way back I crossed the barrage at Gokama and headed home on the east bank. The path on this side of the river was hard to push a bike along and certainly no good for riding.

Back in Kathmandu, I tried to post some letters but had forgotten it was Sunday and the Post Office was closed. The left pedal had almost fallen off my bike so I called it a day and got my hot shower before the regular late afternoon power cut. I tried out a different restaurant for dinner, Utse, recommended in my guidebook as one of the best places for Chinese and Tibetan food. I was tempted once again into spending more than I should have, enjoying a thick noodle soup, Chop Suey, Mushroom Fuyung (omelette) and a large banana split.

Sundarijal – A village scene

Sundarijal – The author having lunch by the waterfalls

1st December 1980: Kathmandu (Rest Day)

There was a heavy mist early in the morning but it soon dissipated to leave a sunny, warm, cloudless day. My social life was good, eating breakfast each day at Astha's and chatting to people I knew as they came in to eat. I even met a couple of people I knew in the Thai Embassy when I went there to get a visa. There were a couple of letters to pick up at the Post Office and read over a snacky lunch at Aunt Janes's, a 1st-floor hideaway with an American decor and menu.

I excelled at shopping by managing to find two rings to put on my travel bag straps, it was just a case of looking in enough shops and persevering. A visit to the British Council failed to reveal when Prince Charles was going to arrive in Nepal, (Subsequently, I learned that the preparations were for a royal visit starting on the 6th of December). Then, with a visit to Thai Air to reconfirm my flight out on the 8th of December, my errands for the day were complete.

Back to Astha's for dinner. Its main virtue was that it was cheap and friendly, but that night it was deserted, so with no one to chat with I retired early.

2nd December 1980: Kathmandu (Sheopuri)

No time to socialise over breakfast today; I was up early and on my way before 8 o'clock. My project for the day was to reach Sheopuri, the highest mountain peak in the valley. At first, the thick mist made cycling rather damp, but just as I reached Budhanikantha the sun broke through and it became warmer. With the day warming up, I was concerned that whisps of clouds were starting to form on the mountains.

I parked my bike in the village square and engaged a boy to look after it for 1½ rupees.

Walk to Sheopuri

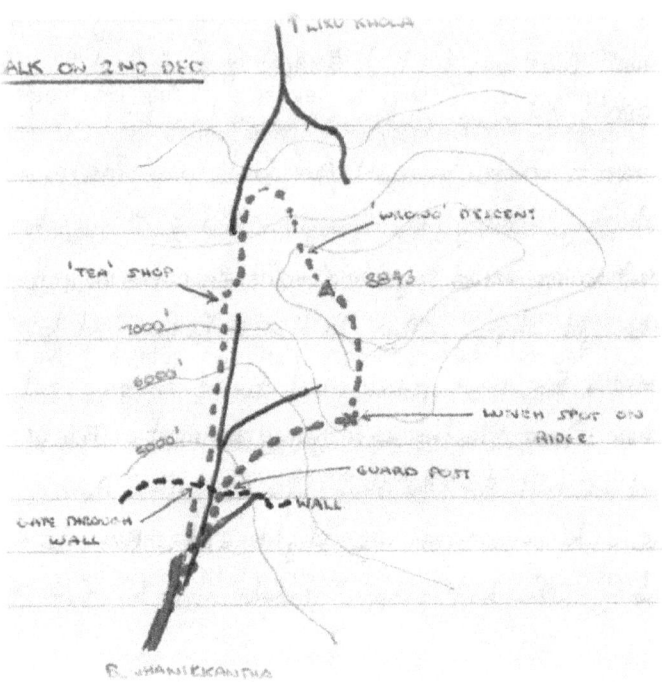

When I started up the main street I was already at 5000 ft. But just 15 minutes into the walk I was stopped by a gate across the path. A boy ran up and told me that the path to Sheopuri was through the gate and that I would need 2 rupees and my passport to get past the soldiers on the other side.

> *Later I found out that the gate across the path was just to stop or control the amount of firewood that the villagers removed from the hillside.*

I pressed on with the boy, past the soldiers who ignored us, till he pointed to a path ascending to the right. Of course, I had to give him a tip, and undertaking a walk like this without a detailed map, I was at the time grateful for his help. It was a stiff climb up, but all the time the cloud cover was increasing so I pressed on. After about two hours I reached a grassy ridge top and was pleased to see that there were fewer clouds on the other side of the mountain.

Budhanilkantha - the village with Sheopuri behind

Just as I was finishing eating my lunch the sun came out and luckily I noticed my shadow; it was telling me that I had taken a right turn in the clouds and was now sitting on a north-south ridge, whereas I had thought I was on the pass into the Liku Khola valley. This meant that I had to turn left to reach the summit whereas otherwise I would have turned right and got completely lost.

A bit more climbing brought me out on the sunny summit of Sheopuri. At 8943 ft. it was well above most of the clouds. My efforts were rewarded with great views.

Sheopuri – From the viewpoint

Whilst I was sitting watching the changing mountain scenery a well-dressed Nepalese man came up and we started chatting. He was collecting plants, in particular, a herb related to coriander. When I stood up to go he offered to accompany me; but he didn't know the route and had a poor sense of direction. The result was that we descended far too far to the north and missed the pass into the Kathmandu Valley.

On the way down the botanist pointed out to me the signs of leopards that live in the area, and gave me some 'jungle fruit', small seeds with a sweet aftertaste.

Eventually, we had to leave our good track (which was not much more than an animal track) and head into the jungle to our left. It was a miracle that after cutting myself to shreds we emerged onto the main track down to the Likku Khola. At this point, the botanist was all for going right but I convinced him we had to go left and uphill to get back to the pass. After slogging back up a thousand feet we reached the pass and descended on the correct side.

Sheopuri - The author at the viewpoint

A short way down we came to a house where we were served arak, distilled chang millet beer; it was heartwarming stuff! Knowing that we were on the right path we raced down and out through a small gate in the wall. It turned out that my helpful boy earlier in the day hadn't shown me the correct path.

I said goodbye to the botanist I had rescued and was pleased to see that a boy was still guarding my bike over eight hours later! I cycled fast to get back to Kathmandu but even so, it was after dark when I got back to the hotel; luckily this time with two still functioning pedals!

3rd December 1980: Kathmandu (Bhaktapur)

After another long breakfast saying goodbye to people, I walked to the Thai Embassy and picked up my visa. To get to Bhaktapur I took the trolly bus built a few years earlier by the Chinese; it was cheap and much easier than cycling.

A short walk from the terminus took me to the Durbar Square. I sat in the sun eating peanut butter and marmalade sandwiches that I had prepared the night before.

Bhaktapur - Dhairab Nath temple

The tourist office published a three-hour walking tour of the town which I followed. From Durbar Square the route took me past the Nyatapola Temple to the Narayan Temple in Sukuldhoka. Heading out of town I visited the Dattatraya Temple. I rested for a while drinking tea in the temple-like café that had been built overlooking Durbar Square, and ran into two people there who I knew.

Bhaktapur - King Malla statue

Bhaktapur - Nyathpola Square

I found Bhaktapur very interesting. Despite its bad press in my guidebook, it was just as filthy as Kathmandu but it hadn't been touched much by tourism.

Bhaktapur - Durbar Square

4th December 1980: Kathmandu (Rest Day)

Someone I knew was leaving the Kathmandu Guest House so I was able to arrange to move back into the room in the annex I had occupied before the trek. After a lot of toing and froing everything was moved across leaving time before lunch to write some Christmas postcards.

I was pretty fed up with meals that were Chinese tasting by now, so spent rather too much having a pizza and curd in KC's restaurant. The remainder of my rest day was spent looking at souvenirs and trying to decide what, if anything, to buy.

Even after overeating at lunch, I was ready for a filling meal at Astha's in the evening but I was trapped on a table with a loud couple and another man who was dead quiet. I spilt a bottle of beer over them!

5th December 1980: Kathmandu (Nagarkot)

Another very foggy morning with the promise of a fine day to follow. I caught an early morning trolley bus back to Bhaktapur; it was crowded with school children and farmers so I had to push to get on board. Then I set out on the trek to Nagarkot. It started with a gently sloping walk over an alluvial plain and soon I found myself at the city waterworks at the foot of the hills. It was here that my guidebook suggested that there was a shortcut up the hill which avoided the lengthy winding ascent taken by the road. Some boys tried to tell me that the track didn't go to Nagarkot, but I ignored them; I had had my fill of being led astray by the advice of boys.

The path started to go up and down a bit as it followed a water pipeline up the valley. When I reached the dam that was feeding the pipeline there was a stiff climb up to the main road, joining it above all the hairpin bends. I was however disconcerted to find that the milestone by the side of the road indicated that I was still 8 km from the top by road.

Nagarkot - Village with mountains behind

I plodded on, but the road was hard to walk on. So I diverted onto the older track that ran in parallel to the surfaced road and passed through villages on the way. When I reached the base of the final ridge I had to leave the road again as it took a long loop to gain height; instead I had a short stiff climb up to the lodges.

I was in luck as it was a cloudless day, and whilst the hills were a bit hazy in the midday sun, the mountains were all visible including Everest. The climb had taken me three hours, exactly what the guidebook had indicated.

Nagarkot – The view of Gauri Shankar

I bought my most expensive Nepalese soft drink; a rip-off as the restaurant was on a surfaced road and didn't have to cover inflated transport costs. I was told that the next bus back to the valley was at 2:30 p.m. That gave me time to walk to the main viewpoint, take my pictures, and eat my sandwiches. I was a bit thirsty as I had put too much chlorine in my water bottle but I couldn't afford another drink at the inflated prices. At 2 p.m. I heard the bus go past and head off down the mountain!

I didn't have many options; reluctantly I set off to walk back down to Bhaktapur, following the same route as I came up to be on the safe side. I raced down with only one rest stop and made it in time to catch the 5 p.m. trolley bus from Bhaktapur back to Kathmandu. Unsurprisingly I could hardly walk from the bus stop up to Thamel; I had probably trekked close to 29 km and climbed about 3,000 ft. that day.

After a relaxing hot shower, I tried out the newly opened Rum-Doodle restaurant opposite the Guest House. I enjoyed a well-deserved meal including a delicious steak.

Kathmandu - Washing near Bhimsen Tower

6th December 1980: Kathmandu (Rest Day)

I was just a bit stiff the following morning and was in no hurry to go anywhere! There was always washing to do, and then I sat in the sun on the Guest House lawn writing. After a light lunch of banana juice and an apple pie, I set out to find a thangka[4] that I liked. After getting a lot of sales talk, I found someone who was helpful and seemed to be knowledgeable about thangkas. I selected one that wasn't too drab but still looked authentic. It was a major purchase on my limited budget but ended my search for a Tibetan souvenir.

During the early evening power cut I walked to the Kebab Corner restaurant which had appeared attractive when I had gone past in the daytime. But I saw dressed-up waiters and posh clientele so retreated to the more budget-friendly Asthas.

7th December 1980: Kathmandu (Last Day)

On my last day in Nepal, I had breakfast with a Swiss couple who were on my truck out from London. Then two other people I knew turned up after trekking so I sat about a bit longer chatting. It was a typical rest day morning, filled with washing and writing and then a trip to the Post Office and the bank. I made a few small purchases, including a pair of coat hangers to better air clothes in tropical climates.

In the evening I ate for the first time in Jemaly's with a few fellow Encounter Overland travellers. I had a really good three-course meal but as always it cost more. After having a final Coke in the Roxy bar I returned to my room to finish packing.

---

[4] A thangka is a Tibetan Buddhist painting depicting a Buddhist deity or scene.

Kathmandu - Flying out

View of Everest from the plane

THAILAND

Bangkok was a noisy city with no real centre or focus. The hotel where I stayed had in the past been renowned for drug dealing but in fact, turned out to be quite safe and pleasant. In a time before yearly guidebook updates any information about hotels quickly became out of date. The hotel was however some way from the river and finding my way around on the excellent cheap buses was a must. I soon exhausted ideas for sightseeing in the city and my two trips out into the countryside were far more fun.

The Thais were industrious and helpful, but perhaps a bit characterless. The temples (Wats) were well-kept, mostly modern, and brightly painted. But the only aspect I personally found spiritual was some of the very large Buddha images.

8th December 1980: Kathmandu - Bangkok

I had one last breakfast in the Kathmandu Guest House before selling my blanket to the hotel and jumping into a taxi to the airport. I was able to exchange my remaining small change before leaving.

My flight was 30 minutes late departing because a warning light came on at our first attempt to take off. Of course, we didn't know if it came on again at the second attempt, but we got safely airborne and took off to the north giving excellent views of the mountains from the window seat I had chosen. The flight had one stop in Calcutta on the way to Bangkok. I enjoyed the in-flight service with tasty food, and the complementary wine and spirits even more so.

Bangkok airport (Don Mueang) was modern and organised. The first few breaths of the hot humid air came as a bit of a shock as I was acclimatised to Nepal's mountain weather. There was an inexpensive air-conditioned shuttle bus that would take passengers to any city hotel. On boarding the bus, I gave my destination as the Atlanta Hotel and sat next to another budget traveller. He was going to try the Malaysia Hotel, even though the airport hotel desk had told me earlier that it had no vacancies. I decided to get off the bus with him and give it a try. The bus driver was a bit upset when I didn't get off at the Atlanta, but the Malaysia hotel turned out to have a room we could share.

Even in 1980 the Malaysia Hotel built for the Vietnam R&R trade was looking strangely dated. The notice board in the foyer was quite an institution and a good source of information. It was the type of establishment where you debated as to whether your valuables would be safer left in the room or entrusted to the hotel safe! The hotel had an inexpensive restaurant where I was able to buy a cheeseburger and a big bottle of Coke.

We had gained 90 minutes flying from Nepal to Thailand so it was nearly midnight local time before I felt tired and tried to get some sleep.

The Malaysia Hotel on Soi Ngam Duphi was one of the original hotels recommended in the first Lonely Planet guidebook. Back in the Vietnam days, it was quickly thrown together for the R&R trade, Then the war ended and they would have had an empty hotel had they not cut prices to the bone to fill it with back-packers. The Malaysia was a working test on how long a building could hold together with much abuse and no care.

9th December 1980: Bangkok (Orientation)

I had a very disturbed night due to the heat and the frequent trips by my roommate to the bathroom; I too felt a dose of the trots coming on. A restaurant across the road served a good breakfast of omelette, fruit juice, toast and coffee. It was a substantial meal that gave my stomach something to work on.

Bangkok – Main railway station

I purchased a copy of the very informative bus timetable; buses had a uniform one Baht fare for any journey in the central area. A No 4 bus took me to the Railway Station. The bus wasn't airconditioned, but it was bearable inside as long as we kept moving. At the station, I picked up a train timetable, and after checking the departures to Malaysia I joined the Advance Reservations queue. When I eventually worked my way to the head of the queue I found I had to have a number before I could be served; so I went to the back of the queue again.

Two girls who were on the same flight as me the previous day turned up whilst I was waiting; they were easily recognised as one had a leg in a plaster cast. I told them that they needed a number before joining the queue, but when my number turned up we decided to book all three tickets together. We were unable to get a sleeper reservation all the way through to Penang in Malaysia, it would be necessary for us to move to a coach car in the morning at Hat Yai on the way south to Butterworth.

I made my way down dusty noisy streets from the station to the Post Office where I had to queue again to buy stamps. I decided that ordering a quick lunch from the appetizing roadside food stalls was too difficult and potentially not safe. I walked through my first Asian food hall, with many traders combining to serve complete meals, but in the end, my lunch was just a Coke bought on Oriental Pier and drunk on the ferry.

The ferry gave a fast ride upriver to the palace area but I didn't see any of the canal life I was expecting; Srinigar had more happening on the water. On my first day in Bangkok, I wasn't aiming to do much sightseeing. Instead, I headed to the Thai Student Travel office opposite the Viengtai Hotel. They sold me a ticket for a day trip out of the city to Ayutthaya the next day. A visit to the Tourist Office yielded information on visiting Lop Buri, and the address of the Garuda airline offices.

Food could be very cheap in Bangkok. I visited the Lisboa restaurant opposite the hotel for my evening meal. It was well cooked but was a poor introduction to Thai food; the menu was designed instead to appeal to international backpackers.

10th December 1980: Bangkok (Ayutthaya)

My alarm was set for a 7:15 pickup from the hotel, but I received a phone call after I had gone to bed telling me the start time had been put back to 8 a.m. That meant there was time for a quick breakfast before boarding an air-conditioned mini-bus for the 85-minute journey to Ayutthaya. This was my first experience of air-conditioned cars; the ice-cold break from Bangkok's humidity was welcome.

Ayutthaya was the capital of Siam until its destruction by the Burmese in 1767. The various Wats, dating from the late 14th century, were either pleasantly ruined or were colourfully restored. On the tour, I visited six of the Wats including Wat Phanan Choeng with a big seated Buddha, Wat Phra Sri Sanphet with three good chedis, and Phra Mongkol Bophit with a huge bronze seated Buddha. I found the large Buddhas rather eery, but was impressed by how clean and tidy the Wats were; a contrast with the lived-in look of India's Hindu temples. It was also interesting to see the mix of Thai, Burmese and Cambodian styles of architecture in Ayutthaya.

Ayutthaya – Chedis at Wat Phra Sri Sanphet

We were taken to lunch in a river-side restaurant and offered a full meal of curry, sweet-sour fish and meat, fried chicken, and soup. From there a fast river taxi sped us to Bang Pa-In. This was a famous royal summer palace built in the 19th century in a hotchpotch of architectural styles. Undoubtedly the best pavilion was the Chinese one, a gift to the King from rich traders in 1887. Its design was best summarised as a tasteless Victorian monstrosity.

Bang Pa-in - The Chinese pavilion

Back in Bangkok, I took a dip in the hotel pool and chatted with a few guys about potential routes to Sydney. For dinner, I walked with my roommate to the Talad Nam Restaurant on Silom Road. It was a long walk but we were rewarded with an excellent, albeit relatively expensive, Mexican-style meal.

11th December 1980: Bangkok (Sightseeing)

After a toast and egg for breakfast, I set out by bus to visit the concrete temple of Wat Saket on an artificial mound; the only hill in Bangkok. Bangkok was such a mess that even this viewpoint couldn't offer an attractive view of the city. However, I ran into a student who wanted to show me around. Such offers were common; I met other people being shown around by a "free" guide working for tips from shops; but I liked to feel I was street-wise after my experiences in Srinagar, Kashmir.

Bangkok – A city view from Wat Saket

After looking at the Buddhas in the temple at the base of the mount we took a bus to the government jewel factory. There I had to look interested in a few rings to get a 'free' Coke, but the thought of spending $500 on my index finger was quite incongruous with my backpacker lifestyle.

In a brief escape from shopping opportunities Wat Benchamabophit, the Marble Temple, was our next stop. This temple looked much better from the outside, however, I found it quite moving to just sit on the floor at the feet of the Buddha. But my guide was all for moving on. He was saying that the other temples were not open and suggesting that I look at shops instead, to which my response was to part company.

Bangkok - Wat Benchamabophit

I was now becoming quite proficient at finding my way around on the buses. Returning to the river I popped into the student travel shop to find out if I could visit the Philippines cheaply on the way to Australia. That wasn't an option; I would have to follow the established 'hippie' trail, down through Singapore and Indonesia.

Moving on to the Royal Palace, the royal temple Wat Phra Keo was closed for an official function but I was able to wander into a small part of the palace grounds and take some photographs from the outside. In contrast, Wat Pho, the Temple of the Reclining Buddha, was open and bustling with monks. I found the reclining

Buddha the least interesting sight as it was all a bit dismal and tatty. Apart from the main sanctuary with the famous Reclining statue, there were also many interesting smaller temples and well-maintained gardens.

Bangkok – Wat Pho

On the other side of the river, a short ferry ride away from Tha Tien Pier was Wat Arun. The feature of interest here was the 86m high prang, or spire, decorated with ceramics and porcelain. Unfortunately, when I got there, the sun was in the wrong direction for good photography.

I ended my city tour with an express ferry from Tha Trien to Central Pier from where it was a short walk to Silom Road and the Central Department Store. Wandering around in the air-conditioning, it was just like an English department store except there were five young sales assistants behind each counter and lots of paperwork to be completed with each sale. The prices were fixed so I looked at the cost of Thai silk, but in the end, just bought a few necessities. After exploring Surawong Road I caught a No 4 bus back along Rama IV road to my hotel.

That evening I had a filling Chinese meal, but was still disappointed that I had not been able to sample any authentic (spicy) Thai food.

The daytime temperatures when I was in Bangkok were in the low 30's with 76% relative humidity. It was quite a contrast from Kathmandu.

12th December 1980: Bangkok (Lop Buri)

I had to skip breakfast and brave the rush-hour buses to get to the station in time to catch an early train to Lop Buri. The 3rd class coach was quite impressive with padded seats and no Indian overcrowding. The train left on time and kept on time for the 154 km journey. It wasn't a much-used railway line and I was amazed to see people walking along the tracks and even pushing themselves along on makeshift wheeled trollies. I was able to buy plenty of cheap food and drink, some from the restaurant car and some from vendors who jumped on board at the frequent stops.

Train Ticket to Lop Buri

Lop Buri was a Khmer capital dating from the 10th century. Some of the ruins date from this period, and some from the later period of Thai rule under King Narai of Ayutthaya in the mid-17th century.

I started my days sightseeing with a bit of duff map reading and got completely lost. With hindsight, I realised that I had started at the ruins of the Wat Phra Sri Mahathart monastery, though that was not my plan. Then more by chance than planning I found the Narai Ratchanives Palace. It was built by King Narai the Great, the king who ruled Ayutthaya from 1656 to 1688. He ordered the palace built in 1666, but now it was not much more than a set of walls of limited architectural interest.

When I oriented my sketch map correctly I was able to get back on the rails and reset my tour in the marketplace. The dominant interest there was the Khmer ruin of Prang Khaek, the oldest monument in Lop Buri and one of the oldest Khmer-style Hindu shrines in Thailand. Finally, on my way back to the station I looked at what I considered the best ruin of them all, Phra Prang Sam Yod. This 13th century Hindu shrine was in excellent condition.

Lop Buri - The market and Prang Khaek

Satisfied with what I had seen in a long busy morning I caught the 1 o'clock train back to Bangkok, picking up goodies like fresh pineapple chunks as compensation for missing out on lunch.

When I got back to the hotel I found that my roommate had left, and was even more surprised to find a friend of his in his place! Back in my airconditioned room, I busied myself catching up with the diary and finishing a letter home. Eventually, I had to give up and I popped across the road for dinner.

Lop Buri Pra Prang Sam Yod

Lop Buri Station

13th December 1980: Bangkok – South Thailand

Yet another rough night with a fever; probably a result of tasting so much local food on the train. I still had a temperature when I got up, but this was not a day for resting in bed, I was leaving the Malaysia Hotel to go to Malaysia!

Eating breakfast was a challenge but some familiar food may have helped my stomach. After paying my share of the hotel bill I took the easy option of a tuk-tuk to the station with my bags. I was feeling a bit frail and my luggage was noticeably heavier now I wasn't wearing my boots!

Leaving my bags in the station cloakroom, I exchanged some Malaysian dollars at the station bank and then set out to do some final sightseeing. It was disappointing to find that the snake farm was closed on a Saturday, but I was able to buy myself a snakeskin wallet as a souvenir from a shop across the road. Then after posting a letter at the GPO, I went back to the Central Department Store to buy silk ties.

Having been impressed by my evening meal at the Talad Nam restaurant I returned there for lunch. This time I ordered seafood in curry sauce. It arrived wrapped in foil and it was seriously hot and spicy. It was so hot I had no idea what fish I was eating. But I was happy to have finally found some real Thai food.

My carriage on the train to Butterworth

Returning to the station I had to wait around till the train to Butterworth was ready for boarding. The accommodation in the sleeper car was quite spacious with only one berth on each side of the corridor. The drinks on board were

240

cheap, as they had been on the train to Lop Buri, but the food ended up being expensive; I was sure that the waiter must have overcharged me.

We were well away from the built-up suburbs of Bangkok and were travelling over flat waterlogged jungle and paddy fields as the light faded. When it was dark, the coach was transformed by the attendant, curtains and sheets appeared, the seats folded down to make a lower berth, and the upper berth pulled down from the roof. I sat chatting with the two English girls for a while and then we all went to bed.

The berths were surprisingly comfortable even though the train seemed to spend most of the time stopping and starting due to adverse signals and the token single line working. I suppose that if the train went any faster in the night it would knock down too many people and animals!

The International Express nearing Malaysia

MALAYSIA

The first thing I noticed entering Malaysia was the large Chinese population. This led to Chinese hotels (bare rooms with a minimum of furniture), food halls, and the busy Chinatown business communities. The Chinese running the Tye Anne Hotel where I stayed on Penang Island were some of the few people I encountered with happy faces; in general, the Chinese did not smile or engage with tourists.

It was a disappointment to find that the tropical island of Penang didn't have the crystal-clear water I was expecting. The beaches were sandy but the sea was cloudy if not polluted.

Food was once again cheap, especially if you were hooked on a diet of Nasi and Mee Goreng. The breakfast at the Tye Anne with Chinese porridge was another culinary high spot.

In Penang, I encountered my first torrential tropical afternoon downpour.

14th December 1980: Thailand – Penang

Sleep on the train was interrupted regularly but the gentle rocking soon sent one back to one's dreams. When I finally woke to daylight, the scenery was much as it had been the evening before, so I didn't miss much in the night! We were served a standard breakfast of fried eggs at an exorbitant price.

When half the carriages were removed at Hat Yal there was a big scrum to find space in the train; I ended up sitting on my suitcase for the one-hour journey to the Malaysian border. The border station at Padang Besar was chaotic, with suspected 'hippy' types being given short-stay visas at random. I was lucky and got the maximum stay of 14 days.

It isn't clear why there were fewer passengers on the train after the border, but I got a seat and was able to complete the journey to Butterworth in relative comfort. On the Malaysian side, the train passed at first through lush tropical jungle but soon we were back to civilisation with paddy fields and rubber plantations. Here the paddy fields were larger and the main season rice planting was already sprouting green.

The stop at the border was longer than scheduled, so as a result, we arrived at Butterworth late. As soon as we got off the train there was a rush to get onto the modern ferry to Penang. The trip to the island was free; it only cost to come back to the mainland. The sun had by now all but set, and Penang rose as a grey mass from the sea into the clouds.

From the ferry port, I took a rickshaw to the budget hotel area. The rickshaws in Penang had the passengers sitting in front of the cyclist; which didn't seem as safe, particularly as they weaved through heavy traffic after dark. The New China Hotel and several others nearby were full. I picked up a second rickshaw to take me down Leboh Chulia. Still, everywhere I tried was full, so when the pleasant guy in the Tye Anne offered me a bed in the corridor I took it.

That evening I ate at one of the most popular Indian restaurants in town, Dawood, where I had a tasty curry.

George Town waterfront

15th December 1980: Penang (orientation)

There might have been some security issues sleeping in the hotel corridor, but I had a surprisingly good sleep. One attraction of the Tye Anne was that it was renowned for its excellent breakfasts served downstairs; each morning I enjoyed the first-class porridge.

The hotel offered me a bed in the noisy dormitory which I took to avoid wasting any more time searching for somewhere else (and inevitably finding somewhere more expensive). With my accommodation sorted I set off to explore Georgetown. My first stop was St. George's Church, the oldest purpose-built Anglican church in Southeast Asia. Consecrated in 1819 it looked as if it had been transported stone by stone from England. Sitting quietly in the church I felt a lot closer to home than ever a letter or postcard could achieve.

Georgetown - Fort Cornwallis

The Tourist Office was able to provide me with some general information to supplement the brief description of Georgetown in the Lonely Planet guide. Fort Cornwallis turned out to be unimpressive, except for the 400-year-old Dutch canon, but it was a good viewpoint. After changing some money so I could buy aerograms in the Post Office I decided to take a ferry back to the mainland. This would allow me to take photos of the island from the water by daylight and also to enquire about onward trains to Singapore at Butterworth railway station.

`Penang – A view from the ferry

Back in Penang in the afternoon, I took a No 11 bus to the Aquarium. There was plenty to look at in over 40 tanks, though not all the fish were from Malaysian waters. It was most interesting and well presented but plagued by children racing around the tanks at five times the speed I wanted to go.

On the way back to the Tye Ann I researched the options for my evening meal and also purchased 4 ft of chain to secure my bags for when I was sleeping in a communal dorm. Later that evening I returned to the restaurant I had selected, the Hong Kong Chinese restaurant, where I ate chicken satay using chopsticks, to slow me down! After purchasing a flavoured ice pudding I went to the Hong Kong Bar, one of the many pubs that catered for seamen and travellers. I had a good time chatting to some other travellers and drinking some fairly respectable beer.

16th December 1980: Penang (Tanjung - Bungah)

With my day sack stuffed with swimming togs and a towel, I headed for the Pranga bus stand to catch a Blue Bus around the north side of the island. The bus I boarded stopped short at Tanjun–Bungah so rather than wait for the next one I bought a paper, had a drink, and then set off to walk along the coast to Batu Ferringhi. It was hot, but not too unpleasant for walking.

I stopped at several places along the way to take in the views, then when I reached the best beach marked by a small cluster of hotels I swam in the Andaman Sea. The water was cloudy and had a lot of rubbish floating in it, quite a disappointment given how idyllic the beach looked.

Penang - Batu Ferringhi beach

Refreshed I pressed on and by the early afternoon had reached a village with several restaurants where I refuelled on a filling Murtabak (curry in fried pastry). I thought I had reached Batu Ferringhi but had actually walked along the entire north coast to Telok Bahang. I must have been thick not to have noticed from the bus ticket, road signs or mileposts that I wasn't in Batu Ferringhi; I put it down to the heat!

The bus I caught back once again terminated at Tanjung-Bungah. When I changed buses I lost my window seat and I ended up standing all the way back to Georgetown. With all the exercise I was losing weight and my trousers were falling down, so I had to haggle for a leather belt from a shop on my way back to the hotel.

There were three new faces in the dorm (of five beds) when I got back to the Tye Anne. After a lemon juice, a shower and clothes wash I felt ready for my evening meal in a food hall. From one Chinese-run stall I ordered the local soup Laksa and from another the most delicious fried noodle dish. After ordering from the various food stalls I sat down and waited for it to be delivered to my table. The tricky thing was remembering to go around and pay the vendors before leaving.

Penang- The coast near Telok Bahang

That evening I was temped back for another drink at the Hong Kong Bar. It was there that I was introduced to the "Aussie" style of payment; leaving my change on the bar ready for the next order.

I was starting to like Penang. Not just for the excellent food, but also because it was a fascinating Chinese town. The tropical heat was becoming less oppressive and the day-to-day activities, particularly eating, were becoming more interesting.

17th December 1980: Penang (Botanical Gardens)

A quiet Wednesday was in order after my exertions the day before. It started with a visit to St George's Church for the morning communion service followed by a short chat with the English vicar. My search for the British Council was futile, it was not where it was shown on the Tourist Office map. I returned to the Tourist Office who admitted it was shown in the wrong place. With updated directions, I found it the second time and sat reading newspapers till lunchtime. The chicken rice I ordered for lunch was not too inspiring and I slept it off with a siesta back at the hotel.

For my main outing for the day I chose to visit the Botanical Gardens, an easy ride on a No 7 bus that passed right outside my hotel. By a strange coincidence, I found the two English girls from the Bangkok train on the same bus!

Penang – The Botanical Gardens

The gardens were pleasant, with lawns surrounded by jungle-covered hills. It was however a bit too popular even mid-week.

Back in Georgetown, my final mission was to cross over to the mainland and buy an onward train ticket. The earliest I could get on an overnight train to Kuala Lumpur was in four days.

Although I didn't have a way to play music, I took advantage of the lax copyright laws to buy two pirate cassette tapes, of music I had listened to in the overland truck.

During the day I had noticed a restaurant advertising Gado-Gado; an Indonesian dish I was keen to try. I headed back there for my dinner and was disappointed to find that they didn't serve it in the evening; instead, I enjoyed a delicious Mee Jawa Goreng (fried noodles). For the rest of my meal, I headed to the Prangin Food Hall and had another Laksa and a bowl of Nasi Gorang (fried rice). I observed that on a slack day, not all the food vendors opened their stalls, and was amused to see that a record shop was open for businesses nearby to provide music for diners. My complete meal cost less than £1.

Penang – A ferry ticket to Butterworth

18th December 1980: Penang (Gertak Sangul)

I packed my swimming togs again and set off to the Prangin bus terminal from where a No 67 bus would take me down the East Coast and around the south of the island. The bus wasn't very frequent, but eventually one turned up. It was a pleasant journey as gradually the coastal development thinned and the jungle took over. The bus conductor showed me where to get off for Gertak Sangul Beach. I soon found myself a delightful isolated spot to set up, away from the main beach which itself was hardly crowded.

Once again I was disappointed to find the water was cloudy, though it was a lot cleaner than it had been on the north coast. I spent a relaxing time swimming, writing and crab-watching.

Penang - Gertak Sanggul Beach

Mid-afternoon I packed up and had only a short wait till a bus came by to take me back to Telok Kumba. In another one of those strange travel coincidences, when I popped into a restaurant to get a drink I ran into a girl who was staying in my dorm. I happily finished off her Mee Gorang for her; I had had no lunch. I changed to another bus that would take me past the Snake Temple but I found it disappointing; it was modern and had very few snakes.

That evening there was a tropical storm which made it feel nice and cool. After a dish of sweet-sour prawns in the Hong Kong Restaurant, I moved on to an Indian restaurant and had a delicious Murtabak.

Georgetown - Street scene

The timing of my onward rail ticket would result in my being in Singapore over Christmas. I was increasingly concerned that this might make it difficult to get a visa issued for onward travel to Indonesia.

19th December 1980: Penang (Penang Hill)

Out with my walking boots for a climb up Penang Hill. The path started by the Botanical Gardens, and at the start, the route was well marked, both by signs and a trail of litter. Leaving the town behind there were lots of jungle noises; a reminder of how many animals call the hills their home. I also encountered a variety of butterflies; some that I saw had a wingspan of over 9 inches.

Penang Hill - View from the summit

There were only two stiff climbs to get to the top of the hill; it was child's play for someone fresh from trekking in Nepal. But in the high humidity, the sweat was fair pouring out! I reached the top (2,700 ft) after about three hours; in time to reward myself with a lunch of Nasi Goreng and a 7-Up from the tea room.

The views were a bit hazy, but the temperature at the top was very pleasant and it wasn't too crowded. I took a stroll on the clearly labelled paths down to the funicular tunnel and back. The fare for a one-way ride down on the funicular was $2 which was too much for me. So I set off to walk down to the middle station where the fare was only $1. But I was thwarted. At first, I was able to follow the railway down the hill but when I reached the railway viaduct I was forced to contour and ended up back on the same path I had come up on.

I decided to cut my losses and return the way I had come up. Well, it wasn't exactly cutting losses as I saved money!

The cloud cover had increased and it had started to spit with rain occasionally. With that incentive, I made good progress and got down in two hours.

Penang Hill Funicular Railway

Once again I enjoyed a great dinner at a backpacker price; fried noodles, mutton korma and pineapple.

20th December 1980: Penang (round the island)

Before heading out to circumnavigate Penang Island I had to buy a new padlock; my cheap Nepalese padlock had seized up, it wasn't designed for humidity perhaps! I also had to go to the Garuda airline office to adjust the reservation I had to fly out of Singapore to Indonesia to give me more time to arrange a visa over Christmas. After that, I was free to start my trip around the island, catching a No 66 bus to Balik Pulau on the western side of the island. I had to wait in the bus for a long time before it set out and it got quite stuffy inside.

After Telok Kumbar the bus took a relatively new road that had been constructed up the west side of the island. It didn't follow the coast, and the route was much more hilly with forest-covered ridges to cross.

Titi Kerawan Falls

In Balik, I had to change bus again to continue up the west side of the island. The No 76 buses were far less frequent, and my bus, when it turned up, was quite an antique with an ant nest in the floorboards and broken seats. An old lady annoyed by the noise her chicken was making on the bus just broke its neck!

I asked the conductress to drop me off at Titi Kerawan Waterfall, which she did, giving me a two-hour break before the next bus. I had a pleasant time sitting by the freshwater pool and had a refreshing dip.

Back on the next bus, we ground our way up into the hills before dropping down to the sea on the north coast at Telok Bahang. From there, a blue bus then took me back to Georgetown completing the circumnavigation of the island.

It was my final evening in Penang so I had planned to splash out on a special evening meal but my chosen restaurant was full. So instead I settled for a Murtabak (an omelette pancake) and Mee Jawa (noodles in a spicy sauce).

21st December 1980: Penang – Kuala Lumpur

There was time for a quick last bowl of porridge for breakfast before I hurried off to the early Sunday service at St George's Church. Christmas Day was only four days away and I was missing the singing of carols. It was a good service and nice to sing some familiar hymns; the organist was blind!

Back at the hotel, I discovered that one of my dorm roommates was from Milton, just south of Abingdon in the U.K. I had a long chat with him about places to visit, then headed downstairs for a 'safe' lunch as my tummy was a bit off.

After paying my hotel bill I chained my bags in the corridor, arranging to collect them later in the day when I would be leaving to catch the evening train.

It was a hot day, and I wasn't sure where or when I would next have a shower, so I looked for ways of passing the time indoors. For most of the time, I wandered around air-conditioned shopping centres. One of them had an escalator, probably the first in Penang judging by the frightened looks of those using it. The heat burst with a tropical storm; rain so heavy it flooded the roads despite the big storm water drains.

Searching for more Christmas spirit I went to the local Uniting Church carol concert. It was a bit of a farce due to the lack of any visible organisation, but it did give me a chance to do some gusto singing.

I picked up my bags at the hotel and then proved how light they were by walking to the ferry. The sleeper car to Kuala Lumpur was just passable, not up to the standard of the International Express. The train left Butterworth at 10 p.m. but didn't fill up till an hour later. It was very noisy but I managed to grab some sleep before getting up at dawn in anticipation of our arrival at K.L.

Kuala Lumpur - Railway Station

22nd December 1980: Kuala Lumpur - Singapore

Unfortunately, the train was running late. It was an hour or so before we emerged out of the plantation and jungle green into a grey drizzly Kuala Lumpur. As a result, I missed the fast express train onward to Singapore. I reckoned that I didn't stand much chance of getting a sleeper berth for the second leg of my journey on a later train; one look at the crowds on the platform was enough to tell me that. I only had one viable choice if I didn't want to overnight in K.L. and that was to brave the crush on the slow train that left later in the morning.

After purchasing a second-class ticket I had a brief look at the outside of the station, a unique mix of Eastern and Western architectural styles. I bought some drinks and biscuits which was just as well because the slow train was packed solid. I had to sit on my suitcase for an hour before I got a seat, and even then I was cramped up with two adults and a child on the one seat.

Arriving in Singapore over the Causeway

Luckily it was pouring with rain most of the way so it wasn't too hot inside the overcrowded carriage. The scenery was pretty much the same all the way, palm groves and rubber plantations as far as the eye could see.

When the train reached Johor Bahru, the final stop in Malaysia, we had to pass through Malaysian immigration. The train was thoroughly searched before crawling across the causeway into Singapore. When the train terminated in Singapore there was a slow queue to get through immigration, but finding a bus was easy and cheap. I headed to Airmaster Travel on Princep Street, a crash pad recommended by Lonely Planet. As such accommodation was technically illegal the dorm was hidden away behind a budget travel agency; you had to walk through the shop to get to the back. I was impressed by the friendly residents with clean bunks, kitchen and washing facilities. But to get a bed I had to spend my first night sleeping on the floor. After eating a Chinese meal with some of the others I crashed out.

The dorm behind Airmaster Travel.

SINGAPORE

A tightly packed city with innumerable shopping centres, blocks of flats and crowds of people. Nearly every afternoon it would rain, heavily. Unfortunately for someone who liked to get away from the mob, there were few opportunities in Singapore. Their economy was based on people buying things; things that I hadn't the money to afford!

Passing through in a few days it was hard to form an impression about the locals, I met so few. The food halls were however a superb culinary mixing pot, and I received the best haircut of my life on Christmas Day!

The city was spotless, litter was unheard of, and with a closed community that made the place a bit characterless and potentially hostile.

23rd December 1980: Singapore (orientation)

After visiting a local café for toast and tea I set off on the familiar search for the essentials of travel, the G.P.O., the Tourist Office, and the Indonesian Embassy. A bus took me to the centre of the city near Clifford Pier, and then it was that I realised that my plans were likely to be thwarted by it being Election Day; most of the shops and offices were closed.

Singapore's waterfront was a strange blend of old and new, with the view being dominated by a new bridge they were building to Sentosa Island.

Dispirited, I walked back to the crash pad via the Anglican St Andrews Cathedral and a shop where I bought a copy of the bus timetable. Singapore had lots of buses but their routes seemed to be more aligned with the needs of commuters than getting around the town and its one-way system. The lack of litter, in particular in parks, took some getting used to.

Armed with my bus map I set out to find the Tourist Office, but it was closed. I walked down half of Orchard Road and failed to find the Indonesian Embassy, but I did find the Cold Storage supermarket where I could buy some supplies (including Alpen Muesli).

Once again back to the dorm where I found an old tourist brochure that confirmed I was looking in the correct place for the Embassy. So I set out again, this time walking the other half of Orchard Road. Finally success!! I found the Embassy and Garuda offices in a building that looked just like a shopping centre. There were so many large concrete shopping complexes, individually well-designed but collectively characterless. I admit to buying a McDonald's to celebrate a small success; it was amazing to see how the staff rushed around trying to contain the inevitable litter generated by junk food!

In the evening I had a meal at the Satay Club down by the water. It was a food hall that unsurprisingly specialised in satay which I enjoyed with fried rice. Back in the dorm, the conversation went on into the small hours. We all chipped in $10 to buy food for a Christmas party.

Singapore River

Singapore from Central Park

24th December 1980: Singapore (ChristmasEve)

How better to celebrate Christmas than by cracking open my box of Alpen muesli and reviving memories of breakfast on the Encounter Overland truck! Businesses and offices were open again and my first trip had to be to the bank to get some cash, and then to the G.P.O to collect letters.

Then it was time to join queues. First I queued in the Indonesian Embassy to hand in an application for a visa, and then again in the Garuda Office to confirm my onward flight to Indonesia. With the waiting over I went back to Cold Storage and bought goodies and booze for Christmas, which I took back to the dorm.

After changing out of my 'Embassy' clothes I jumped on my fourth bus for the day, getting off in the High Street for a short walk to the Telok Ayer Food Hall. With another tasty Murtabak to fuel my sightseeing, I braved the afternoon rain to phone home from the nearby Telecom Centre. Unfortunately, they didn't accept my little used English credit card and I had to pay upfront in cash for a 3-minute call.

Singapore - Old Chinese Quarter

As the rain had set in for the day I had to ditch my plan to visit the Japanese Gardens. Instead, I tried to get a bus to Chinatown but it was difficult as there were few cross-city services. It took me longer to get to the People's Park Centre by bus than it would have taken to me walk, but I arrived substantially drier. The Centre was a brutalist concrete replacement for areas of the old Chinatown that had been demolished in the name of progress. I wandered around in the dry for a bit, but then the rain eased enough to take a bus to Central Park. A short walk over the hill took me down to the Airmaster Travel Centre and the dorm.

We all went out for an evening meal in a vegetarian restaurant on Serangoon Road. They served Masala Dosa, an Indian pancake roll that was eaten by hand. At 10:30 I took a bus to the Cathedral. The church was full for Midnight Mass, a service that wasn't particularly moving, but it was at least the sort of Christmas celebration that I was used to.

25th December 1980: Singapore (Christmas Day)

Christmas at Airmaster Travel was marked by a relaxed start. We tidied up the dorm and started preparing the food. In a sudden move, I decided to have my hair cut for Christmas. I popped around to the Indian barber next door and had the best cut in my life, including a scalp and back massage. Feeling much more presentable I returned to the dorm to wash my hair.

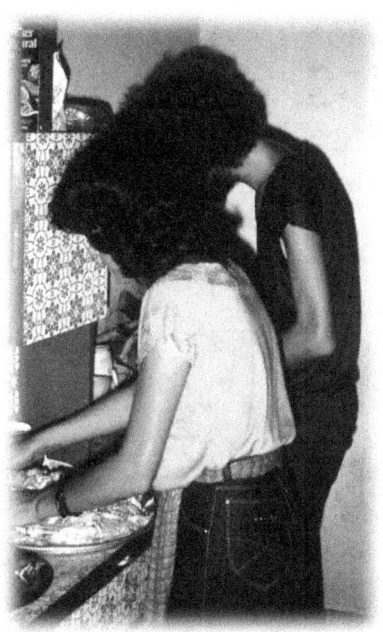

Singapore: Preparing our Christmas feast

Our feast was ready by mid-afternoon and the party started. Airmaster Travel had lent us a Hi-Fi system so we could have music and also donated a Christmas Cake, a big tin of Quality Street chocolates, and a parcel of goodies. In an act of unrestrained gluttony, I demolished my present to myself, a box of Milky Tray chocolates. Dancing continued until the small hours.

Singapore - Christmas at Airmaster Travel

Singapore - In the rain, from Sentosa island

26th December 1980: Singapore (Boxing Day)

Everyone was feeling a bit rough the next day, but I had to be up early to beat the crowds at the Indonesian Embassy on my final day in Singapore. After collecting my visa I took a bus to the Botanical Gardens.

Singapore - Orchids in the Botanical Gardens

This was a very well-cared-for park with many of England's house plants growing outside in the open and growing much larger. There was a large display of orchids that were not in a greenhouse and a section of preserved natural jungle.

After lunch back in town (Mee Goreng and Chendol) the afternoon rain started. But I refused to be beaten by the weather on my final day's sightseeing. In a torrential downpour, I took a bus to the World Trade Centre, from where it was possible to either take an expensive cable car across to Sentosa Island or a cheap ferry; I took the latter.

Sentosa was just an over-developed pleasure ground, but it was an excellent place to spend a rainy afternoon. I ended up walking around because the shuttle buses were full on a wet day. There were two good museums, one on the history of the harbour, and the other on WWII in Malaysia.

As usual, the rain dried up later in the afternoon and it was fine when I returned on the ferry to the mainland. Back at the dorm, I packed my bags and then ate with the others in the Albert Street Food Hall enjoying some excellent fruit juice.

JAVA

With the Indonesians, I was once more back amongst simple and friendly people. Jakarta was as terrible as the books described. I just wished I had been warned of the rigours of Indonesian train travel in advance.

In contrast, Yogyakarta was a relaxed attractive town with pleasant inhabitants and a slow pace of life. There was also lots to see and do in Jogja and perhaps a bit less rain. The temples in Central Java were old and interesting and I had lots of fun exploring the historic sites at Pramborian and Borobudur.

In Java, I stayed in simple Losmen, with just a few rooms, a family atmosphere, and a tank to wash from (a mandi). My enjoyable stay in Yogyakarta was rounded off by finding a pleasant roommate and a large circle of fellow travellers.

27th December 1980: Singapore - Jakarta

My plans for an early getaway didn't go down too well in the dorm. When I finally walked out the front door my luck changed as a bus turned up straight away and whisked me off the the airport. Singapore Airport was smart and well organised so progress through to the spacious departure lounge was swift. That left plenty of time to use up my remaining change and buy a coffee and a Danish pastry for breakfast. The flight to Jakarta boarded and left on time; it was a DC10 and I had a window seat; the plane was not full. There were good views over Singapore and southern Malaysia as we took off.

Singapore Airport

The inflight service wasn't as bad as I was expecting from Garuda; there were even complimentary drinks. Arriving in Indonesia, Jakarta Airport was very quiet compared with Singapore. The inbound Customs Officers were only interested in locals, so with the benefit of a 30-minute time zone change, I was out of the airport by midday local time.

Approaching Jakarta Airport

I lugged my bags past the waiting taxi drivers to the bus stop where I picked up a decrepit bus with a price to match; there was a fixed fare right across the city. It deposited me at the Banteng Bus Station, where a helpful man showed me how to get to the Gambir railway station. I planned to catch an overnight train so I would not have to stay in Jakarta. However, it soon became apparent that getting train tickets was not going to be an easy business; there were long queues of people sitting in front of empty ticket booths. So I reverted to Plan B and decided to stay a night.

The accommodation of choice was Wisma Delima at No 5 Jalan Jaksa, not far from the station. This was my first losman, a single-story homestay with a central courtyard. And it was also my first wet bathroom with a mandi, a big water trough with a dipper. I ate at the losman to avoid going out in the rain and played cards with three other travellers. It rained all night.

28th December 1980: Jakarta – Cirebon

After racing to the station first thing, I found out that they only sold tickets one hour before a train was due to depart! Tourists were however able to get a reservation in advance from the Station Master, but he wasn't going to turn up at work till mid-morning!

I walked back at a more relaxed pace to the losman to have breakfast and seek solace from others. When I returned to the station I was in the company of others who were on the same mission escape to Jogya. We found out that 3rd class tickets were unreserved, 2nd class had queues (bad at 7 am and worse by 10 am), and first-class could only be bought at Kotu station So we jumped on a bus to Kotu, and came back by taxi when we discovered that there was no 1st class on the slow overnight train.

With some difficulty, we tracked down the Station Master and obtained four ticket reservations, for myself, for an Australian (Peter), and for two Finnish girls.

Back at the losman, the man who had helped me the previous day, was back again offering to go with me to the National Museum. I cleared my room and went off with him as a guide. There were a lot of good exhibits but the presentation was poor and cluttered. And that was all my sightseeing! A short walk down the main street, Jalan Thamrin, was enough to convince me that there was nothing else for a tourist to do in Jakarta on a Sunday afternoon.

I met up with my fellow travellers at the losman and we staggered to the station with our luggage. Our reservations were valid and we were able to buy 2nd class tickets. When the train arrived it was mostly 3rd class with a refreshment car and a couple of 2nd class coaches at the rear. The seats were padded but not reclining and a pillow could be rented for a touch of luxury if you wanted one.

Jakarta – The National Museum

It was the start of a long, long night and I got little sleep; I just listened to my two cassette tapes over and over again on my headphones. In one moment of drama, a lady passenger had her bag stolen by a thief who climbed down from the roof. By 1 a.m. we had reached Cirebon on the North Coast of Java, and the engine broke down! It took three hours for them to find a replacement during which time we managed to grab some sleep.

29th December 1980: Cirebon – Yogyakarta

The slow night train lived up to its name. By dawn, we were running a good seven hours late and had lost our place in the rhythm of single-track working. The day passed dozing and drinking but with no food, till we pulled into Jogya mid-afternoon. Peter and I parted from our female companions who were heading for a room with a private bathroom, whilst we looked in at the best losman in town, the Kota. Unsurprisingly it was full, so we did a Joseph and Mary act around town (well more an Adrian and Peter act) till eventually we found a vacancy in a simple but well-located losman not mentioned in our guidebooks.

Purwokoto Station

Central Java from the train

Central Java - Paddy fields viewed from the train

Losman Jogya was in a side alley so it was quiet. The owners were friendly and the price for a double room was good reflecting the quality of the courtyard and shared mandi. Once we had had a shower (well actually a splash of water from the mandi) we ate in a restaurant popular with travellers, Superman's, on the same alleyway as our losman. They served good pseudo-western food at a reasonable price; I could see why they were popular. It was fun watching the geckos climbing up the walls in search of insect dinner.

After so little sleep on the train, we were early to bed and slept well.

Jogya - Losmen Jogya

Jogya - Main street

30th December 1980: Yogyakarta (rest day)

It was a bad idea, but we got up early to try and find another, better, losman before breakfast. But we had no luck and so were resigned to staying put. At least Superman's and our breakfast was only a few doors away!

The heat was sticky and sapped my energy so I didn't do much in the morning, just a slow walk down to the G.P.O to buy some aerograms.

Losman Jogya on Gang Sosrowijayan

There were batik shops on every corner with some lovely designs; I popped into a fixed-price shop and was surprised to find how cheap they were.

Peter and I met up for lunch at Helen's, a place I spotted on the main street (Jalan Malioboro). It served comfortable traveller food and iced fruit drinks.

The afternoon was just an extended siesta chatting to the boys in our losman and coming to like the place despite its obvious shortcomings.

We returned to Helen's for dinner, where I finally got to taste an excellent Gado-Gado. After only one day in Jogya, we started to see familiar faces as the backpackers congregated in just a few places. The evening, we had to scratch a planned visit to the Kraton, the Sultan's Palace, by night when the heavens opened sending us scuttling back to our losman.

31st December 1980: Yogyakarta (Borobudur)

It rained through the night which finally put pay to any remaining ideas we had to upgrade our losman. Suerman's came up with some passable porridge for breakfast then I did some washing whilst Peter arranged a flight.

We walked across town to the bus station intending to catch a bus to Borobudur. On our way there we met two Danish girls, Ingri and Elizabeth who were just as lost as we were and attempting to catch the same bus. When we got to the station the buses were clearly labelled and it was easy to catch the right one for the one-hour journey to Muntilon. Then there was an easy change onto a crowded local bus to Borobudur.

The small village of Borobudur has a huge terraced Buddhist monument dating from the late 9th century A.D. It was in a very different style from anything I had previously seen, with terraces of beehive structures containing Buddha images.

Borobudur - Approach to the temple through the village

We took the bus back to the smaller but pleasant Mendut Temple outside the village. After buying a selection of tropical fruits including pineapple, jambu, mangosteen and mango we sat beneath a shady tree eating our lunch.

Borobudur Temple

When we got back to Muntilon we had a lot of trouble finding a bus going to Jojya with empty seats. So we took a Colt shared minibus for a bargain price. It was a good journey but we had to push start it once.

It was the last day of 1980 and it was starting to look as if we weren't going to be able to party and welcome in the New Year. So we asked the Tourist Office for suggestions, forgetting that we were in a Muslim country where alcohol was not freely consumed. They sold us each a ticket to the Hero English Meeting Club which was going to have a 'celebration'. Ingri, Peter and I had an early evening meal and then dressed up and set out in a becak trishaw.

The hall was in the Back of Beyond, and as soon as we stepped inside we were aware we had made a BIG mistake. But there was no escape. When we went outside for 'air' we were watched like hawks being one of the few foreigners present. At 9 o'clock the speeches started. We couldn't keep a straight face; they were taking everything so seriously, and there was only tea to drink. In the end, we just couldn't take it any longer. We slipped out on the pretence of going to look for some beer, grabbed a becak and made a swift getaway.

When we got back we found that Superman's had closed. It was 10 p.m. and we still hadn't found any alcohol, but we were not going to give up. We set off on a search down Malioboro till we found a café that was open and serving beer. We drank ourselves silly, whilst others we had met around town came past and joined us! Our celebration ran on till 1:30 when the café chucked us out. The owner wouldn't give me the right change so I took back a 1000 rp note which made my evening's drinking quite cheap. Back at our losman, we carried on chatting for another hour or so.

Invitation to New Year (sic) Eve Party

1st January 1981: Yogyakarta (Kraton)

Unsurprisingly I woke with a good hangover and suffering from a lack of sleep, but all three of us were in Superman's for breakfast by 8:30. After the usual domestic chores, Peter and I set off with Ingi to visit the Kraton. There was a fair in the North Square and we were ripped off buying Cokes in a cafe. Then we found that the Sultan's palace was closed.

We jumped into a becak and headed round to the Fragrant Garden or Water Castle. This was an area of palace ruins that was taken over by batik workshops. After wandering around, Ingri bought some small and in my opinion tatty pictures. A bit of rain didn't help the generally drab scenery, and what might have been attractive was spoilt by over-enthusiastic concrete restoration.

Jogya - Water Castle

We split up; Peter and I took a look at a batik material factory and then a shadow puppet factory. Then Peter needed to go back to the losman to pack, so we took a particularly frail becak for the short trip. Ingri and Elizabeth came round and left their packs in my room whilst we all went down to the Malioboro restaurant for lunch. That afternoon Pete set off to Denpasar and the two girls to Jakarta. We swapped addresses and then I was on my own and broke (the banks were shut). An ideal excuse to get my writing up to date.

I could only afford a snack that evening at Superman's but as usual, someone I knew turned up to chat with.

Peter and Ingri having expensive Cokes

2nd January 1981: Yogyakarta (Prambanan)

My first task for the day was to make myself solvent, taking a becak to the bank which offered a good rate for US$. On the walk back I bought a bus ticket to Denpasar at the Aziatic Hotel. I figured that an air-conditioned bus with reclining seats couldn't be worse than the overnight train from Jakarta!

After a refreshing lemon juice from a stall in our alleyway, I took a becak to the Bus Station and a nice coach out to Prambanan on the road to Solo. Prambanan is the biggest Hindu temple complex in Java, but surprisingly I had difficulty finding someone who could direct me to it.

I was misdirected to a minor temple complex some 2 kilometres away. It was a hot day with a strong wind, but it was fascinating to walk over the paddy fields and see all the local life. The monument, when I reached it, was deserted.

Yogyakarta - Fruit Stall

On my way back I spotted the main temple above the trees. It had similarities with Khajuraho and was unfortunately swarming with irreverent Indonesian tourists. I was uncomfortable with how religious sites could so easily turn into tourist attractions. I met two English travellers and joined them taking a Colt shared minibus back to Jogya.

Even though my stay in Indonesia was short, I made a determined effort to learn the language. Walking to the losman on the way back from Prambanan I managed to order some fruit from a stall using just Indonesian.

3rd January 1981: Yogyakarta (Shopping)

A miserable day raining on and off, leading to my cancelling any ambitious plans I had. In a blitz on catching up with my correspondence, I wrote ten postcards and one letter. At lunchtime, I negotiated with a becak to take me to the G.P.O. to post the fruits of my morning's writing, and then on the way back go to the fixed-price batik shop. I bought an expensive hand-produced shirt, some material for Mum, and a tablecloth; all for just over 50 US$. On a separate expedition between showers, I bought two cheap batik shirts from street stalls and then washed them to get rid of some of the residual wax.

After an evening meal back at Helen's I wandered down to the North Palace square where a big circus and fair was being held. I was swept along by the crowds. It was very noisy because each stall had its own P.A. blaring away. The museum in the Kraton had displays on batik and wax dioramas of court life which I found interesting.

Yogyakarta - Gamelon orchestra in the Kraton

4th January 1981: Yogyakarta - Denpasar

It was my last day in Java and Yogyakarta. The morning was spent packing, and playing chess with one of the losman boys; the latter resulted in a comprehensive defeat for me.

Just before midday, on a hot sunny day, I walked down to the Sultan's Palace area of the Kraton; I was quite surprised to learn that Jogya still had a Sultan. The guided tour of the pavilions was inexpensive, but the displays were not as good as I had seen the night before in the museum. However, the architecture of the palace was interesting for its blend of Hindu, Buddhist, and Contemporary styles. The high spot of the tour was a classical dance rehearsal complete with a Gamelan Orchestra.

Check-out from the losman was 2 p.m. after which I enjoyed another Gado-Gado at Helen's. There was plenty of time to kill chatting in the losman till later in the afternoon when I boarded the coach to Bali at the Aziatic Hotel.

The Cakrawala coach did a tour of the town gradually picking up passengers, but when we finally left it was hardly full; I had a double seat. It was a nice modern clean coach, and there was just one other traveller on board, a Swede.

On the other side of Solo, we stopped for rice and curry which was included in the ticket price. It wasn't a gourmet meal, and when we got back onto the coach two people had gone missing along with one man's luggage.

Though it was quite early in the evening there was little to see out the windows and most passengers settled down on the reclining seats to grab some sleep. The driver drove like a maniac and it was best not to watch. I slept fitfully till we arrived at the primitive Java-Bali car ferry at dawn.

We stopped soon afterwards for a token breakfast in Bali then pressed on through attractive paddy fields to get to Denpasar at 8:30 a.m.

Bus ticket from Jojya to Denpasar

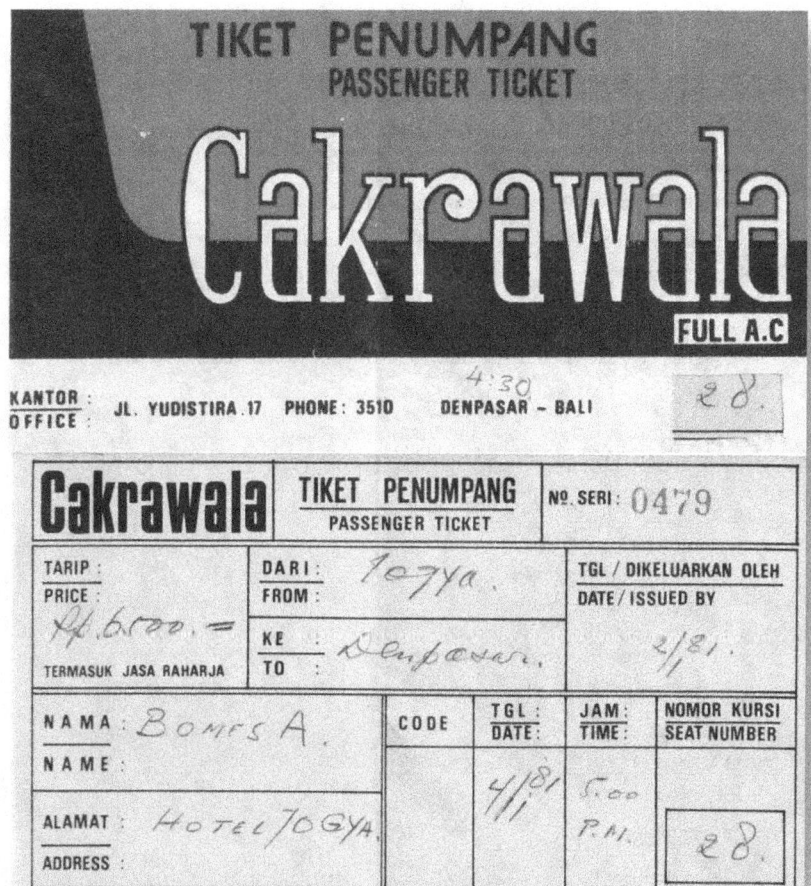

BALI

Compared with the Javanese train, the overnight bus to Denpasar was a relative luxury. It was a good start to my time in Bali, a relaxed end to the rigours of overland travel. The losman I stayed in in Ubud allowed me to experience the real life of Bali well away from the tourist beach culture at Kuta Beach.

Balinese life revolves around their religion; they are Hindu, and they have a great feeling for beauty which is reflected in their temples, gardens and houses.

With its mountains, terraced paddy fields and temples there was no questioning the island's beauty. But it also had something special that attracted the tourists and seemed to survive despite them. I put it down to the universal presence of religion in their lives but it is something I found hard to understand or express.

Once again I met many other fellow travellers in Bali, often people I had met earlier on my trip. It was fun to compare notes and impressions.

5th January 1981: Denpasar – Ubud

My chosen destination in Bali was Ubud, a centre for traditional crafts and dance far from the beaches. But the coach from Jogya didn't stop at a particularly convenient place in Denpasar. I had a fair walk in the blazing sunshine to where Lonely Planet had marked "Ubud Bemos" on their sketch map. When I got there my requests for "Dimana ada bemo Ubud?" were met with blank looks or conflicting directions. One thing was certain, there were no bemos (shared pickup trucks) going to Ubud from where I was. After wandering around I was rescued by a bemo going to Gunung Kawi which took me past Mas and then transferred me onto an Ubud bemo. It all went very smoothly and only cost a bit more than a bemo direct from Denpasar.

At Peliatan, just before Ubud, I decided on impulse to jump off the bemo and go to the Mandala Homestay mentioned in the Lonely Planet guidebook. It was a quiet family home, surrounded by village and jungle, run by a man who made genggong (a type of Jew's harp used in Balinese music). He gave me a recital before even showing me the room he had available!

Bali - Outside the Mandala Homestay

It was just a kilometre walk into Ubud to the popular restaurants. I had a rather expensive meal there, before going over the paddy fields to the Monkey Forest. From there I got lost trying to make a shortcut back to Peliatan as my only map was pinned on the wall of the homestay.

One other person was staying in the homestay, Christian, a German. We both went to a cheap but good warung (family-run restaurant) in the village for dinner.

6th January 1981: Ubud (Denpasar)

Ubud was a mosquito paradise; I had to burn a coil all night. After an excellent night's sleep, I was woken by the sound of a genggong being tested. Breakfast was a free plate of banana cake together with tea; a thermos of hot water, tea and sugar were always available. My room had a private mandi which made it easy to wash clothes, and when I had caught up with domestic tasks I walked out onto the main street and jumped on a bemo to Denpasar.

When the bemo stopped I found out that the terminus was in the Kereneng Bus Station, a long way from where I was looking the previous day.

The Tourist Office people weren't very helpful so I found my own way to the bank, then wandered around the town centre. After a Chinese lunch, I researched where the motorbike hire shops were in preparation for a planned trip around the island.

Slide 1: Bali - Denpasar Market

Before the afternoon rain started I managed to buy a batik temple scarf (worn around the waist) and I reconfirmed my onward flight to Sydney in ten days time.

The contrast between Peliatan's quiet muddy streets and Denpasar's chaotic noisy traffic confirmed that I had made a good choice to stay inland.

Once again I visited the local warung in Peliatan to enjoy a veritable feast of 'tomato' soup (with noodles and meat), black rice pudding with fruit salad, and chocolate; tasty home cooking for just 700 Rp.

7th January 1981: Ubud

The traffic in Ubud may have been quiet, but the wildlife at night certainly wasn't. As I lay in bed I could hear the dogs socialising, frogs croaking in the stream, the sound of jungle birds, rain on the roof, and odd strains drifting across from the village band rehearsing. The day started with some more banana bread then a short walk up to Ubud to finish breakfast with porridge and thin coconut pancakes from Chawati's warung.

My business acumen first thing in the morning was never that good, and I demonstrated it by paying too much for a red/brown woven sarong. During the best part of a rather overcast day, I wandered around Ubud down to the old bridge and back to visit the Art Museum. The latter was very nice, but I got the impression that artists only took residence in Ubud in the 1920s.

Bali - Ubud main road near the river

It was good to sit down for a while, resting my feet whilst sipping a hot orange juice. Then I was back on my feet again tramping across the paddy fields towards

Pengosakan. Soon I was lost and got very muddy. I found a shortcut footpath back to Peliatan by following the girls carrying rice home on their heads from the mill. However, on the Peliatan side of the stream, I lost the path and only got back onto the street by walking through the grounds of a house!

The rain which had been threatening all afternoon finally started at 4 o'clock when I was safely back in the homestay.

Bali - Ubud paddy fields

I had a good chat with the 65-year-old man who was in charge of the losman, I wasn't sure if he was the family father or grandfather. I was taken aback to find that he didn't expect any payment for the room. He also told me that some of the locals thought I was an Indonesian! He was happy to look after my bags whilst I toured round the island by motorbike.

That evening we were back again in the Warnung Jero Arsa for gado-gado, satay, and another helping of their delicious black rice pudding.

Bali - Map of Ubud

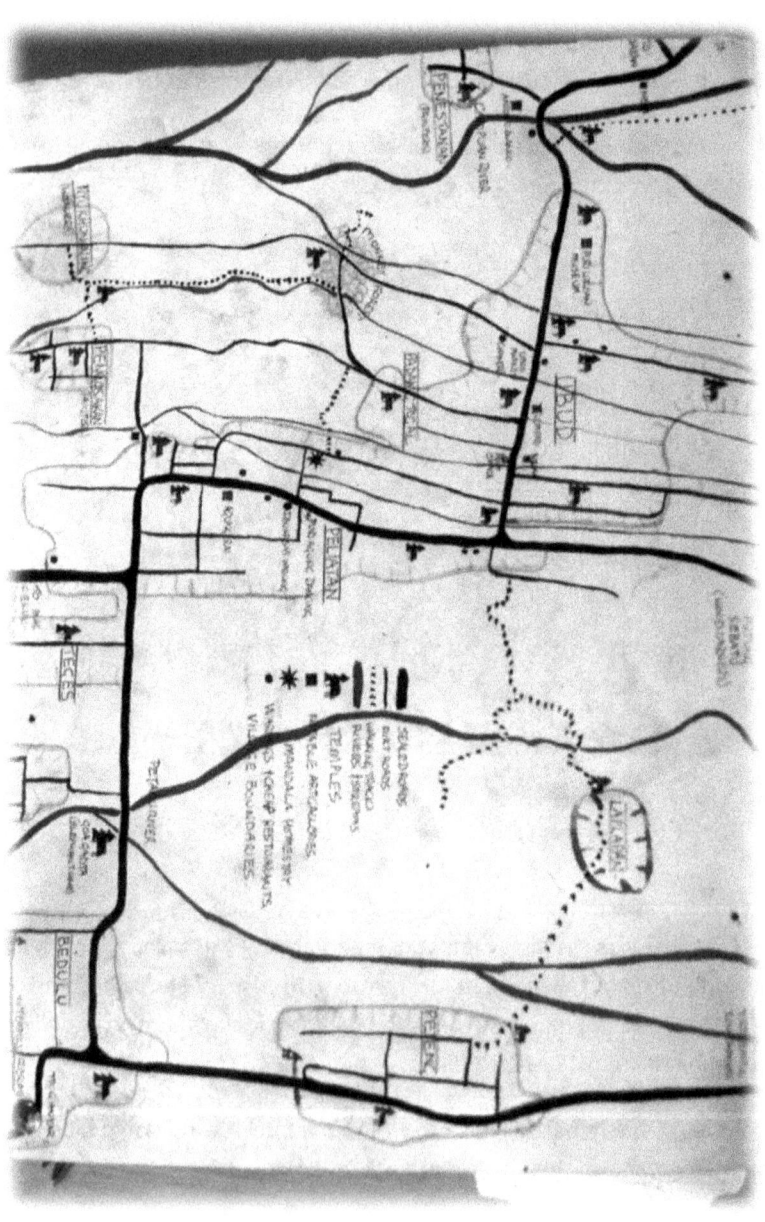

8th January 1981: Ubud – Tirta Gangga

I was rested and now ready for a motorcycle adventure around Bali; no more lazy breakfasts for a while! I slotted quickly back to my old habits with an early start, bags packed and out the door by 7:30. As arranged, I left my suitcase and kit bag with the losman, cramming all my essential belongings into my day sack and a plastic carrier bag. The first bemo that came past only went as far as Mas so I had to change to get to Denpasar. The second bemo driver seemed more preoccupied with finding petrol than delivering us to our destination.

To get to the bike hire shops from the bus station, I caught one of the scooter trishaws that plied a circular route around the town. I quickly found a respectable-looking bike hire shop but it took a long time to haggle down the advertised daily rate to something more reasonable for a longer hire. I convinced them that I didn't need to fork out for Balinese insurance as I had an International Licence. Soon I was riding away on a Yamaha Rx100 and heading through Glianyar on my way to Klungkung.

Bali - Klungkung Kertha Gosa and the Water Palace;

The Kertha Gosa (Hall of Justice) in Klungkung was rather run down and a disappointment; the lunch I bought in a touristy restaurant was a rip-off. All in all, not a great start to my island adventure. The next stop was the bat cave and temple, Pura Goa Lawah. This lived up to its name with plenty of bats, and even one snake.

Bali - Klungkung bat temple

The road west to Amlapura passed over fresh lava fields from an eruption of Mt. Agung twenty years earlier. On the coast side of the road were pretty beaches dotted with fishermans' huts. I pressed on as the weather was turning from hot and sunny, with increasingly ominous rain clouds. My stop for the night was the Water Palace at Tirta Gangga in the shadow of the Mt. Agung volcano.

The palace was little more than a few ponds but the adjoining losman, Dhangin Taman Inn, was positively picturesque. There was a nice open lounge overlooking the ponds and food was available all the time (at a price).

Bali - View west to Pandangbai

Bali - Klungkung mountains

I fixed the electrics on my bike (the battery wasn't securely connected), then had a quiet evening. Relaxing on the pavilion with the other guests (mostly English) and writing my diary by the light of a hurricane lamp as there was no electricity. A lot of strange insect life was attracted to the light. Then to bed by oil lamp where I slept surprisingly well in the shadow of an active volcano!

9th January 1981: Tirta Gangga (Besakih)

I woke to a fine morning and the clouds had lifted from the lower slopes of Mt Agung; it looked like a good day to visit the mother temple at Besakih. The back road to Klungkung was higher up the slopes of the volcano and it was more hilly than the coast road I had used the previous day. It enjoyed excellent views of the volcano, so I stopped several times to take pictures. Consequently, the clouds were already starting to settle on the mountain by the time I got to Besakih.

Tirta Gangga - Water Palace

Bali - Mt. Agung from Klungkung Road

The last few kilometres to the temple were crowded with overloaded trucks and bemos transporting worshipers to a temple festival. The packed car park must have contained a fair percentage of all the island's bemos! I drove my bike up to the temple through crowds of people carrying their offerings.

As a foreigner, I had to pay an entrance fee or donation, but at least in return, I was shown how to wear my sarong correctly. As I walked around the temple I was able to watch the many blessing ceremonies. Although the temple had extensive views over the south side of the island I didn't climb right up to the top of the hill as the day was clouding over fast. Instead, I followed the crowds to find out what happened after the religious ceremonies and found a large communal picnic in progress.

Map showing my tour around Bali

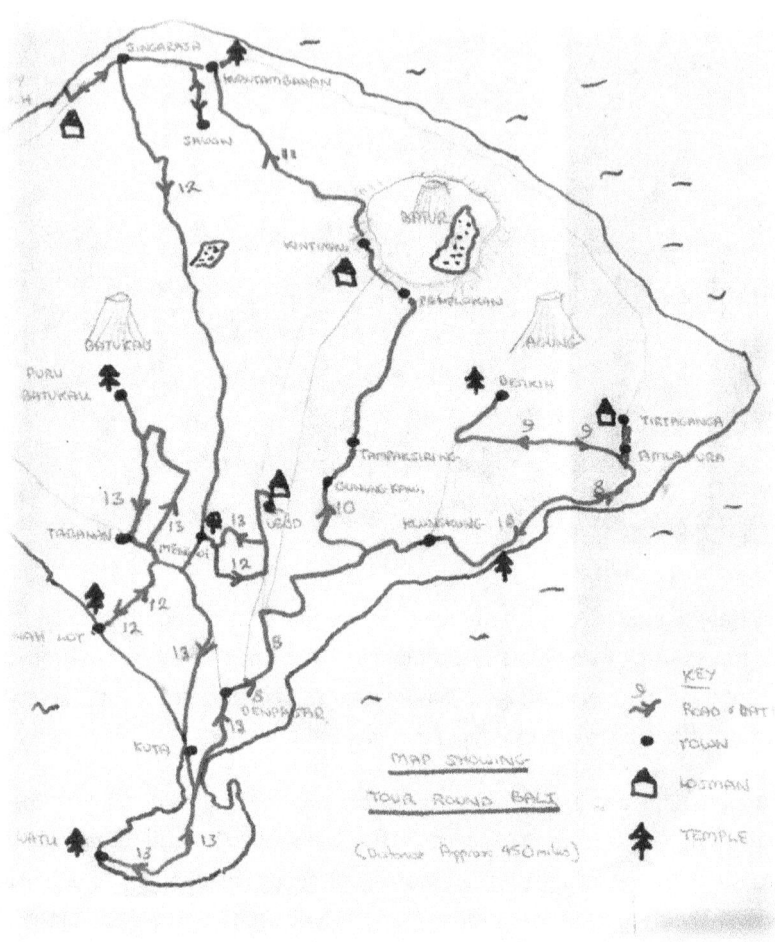

Bali - Besakih temple feast picnic.

Soon after midday, I set off back to Amlapura under threatening skies, but my progress was thwarted by the heavy pilgrim traffic. As I neared Amlapura I saw heavy rain over Tirta Gangga so I delayed by looking around the town for a bit and managed to get back to the losman in the dry.

To clean off the travel grime and soothe my sunburnt limbs I had a dip in the pool. It was lovely to sit in the warm clear water watching the small fish swimming past. The rain came on quite heavily so, once again, I sat again on the verandah writing. In the evening I was still there, talking with an Australian couple, and eating the expensive but unspectacular food.

> *The volcanos sloped down steeply on the north side of the island, and with prevailing northerly winds this meant they were perpetually in the cloud.*

10th January 1981: Tirta Gangga - Kintimani

After checking out from the Dhangin Taman Inn I retraced my route down the coast road to Klungkung. The weather was a bit undecided about what to do, but the cloud was down on the mountains which was not a good sign. After Klungkung I drove through Gianyar to Tampaksiring. The Gunung Kawirock rock temple carved in the side of a valley was impressive but it was a hot walk climbing back up to where I had left the bike. Just a bit further up the road was the holy spring and temple of Pura Tirta Empul; nothing special and spoilt for me by the Sultan's flash modern house next door.

Bali - Tampaksiring - The author in the Outer Temple courtyard

The rain eventually started just as I started the long gradual climb up the flanks of Mt. Batur. Unexpectedly there was sunshine when I reached the outer crater rim at Penelokan, and I was rewarded with clear views of the Batur volcano (5600 ft). After buying pineapple and passion fruit I pressed on to a losman in the market town of Kintimani. Although it was only early afternoon the rain set in and it was heavy at times; when it eventually stopped it left us in heavy cloud.

Two Australians turned up at the Losmen Lingga Giri as wet as I was and they had travelled by bemo. We sat around a wood fire and steamed all evening!

Bali - Penelocan - view of Mt. Batur crater

11th January 1981: Kintimani - Singaraja

We were still in the clouds when I woke to a damp cold morning. There was no chance of any more mountain views; I had been lucky to get some the previous day. It was a miserable climate to ride a motorbike, the road was in cloud almost all the way down to the north coast, and there were patches of heavy rain. There was lots of mud on the road making it slippery, and in places the muddy landslides reached right across. I descended at a crawl because the bulb in my headlight had blown.

Reaching the coast and somewhat drier weather at Kubutambahan I turned inland on the road to Sawan. I was looking for the temple of Jagaraga mentioned in my guidebook. The surface of the road was shocking, with more potholes than surface, and I must have driven past the temple whilst keeping my eye on the road. I pressed on till I reached the foot of the mountains passing through villages full of friendly (and probably rather surprised) locals.

View from the front door of my homestay on Happy Beach.

Backtracking I continued on the coast road to Singaraja, a busy but not attractive town that was mopping up after recent floods. Like all tourists, I headed for the nearby beaches looking for accommodation. The best losman recommended by Lonely Planet was full but there was a pleasant room available in the Losman Agung on Happy Beach, sandwiched between the rice paddy fields and the sea.

My motorbike had to be left in the nearby fishing village as the path to the losman was along the narrow black sand beach exposed to the heavy surf.

It wasn't a good day for me. Apart from the depressing clouds and rain, my biro leaked inside my daysack, my sandals broke, and my watch stopped. Things brightened up when I found that two Swedish guys staying in the losman had bought watches in Singapore that they subsequently found they couldn't sell. So I got a new watch from them at a bargain price.

There was a drama during the evening meal when the losman cooks found a metre-long snake in the kitchen. I was also a bit terrified to tell the truth but others lept into action; it turned out to not be poisonous but nevertheless unwelcome.

The author on the motorbike (on a dry day)

12th January 1981: Singaraja - Ubud

A cloudy morning with once again no chance of sunshine as the monsoon broke on the north coast. I decided to head south in search of better weather. Once again the drive over the mountains was in appalling visibility but it was reasonably dry early in the morning.

Bali - Mengwi Temple

Lake Bratan passed by shrouded in heavy rain, but when I descended further I was greeted by bright, hot sunshine.

The water palace at Mengwi was one of the most picturesque I had visited, with a pond surrounding the temple. It was also sunny and that might have coloured my opinion of it after two cloudy wet days.

As the weather was still perfect, I drove down to the coast at Tanah Lot to see the much-photographed temple. There was a motorcycle parking fee at this site and an entrance 'donation'; I was told the money collected went to the government and not the temple. I was rewarded with a fine view of the temple on a rock just offshore with surf pounding against it.

Bali - Tanah Lot

It was now time to return to my losman in Ubud. Without a good map, I took a wrong turn and ended up driving in the wrong direction on a very bumpy surface. Getting back onto the right road involved a substantial detour. As a result, I approached Ubud for the first time from the west. With my bags deposited in the Mandala Homestay, I returned to Ubud for a late lunch in Okawati's Warung; excellent pineapple fritters followed by peanut butter, honey and banana sandwiches.

Back at the Mandala Homestay, I had a different and better room than the last time. More guests were staying in the homestay including one person I recommended it to on my island tour. I relaxed for what was left of the afternoon then had an evening meal with Christian, the German, who had also returned that day.

> Looking around the village of Peliatan one could not help but notice how the locals lived at one with their environment. When it rained they just used large leaves as umbrellas, the jungle provided most of their food (except rice), and they built houses with bamboo.

Ubud - The family temple at Mandala Homestay

13th January 1981: Ubud (Puru Batukau)

I slept through the alarm from my new watch probably because I was wearing earplugs to keep out the night noise. Having returned early from the north coast I now had one final day with the motorbike to go sightseeing. With the weather looking promising I drove cross-country west from Ubud towards Gunung Batukau, the second-highest mountain in Bali.

Bali - Wangaya

The bike needed refuelling so a diversion had to be made to the main road at Tabanan to fill up. Then I picked the wrong route inland from the town, taking a good road up to Marga, but from there I had to cut across on a dirt track to get to Penebal. Back on asphalt, passing the hot springs of Yeh Panes and the prettily decorated village of Wangaya I reached the remote temple of Puru Batukau at the foot of the mountain.

The temple was deserted, there was no one requesting money outside so I made a larger-than-usual donation. I sat for a while in the temple soaking up the complete peace; it was well worth the considerable effort to get there.

I returned to the main road at Tabanan by the correct route then made my way to Kuta on a back road. At the Post Office, I posted my last batch of cards and collected three letters from home. As I wandered up the main street of Kuta researching where the losemen were I ran into two people I knew, Australians that I had celebrated the New Year with in Yogya!

I had shrimp curry for lunch and then got back on the bike to head to the southern tip of Bali. The peninsular south of Kuta was not made of volcanic rock like the rest of the island. It had distinctive vegetation because of the geology and low rainfall. Unfortunately, there wasn't a complete lack of rain because I sped through a puddle and covered myself and the bike with mud.

The clifftop temple at Ula Watu was not as good as Tanah Lot, but what spoilt it for me was the ripping-off of tourists. It was so unlike the Bali that I had come to know; there were inflated 'donations' demanded and touts everywhere.

I escaped back to Denpasar, pausing only to wash the mud off the bike and myself in an irrigation ditch. The shops were all closed, so after handing back the bike, I jumped on a bemo back to Ubud. I had driven about 450 miles on my trip.

Ubud was preparing for a temple festivity the next day. In the evening Christian and I decided to eat in Ubud in the one restaurant, Canderi, that was open. It was so overcrowded it took four hours to get all of our meals.

Bali - View over Kuta from the southern peninsular

14th January 1981: Ubud (Festival)

Galungan festival day in Ubud. All the streets had been swept overnight and were decorated with sweeping bamboo penjors. Every temple altar was dressed with offerings.

In the morning there were blessing ceremonies with women carrying baskets of food around the village. Christian and I walked up to Ubud, but although the temples were decorated nothing particular seemed to be happening. Religion to the Balanese was a personal family thing and not about public gatherings. We were driven by hunger back to Canderi where the service was much better and we had a filling lunch. It was such a good lunch we had to take a bemo back to the homestay!

Later in the afternoon, the Barong came around the streets; great fun for all the children. Other than that, the festival day was a bit of a letdown from a tourist perspective.

Bali - Festival offering outside my homestay

In the evening we ate a Balinese Smoked Duck at our local warung; it was only available on festival days and had to be ordered earlier in the day. The duck was a medium-sized bird with virtually no fat and a unique spicy taste. I finished off the meal as usual with black rice pudding.

Bali - Ubud crowd watching the Barong

15th January 1981: Ubud (Barong Dance)

After grazing on the "Food of the Gods" left at the temple, Christian and I took a bemo to Batubulan to see the tourist version of the Barong dance. It was much less a dance than we had seen in Ubud, and more a storytelling, like the Ramayana, with actors in costume and Balanese music. It was generally to a high standard, and very amusing in parts. I enjoyed the opening scene with a tiger and monkey, and the killing of Kalika in the form of a bear.

Bali - Barong dance - The monkey and the tiger

After the performance finished I searched without success for replacement sandals in Denpasar; everything in the shops was cheap and nasty. Instead, I ended up buying some more bootleg cassette tapes and tiger balm. After a snack lunch, I lay on my bed listening to music. I was feeling a bit under the weather, something that wasn't helped by it being a very hot day. Consequently, my dinner was suitably restrained; egg soup, a Chinese omelette and a special dessert. Afterwards, I set out to walk up to the cemetery where the locals were celebrating but I was so tired I gave up and went to bed.

Bali - Barong Dance - Gamelon Band

16th January 1981: Ubud – Kuta Beach

My stay in Bali was rapidly coming to an end. I had to pack my bags and decide what I was going to take with me to Australia. Some of my clothes were barely better than rags. I said my farewells to Peliatan and hopped for the last time on the bemo into Denpasar en route to Kuta. Luckily I was feeling better and was able to carry my bags.

The catching of two more bemos went without a hitch, and without me having to carry my bags very far. On arrival in Kuta, I planned to look lost and be 'picked up' by someone from a losman with vacancies, and that is what happened. It saved me from lugging my bags around town in search of a room. Conveniently the losman turned out to be on Poppies Gang, a quiet alleyway that I had checked out on my earlier visit. The Losman Kamala Indah was fine for a one-night stay.

> *In the Losman Kamala Indah, I ran into a guy I had met before. It took ages to narrow our meeting down to the 15th of December in the Hong Kong Bar, Penang.*

The restaurant menus in Kuta were far more Western than I was used to. The Tree House Warnung served me a waffle for lunch which I walked off along the beach. Later in the afternoon, I went for a swim. It was a good beach with lifesavers on duty, but I found the heavy surf terrifying.

Bali - Kuta beach

In the evening I went with a group from the losman to eat in Legian. The ride home afterwards on a motorbike was a bit hair-raising.

There was heavy rain in the night and the thunder woke me up.

Kuta - Street scene

17th January 1981: Kuta - Australia

My last day, and a chance to get up late to prepare for a long night flight ahead. At the last minute, I found out that there was a departure tax from Denpasar Airport so had to change another $1 note in the bank. I posted my last Indonesian aerogram then had a shower and checked out of the losman.

> Kuta wasn't as bad as I had feared. Its worst features were the hawkers and touts everywhere, the noisy motorcycles, and the general air of people who wander about with nothing better to do than eat and shop. I found some of the 'impressions' that tourists in Kuta had about Bali amusing but there was no point telling them how wrong they were.

I now looked for ways to spin out the time till my evening flight. Firstly there was lunch to be had in the Dayull restaurant; exploring the pseudo-Western menu. I discovered Turtle Steak, a dry but pleasant-tasting meat. Then back to the losman to check that the bags I had chained to the verandah hadn't walked anywhere. It was not a particularly nice day with lots of cloud and occasional showers, but it was a good day for walking so I wandered down the beach to the airport and back again without getting too hot and sweaty.

Kuta Beach - Losman Kamala Indah

Back at the losman again I met a Pom turned Australian, who had flown in from Melbourne; chatting to him passed the time well. We had a light meal together in the Tree House then I left for the airport by bemo. I showed that I wasn't a tourist by paying the local fare for such a journey!

Denpasar airport was poorly organised and it took nearly two hours to process the passengers on an almost full DC10 flight. My check-in bags weighed in at 22kg but I only achieved that by making my carry-on daysack very heavy. Surprisingly we took off almost on time. The takeoff was on a runway jutting out into the sea; you only got one chance to get airborne.

After serving a hot meal there was a film shown, but I chose to try and grab some sleep in the remaining four hours. There was a spectacular light show outside the aircraft as we flew over a tropical thunderstorm.

After six hours in the air, and 143 days since leaving London we landed in Sydney. The plane was fumigated by a man in shorts and long white socks then I was free to step out and continue my adventures in Australia.

.

Sydney

Daily costs (excluding souvenirs and Travel)
Nepal - £4.50
Thailand - £7
Malaysia - £3.20
Singapore & Bali - £3.20

The overall cost for 41 days - £311

Hotel Costs (per night)
Nepal - £1
Thailand - £1.70
Malaysia - £0.70
Singapore - £1
Java - £1
Bali - £0.66

Australia

I arrived in Sydney on 18th January 1981 and quickly settled into looking for a job whilst exploring my new home away from home. I had a 12-month working holiday visa which meant that I could earn money but was also expected to take trips round Australia. Going on holiday and earning money turned out to be mutually exclusive. Other than the usual tourist expeditions out from Sydney to the surrounding National Parks, I only took one significant holiday.

In September 1981, just over a year after I left the U.K. I went on a Bill King camping adventure in the Northern Territory. The tour took us from Darwin, out through Arnhem Land to the East Alligator River, then through UDP Falls and down to Alice Springs. It finished with the obligatory visit to what was then called Ayers Rock and a more adventurous route back to The Alice via Reedy Rockhole, Palm Valley, and Glen Helen. Lasting just two weeks, this was one of the shortest camping expeditions I did on my round-the-world adventure. Once again I found myself in a Bedford truck but this was a truck-in-a-box modified for greater passenger comfort. We had (and needed) 4WD and the truck was kitted out for safe travel in the outback. We also had a chef who did all the cooking which was lucky as we didn't pass through many towns to buy supplies. The other passengers were predominately Australian and the average age was a lot older than the groups I had been part of in Asia.

Back in Sydney, when I wasn't working or socialising I was attending a WEA Spanish evening class as I was intending to travel at some point to Latin America. I put my new language skills to the test sooner than I had expected. When I overstayed my working holiday visa I was told to leave and given a week to get out of the country. I was able to quickly put together another overland adventure with Encounter Overland by truck. This time I chose to start in San Francisco and head down through Central America to Peru. I was sad to leave Sydney.

I had enjoyed being in Australia on so many levels, but it had also been a distraction from getting back on the road and exploring more rarely-visited places.

NT Trip Darwin - Truck at East Point (top) and lunch on The Track (bottom)

PART 2
San Fransisco to London

Central America in the rain

THE GROUPS' CONVENING

On arrival in San Francisco please rendezvous with your Leader/Driver and the other group members at:

>	Olympic Hotel
>	140 Mason Phone No. 982 5010
>	San Francisco

no later then 7:00 a.m. on ...4TH. MAY.

Single accommodation is around US$ 20 per night; Double rooms from $ 25.

There are various forms of transport available between the Airport and the centre of San Francisco. The Airporter Bus costs around $4 and terminates a few blocks from the Olympic Hotel.

There will be an informal meeting in San Francisco at the Olympic Hotel with the other group members and your expedition Leader/Driver to discuss the running of the trip and to double check red tape matters.

As mentioned on Page 5 of these details, please be in San Francisco at least two working days prior to departure in order to obtain the necessary visas.

4th May 1982: San Francisco – Monterey

The final chapter of my overland adventure started at the Olympic Hotel in San Francisco. It was the meeting point for the Encounter Overland expedition to Panama. It was where I decided to stay on the night before our departure.

After having had a narrow escape from a hotel fire when I was backpacking in Australia, I wasn't particularly comfortable sleeping on the 6th floor of an old building in an earthquake zone. When I was woken by traffic noise at dawn, I was quietly relieved to find that there hadn't been a quake or a fire in the night.

Sixteen other expedition members were joining me on an overland adventure through Central America; 4 guys, 10 girls and one engaged couple. We started the trip with two drivers; one was a trainee learning the route. I was back again on an Encounter Bedford truck, 523 days after saying goodbye to my last one in Kathmandu. After my experiences trucking overland to Nepal, much of what was new to others was very familiar to me. So familiar was it, that I saw little need to describe it in detail in my diary! I didn't even record the truck registration!

San Francisco

On our first day, we did some San Francisco sightseeing, to bed down the truck, driver, and expedition members. We went over the Golden Gate Bridge to the Marin headland where we stopped to photograph the iconic view of the city appearing out of the sea mist. Then we turned back south, passing through San Jose and out to the coast at Monterey.

Our beginners' first night camp was in the Julia Pfeiffer Burns State Park close to Big Sur. I knew the routine so didn't have to learn how to put up a tent. But I enjoyed the hot showers more because I suspected they weren't going to be a regular feature of the adventure ahead.

5th May 1982: Monterey – Los Angeles

No more sightseeing the next day, just a hard day's trucking to get south of Los Angeles. At first, we followed the coastline which was too misty for any good views; then we bounced down the freeway towards San Diego.

It was my first turn to cook for the group so had to go shopping and then prepare dinner and lunch. I found it much easier to buy food in California than in Syria! Sausages with pineapple, one of my favourites, was on the menu. Surprisingly it scaled up well to cooking for 18 not just one! My experiences cooking on the trip out to India had taught me that a full truck of expedition members needed a lot of food!

I sat up late into the night talking which was perhaps a silly thing to do if you had to be first up in the morning to prepare breakfast!`

6th May 1982: Los Angeles – La Bufadora

It was no surprise, but I was bleary-eyed in the morning and catering on autopilot! One of our group needed to visit a bank in San Diego to collect some money. This gave us one last opportunity to shop in the U.S.A. I used the time to buy a bucket, guessing correctly that there would be few opportunities to wash clothes.

From San Diego, it was just a few miles to the border with Mexico. There was a hold-up because the Mexicans couldn't decide if the truck was a truck or a bus! As a result, we ended up eating lunch in a car park just across the border in Tijuana.

Mexican Border at Tijuana 1981 (Photo by ukoboe on Flickr)

It was interesting to observe the different dynamics of the group as it settled down to overland travel. The group was unified from the start. There were no problems getting going in the morning, no complaints about rough camping, everything ran smoothly. Maybe this was because the majority of the group were girls; there were only four eligible males. Two of the men were much older, 38, and heavy drinkers/smokers, whilst the other was a young and somewhat eccentric Kiwi. So I found myself the centre of attention early on, particularly since I knew the ropes and could speak Spanish. I was trying to untangle my romantic life and didn't want anything other than a good friend for the next seven weeks. Asserting that was painful and confusing at times.

Passenger List

... TO PANAMA   4th May 1982   (7 Weeks)

NAME	NATIONALITY	MARITAL STATUS	PASSPORT NUMBER	DATE OF ISSUE	DATE OF EXPIRY	PLACE OF ISSUE	DATE OF BIRTH	AGE	OCCUPATION
..., Jennifer	Australian	Single	M782040	13.07.81	13.07.86	Sydney	26.10.57	24	Teacher
..., Roberta	Australian	Single	M159716	18.04.80	17.04.85	Sydney	17.05.61	21	Nurse
..., Agnes	Australian	Single	M104665	12.05.80	12.05.85	Lima	03.07.57	24	Nurse
..., Elizabeth	Australian	Single	M104664	12.05.80	12.05.85	Lima	31.07.55	26	Nurse
..., Friedrich	Australian	Married	M101780	10.03.80	09.03.85	Perth	14.04.48	34	Maint. Foreman
..., Magda	British	Single	337068B	23.07.76	23.07.86	London	16.07.52	29	Hairdresser
..., Adrian	British	Single	N6550248	22.02.79	22.02.89	Newport	07.03.54	28	Design Engineer
..., Marlene	Dutch	Single	T936236	30.11.81	31.08.86	Davos	11.02.52	29	Teacher
..., Susan	German	Single	D5687807	16.07.74	21.05.84	Konstanz	28.04.51	31	Medical Asst.
..., Paul	New Zealand	Single	R690402	21.07.78	21.07.88	Wellington	01.09.52	29	Watchmaker
..., Silvia	Swiss	Single	3239287	20.05.77	20.05.87	St Gallen	09.02.57	25	Teacher
..., Elisabeth	Swiss	Single	3546144	09.04.79	09.04.84	Liestal	12.10.55	26	Teacher
..., Daniel	Swiss	Single	3432635	11.07.78	11.07.83	St Gallen	26.06.55	26	Engineer
..., Ruth	Swiss	Single	3113495	29.12.77	29.12.82	Durcnten	05.12.57	24	Artist
..., Marlen	Swiss	Single	3432657	11.07.78	11.07.83	St Gallen	31.12.60	22	Nurse
..., ...	Canadian	Single	JC101740	15.02.82	16.02.87	Calgary	05.09.44	38	Medicine

COURIER AND LEADER/DRIVERS:

| ..., ... | British | Single | B162430 | 05.02.82 | 06.02.92 | London | 17.11.56 | 25 | Driver |
| ..., Anthony | New Zealand | Single | R831961 | 11.02.80 | 11.02.90 | Auckland | 28.10.56 | 25 | Driver |

MEXICO

Our Mexican itinerary started with a succession of rough beach camp sites. It wasn't until we got to Mexico City that there was anything historic or interesting to look at.

There were so many Americans around that it didn't seem as if we had changed country. The only clue we had left the USA was the appallingly bad state of Mexican roads.

In Mexico, there was an extreme climatic contrast between the cool mountain weather of Mexico City and Oaxaca and the steamy tropics of Palenque to the south. The only constant was the fact that it rained wherever we were.

Having my luggage stolen inevitably resulted in negative feelings about visiting Mexico but that is jumping ahead in the story.

Following the coast down Baja California, the scenery improved but it was still quite hazy. The day's food shopping at Mexican prices was done in Ensenada. We then pressed on to Bufadora where the blow hole obliged by blowing a bit for us.

We camped nearby; the first rough camping for most of the group, but a familiar routine for me. Having escaped from 'civilisation', I was in great spirits.

7th May 1982: La Bufadora – Baja de Los Ángeles

It was a long but interesting journey down the Baja California peninsula. We started early, driving through sea mist till the sun broke through. Then as we headed south, the ground got drier and unusual cacti appeared by the side of the road. By the time Route 1 switched over to the east side of Baja, the vegetation was dominated by cactus scrub.

As the day ended, we turned off down a potholed side road to the picturesque bay of Bahia de Los Ángeles.

Baja de Los Ángeles (1982 Wikipedia)

We arrived in Bahia just as the sun was setting; the bare hills and still water were beautiful. To cap it all there was a perfect full moon that night. We were dusty and tired after a day on the road with temperatures in the high 30s; a wash in the shallow warm water was the perfect antidote.

8th May 1982: Baja de Los Ángeles - Mulege

I got up early so I could have a quick dip before breakfast while watching the sunrise. I wasn't expecting the water to be so cold. As we set off up the hill, we discovered that there was a cold wind blowing through the truck. We had to huddle together in the back till we were able to stop and drop the canvas sides.

After that early drama, the rest of the day passed without note. It was a hard day's motoring through scenery that became steadily less interesting. We reached a beach beyond Mulgee for the night, early enough for a swim and to collect firewood before dinner. Dead cacti provided a good source of fuel, though you had to stand well clear as they fell, to avoid the spines turning you into a sieve. We slept in the open as there was no chance of rain.

The route taken down Baja California

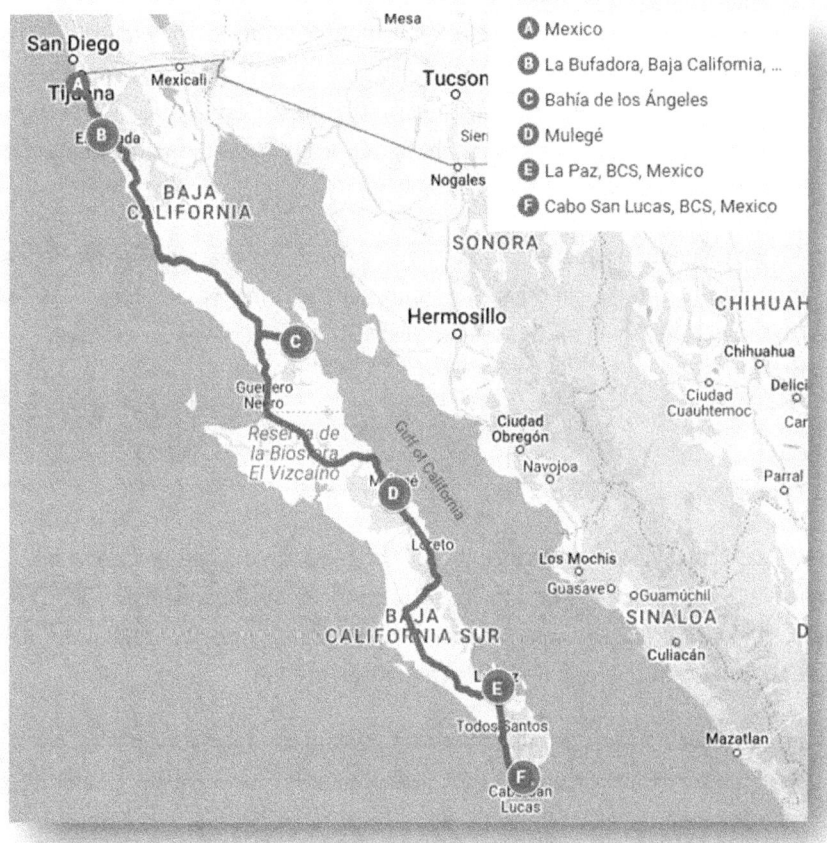

We arrived in La Paz on a Sunday but the ferry to mainland Mexico was not due to depart till Wednesday. This gave us time to kill. All there was to do was to sit around on beaches and wait. The enforced pause had the same effect on the group as did the truck breakdown in Turkey. It was a time to explore, to make and break friendships.

9th May 1982: Mulege – La Paz

There might not have been any rain in the night, but I was annoyed by flies and woken by an enthusiastic cockerel at 5:30. Another boring journey followed, down to La Paz. The endless desert scrub was only broken by an area of irrigated green fields near Cuidad Constitution. I travelled in the front most of the way but it wasn't a big advantage on dead-straight featureless roads. My main task was just to keep the driver awake!

When we reached La Paz there was a short break on the beach before we headed inland to set up camp in an organised campsite. The camp was a luxury for us, with warm showers, washing machines and electric lights. But it was only for two nights!

10th May 1982: La Paz

In La Paz I had my first real chance to practice the Spanish I had been learning whilst in Sydney. On a trip into town with one of the Australian girls, I visited the bank, the post office, and some shops. I was particularly proud of myself for being able to order fruit drinks in Spanish at a roadside stall.

Then we all took off to a beach on the north side of the town for a late lunch and some more sun. The dirt road was so rough that all our washing and cleaning at the campsite was in vain! The beach wasn't worth the effort either. I amused everyone by building a sun shelter; a year in Australia had tought me to respect the sun.

On the way back to the campsite we stopped to watch the sunset and drink margaritas. The sunset didn't happen and the alcoholics in the group succeeded in delaying dinner by ordering more drinks!

11th May 1982: La Paz – Cabo san Lucas

It was time to say goodbye to the showers. We left our comfortable campsite in La Paz and took a short, but incredibly dusty, road down to the port of Cabo San Lucas on the extreme southern tip of Baja California. Our first attempt to camp on the beach was a bit of a failure. We turned down a road that, instead of leading to the beach, went to a new marina that was under construction. We needed to turn round, but the road was too narrow. We pushed on till we got to a wider gateway, pruning lots of overhanging branches on the way; then to turn round, we just about felled a whole tree!

Back on the main road, we found a way down to the shore and were able to relax and have yet another swim. There were many boats anchored in the bay and far too many rich Americans around. We camped for the night in a quiet cove further up the road, away from the town. There was a beautiful moonrise as I took an evening walk along the beach in the cool evening air.

12th May 1982: La Paz – Puerto Vallarta

Finally, the day arrived when we could sail to the Mexican mainland. Our two drivers, Tony and Neil, left us on the beach whilst they went and bought tickets for the ferry. That left us with no shade and no bathers; so we went skinny-dipping in broad daylight! I walked out towards the lighthouse to get some exercise but it was too hot and uncomfortable with a salty body.

Boarding the Azteca ferry took a long time, but once we were on board we raced for the showers and had a quick lunch. The boat sailed late in the afternoon. It was a new clean boat and was half empty. A lot of time that afternoon was spent just relaxing and sitting on the deck. We saw dolphins following us as we sat watching the swell behind the boat. It was a rare chance to relax and collect one's thoughts away from the bustle of the truck and the daily routine. I grabbed a few hours of fitful sleep; others stayed in the bar for the entire trip!

In our first time change of the trip, we lost an hour during the night.

The Azteca Ferry to Puerto Vallarta

13th May 1982: Puerto Vallarta

The next morning there were some pretty rough looks on display at breakfast. I didn't feel exactly refreshed but I did feel better when I got some of my long overdue letters and cards written.

The group had settled down after those idle days on the beach and an overnight party on the boat. Friendships had broken up and new tent partners established. I wasn't prepared for such fickle social grouping, though of course, I had seen it on previous trips.

I had to shop and cook when we disembarked from the ferry in Puerto Vallarta which kept my mind off all the changes in the group. But I was tired and a bit depressed. So when the rest of the group hit the town, I stayed behind in the camp site and caught up on my sleep.

We had left the desert and the cacti behind; Puerto Vallarta was hot and humid with green vegetation. Unfortunately, Puerto Vallarta was also full of Americans on holiday; I couldn't wait to escape from them and resume the real adventure.

One rest day in Puerto Vallarta would have been enough for me, but we stayed a second day.

14th May 1982: Puerto Vallarta

We had a rest day in Puerto Vallarta. I took a bus into town and had a somewhat aimless wander round; The town didn't have any historical attractions worth seeing; it had been redeveloped extensively as a resort for rich Americans. I bought a straw hat, a pair of tennis shoes, and a few oddments before having a restaurant lunch.

By the time I got back to the campsite, I was ready for a dip in the pool and a relaxing afternoon. The still heat, particularly in the early morning, reminded me of India.

In the evening we drove the truck into town for drinks and to bed down the new social groupings. I wasn't too sure where I fitted in, but wasn't too concerned. The drinks were expensive!

15th May 1982: Puerto Vallarta – Punta de Mita

After two nights in Puerto Vallarta, we were on the road again, but only for a short hop up the coast to somewhere our driver Neil described as "Mexico's best beach". He probably meant that it was Mexico's best surf beach, which it might have been; none of us were carrying surf boards to check it out. As for the beach, it was just a rubbish dump; I was completely turned off, perhaps I had been spoilt by the beaches in Sydney. I suspect that I wasn't the only person in the group who was getting a bit sick of beach camping.

I resorted to climbing the local hill to pass the time, and I was surprised to find that it was a quite passable viewpoint. If only I had the pictures from my camera to prove it; but that was not to be! My exercise was followed by a spectacular sunset and a barbeque on the beach.

We had all taken to using mosquito nets overnight as the weather got hotter and the flying wild life became more feral.

Route from Puerto Vallarta to Mexico City

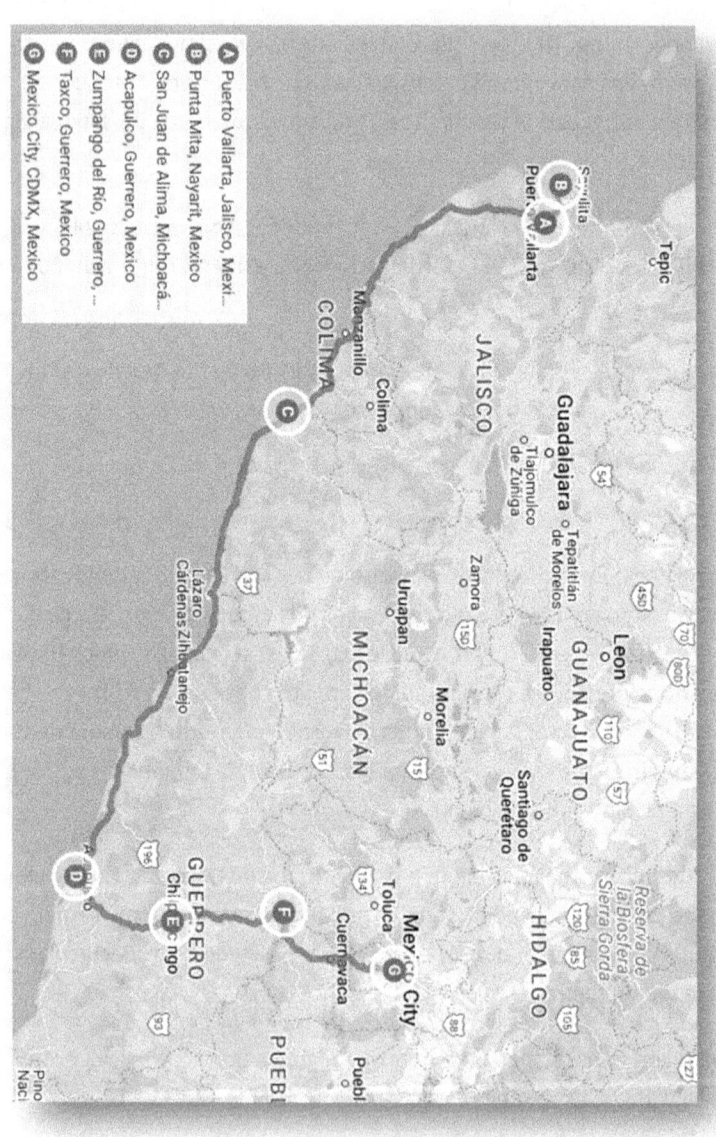

- A Puerto Vallarta, Jalisco, Mexi...
- B Punta Mita, Nayarit, Mexico
- C San Juan de Alima, Michoacá...
- D Acapulco, Guerrero, Mexico
- E Zumpango del Río, Guerrero, ...
- F Taxco, Guerrero, Mexico
- G Mexico City, CDMX, Mexico

16th May 1982: Punta de Mita – San Juan

For the next two days, we were back again to relentless hard driving to get our slow truck down to Acapulco, a distance of close to 1000km. On the first day, I sat in the front. As the weather got hotter and more humid it was hard to keep the driver awake. The road south was uninspiring; except for a brief moment after we passed through Manzanillo, when the banana plantations gave the place a very Malaysian feel.

We had trouble filling up with water and then had trouble with natives who seemed to be a bit high on some substance. It wasn't an easy time in the truck.

When we stopped for the night just beyond San Juan de Alma, a dip in the surf provided little relief from the hot weather; it just left my skin sticky with salt and needing a shower. I wandered up to a nearby brickyard hoping to wash in their water tank but had to retreat when it turned out that the yard doubled up in the evening as a local night club!

17th May 1982: San Juan - Acapulco

With just one stop for lunch, we drove from 7 a.m. to 8 p.m. averaging little more than 50 km/hr. The lunch stop was by the side of a near-stagnant river. We were so dusty and salty that we all washed ourselves with total disregard for cholera and other tropical nasties that could be lurking in the water.

We reached Acapulco in the dark and parked in a campsite on the sand spit of Pie de la Cuesta. There was roaring surf on one side of the spit and a still, freshwater lagoon on the other. We swam in the lagoon without hesitation and without the benefit of seeing the colour of the water!

We had an evening meal to celebrate Roberta's 21st birthday before setting up camp for the night. Just as we finished eating the heavens opened with a storm that had been brewing all evening. This was the heaviest rain we had encountered so far, and like fools, we raced around trying to put up our tents in it. I was soaked but put my pack under the front of the truck to keep it dry. When I got my tent up

I looked for my bag but couldn't see it, but assumed it had been collected up and put in the trailer. To make matters worse the electricity supply went during the storm plunging us into darkness. I stripped off my wet clothes and joined the others in the back of the truck till the rain stopped.

When we had righted all the tents that had blown over and unpacked the luggage again out of the trailer we found that several bags were missing, including mine. Unfortunately, I had packed all my valuables in my pack ready for it to be locked away overnight.

A fruitless search was initiated round the camp, on the beach, and in nearby streets. So Neil and Tony drove the truck to the local police station to file a report, whilst we all went to bed.

Encounter Overland – Information for Expedition Members

SECURITY

No doubt in your consideration you have evaluated the pros and cons of this style of journey and the pros and cons of camping. Security needs to be borne in mind and with proper attention, losses will not occur. Theft can be from one's person or bag when in a large town, or from a campsite. In choosing a camp location this will be carefully considered but personal effects should not be left in unoccupied tents.

Other aspects of security will be discussed and implemented. It is a fact that a journey like this is in some danger of being spoilt by valuables being lost. It is recognition of this fact and the implementation of the proper precautions that will reduce this risk to a small, acceptable level. Although this aspect of security applies throughout the world, it is particularly relevant in Latin America, where a considerable amount of time will be spent in towns and populated areas.

18th May 1982: Acapulco – Zumpango del Rio

Daylight brought no sign of the missing luggage. But during the night someone pinched my thongs from outside the tent, how petty! Liza, Agnes and Ruth had also lost their passports so we set off together into Acapulco. We searched for a hotel that would allow us to call our respective embassies in Mexico City. The bus stopped in the town centre but the smart hotels were at the far end of the beach so we had to take a taxi. The first taxi we approached wanted $5 for the short trip but I asked another one in Spanish and got quoted about an eighth of that price. Unfortunately, we were not able to find a hotel that would help us make the necessary phone calls, so had to head back to the city centre.

Feeling increasingly dejected, my next stop was the American Express office to report the loss of Traveller's Cheques, but they didn't share my sense of urgency and asked me to come back in 30 minutes.

Things weren't looking too good but things were going to get worse before they could get better! We all jumped on a bus to go and find the British Consulate. It was a packed bus with standing room only. In the crush, someone lifted my wallet which contained a small amount of cash that Neil had lent me.

Finally, we found the Marriot Hotel and the British Consulate; except it turned out the Consul was an American! Nevertheless, he did explain where the Immigration Department was so we could report our lost visas. I was broke and had had my fill of bad luck. Collectively we had achieved nothing, so I suggested that we should try and find Neil, our driver. I'm not sure why I thought we could find one man in such a big town; we took a taxi to the Zócalo, drew a complete blank, but found the Immigration & Telegraph building.

A postcard from Acapulco

At this point, our luck finally began to turn.

After a worrying wait, an Immigration official told us that the police statement we had was good enough for them to issue a tourist transit card. Downstairs we were able to send telegrams to report our stolen tickets and credit cards. Then we ran into one of our group who told us that some of our luggage had been returned to the camp site including our passports. On getting back to the truck I found my Traveller's Cheque numbers in the returned luggage. I raced back to the American Express Office only to find them closing for the siesta!

The group had to move on, although I hadn't managed to replace any of my money. We drove out of the town and up into the hills. It was a spectacular climb and we all were relieved to escape from the heat and the thieves of Acapulco. The camp that night was on a narrow ledge above a stream. I thoroughly checked what few belongings I had and found that I had lost all my clothes, my sleeping bag, camera and money. But I still had a lot of reels of unexposed slide film! I was still in a state of shock, having lost so much that I considered indispensable and irreplaceable.

19th May 1982: Zumpango del Rio - Taxco

It didn't take me long to pack away my things the next morning! The plan was to drive to Taxco and spend the day sightseeing there. One of the drivers, Neil, would look after the truck and do the cooking, so freeing us all to wander around the town. Taxco is famed for its silver jewellery which wasn't worth looking at, as I had no money. The best I could do was to sit in the truck, collect my thoughts, and write some letters.

Late in the afternoon we regrouped and took the truck down the hill away from the steep town streets to find some flat land to camp on. Neil prepared his Guacamole but it was quite fiery and few came back for seconds. We gave the substantial leftovers away to the locals!

I went to bed early because, after all I had been through in the past days, I now had swollen glands and felt I was sickening for something.

Taxco *(by Salvador Fematt)*

20th May 1982: Taxco – Mexico City

Mexico City was still a three-hour drive away; a drive that took us up into the clouds and over a pass at close to 10,000ft above sea level. The subsequent descent into the valley was more gradual. As we neared the city the cloud and smog got thicker and the sky greyer.

Mexico City – Panorama *(by Mark Turok)*

We set up in a cramped campsite off Avenue Universidad in the suburb of Coyoacan. There was a supermarket nearby where we shopped for food. It also had a department that sold clothes and it appeared I would be able to pay for them with my English Access credit card which I had squirreled safely away in my bag.

The Bedford truck was not designed for city driving, so we left it at the campsite and took a local bus to Zupata. The Metro we then used to get into the centre was new, smart and efficient.

My first stop wasn't a tourist attraction, but rather the American Express office. I filled out a form and then unsuccessfully tried to get replacement cheques before Monday; it was Thursday and I faced a weekend with no money. I took the Metro across town to the Palace of Fine Arts Station which was close to the main Post Office. After collecting three letters from the Poste Restante I returned to the camp as there was little else I could do with no money

Getting the Metro back to Zupata at the end of the line was easy. Finding a bus from Zupata back to the camp site turned out to be harder. I asked a local for directions and he offered to drive me back in his car. Once again I proved how useful it was to be able to speak a bit of Spanish! Another member of the group avoided public transport, took a 90-minute taxi ride back, and was charged accordingly.

I was cooking for the group in the evening but not before I had enjoyed a nice hot shower.

21st May 1982: Mexico City

I phoned the American Express office from the camp site to see if they could arrange a loan for me, but no offer was forthcoming. I desperately needed something else to wear; I'd been living in the same clothes for three days. The supermarket clothing department had a limited range but I was able to find things that fitted me and which I liked. After some fuss, they accepted my Access credit card, which was lucky as I was down to my last 200 pesos cash (about $4).

With a new shirt on my back, I took the bus and Metro into the city surfacing at Balderas. When I phoned American Express I was told to call back in an hour because they were going "to phone New York". I filled in the time walking up the main shopping street, passing a good handicrafts market on the way. But alas I had no money to buy anything.

Mexico Metro Ticket

I rang back American Express an hour later as requested and I was told that there could be no money or cheques for me till Monday. At that point, just to ensure I was completely miserable, it started to rain. Luckily I had an umbrella that I had bought on credit in the supermarket. I was able to continue my wandering, just looking in the shops was free. I was shocked to find out how much a replacement camera would cost me, more than I could afford.

Mexico City - The National Palace *(by Kipl Turok)*

One free tourist attraction was to look inside the National Palace in the Main Square or Zocalo. The large murals on the walls of the stairwell depicted the history of Mexico from the Conquest through the Mexican Revolution to the present. Then on the opposite side of the square, I went inside the sinking Cathedral. Like all the buildings in the main square, the cathedral was built on top of a pre-Hispanic structure, which was in turn built on soft ground. The resulting subsidence gave the nave a strange tilt; in fact, most of the old buildings around the square had settled at unusual angles.

I still had business to do on the last working day before the weekend. On the way back to camp I stopped off at the Pan Am Airline offices on the main street, Paseo de la Reforma. I let them know that I had recovered my stolen airline ticket and it no longer needed to be cancelled.

It was still tipping down with rain when I got to the campsite, which was now flooded! We had to eat our evening meal sitting in the truck. One of our group, Fred, had decided that the camp wasn't to his liking and had transferred to a posh hotel. I had the loan of his sleeping bag which was lucky as it was cold overnight up at 7,000 ft above sea level.

22nd May 1982: Mexico City

Driver Neil lent me some more money; I'm not sure how I could have managed that weekend without the cash top-ups from the truck. I'd decided that, as I had lost all my warm mountain gear, it was no longer feasible for me to take the Brief Encounter in Peru that I had booked. Machu Picchu would have to wait for another time. I sent a telegram to Encounter Overland cancelling my booking, and another back to England to let my parents know what was happening.

Now I had some money to spend, I retraced my route from the previous day stopping to buy things I had noticed in the shops. I finished up in the Baldaras craft market where I bought a wool blanket to replace the warmth of my lost sleeping bag.

It was a short metro ride to Chapultepec Park and the Museum of Anthropology. The museum collection was too big for one visit but a great introduction to pre-conquest Mexican culture. It was a bit of a shame that I had handed in my Spanish Dictionary with my bag at the entrance, so I couldn't translate any of the explanatory signs. Chapultepec Castle at the top of the hill in the park had a good view over the city and housed a complimentary museum of post-conquest history.

Somewhat unexpectedly there was no rain later in the day and the sun occasionally managed to shine through the smog.

Once again I found it difficult to get back to the campsite by public transport. At the Metro Zapata station, I waited 45 minutes for a bus without success. I suspected that the buses departed from somewhere nearby, but in the end, I gave up looking and just walked. It only took 30 minutes and the route followed the line of the Metro extension being built; there were fascinating civil engineering works to look at on the way.

I turned my new trousers up in the evening before going to bed. But I had a disturbed night's sleep as my tent-mate had the trots!

Mexico City - Rain God Tlaloc outside the Museum of Anthropology *(by Mark Turok)*

23rd May 1982: Mexico City

In a brave gesture, Neil gave everyone a lift into the city in the truck. But that meant we had to go early before the traffic started to build up. As a result, we had an hour to fill in before the start of the performance by the Ballet Folklórico de México which was an inclusion on our trip. The show ran for over two hours and was largely based on regional folk dances. In parts, it was very interesting, but the Art Deco interior of the Palacio de Bellas Artes in which it was held was also well worth seeing.

When the performance finished, we drove out to Teotihuacan, the most important and largest city of pre-Aztec central Mexico. Lunch was taken in the car park and then we were free to look around. It was a big site to explore, but at least I didn't have to stop to take photographs! Teotihuacan was far more impressive than I had imagined, particularly when viewed from high up on the pyramids. We were generously given about four hours to look around which gave us time to explore the entire main site and also some of the interesting ruined residential buildings, many of which also had well-preserved murals.

Teotihuacan - The Great Avenue from the Pyramid of the Moon *(Ammex Asociados)*

Teotihuacan - Temple of the Quetzalcoatl *(Ammex Asociados)*

> *I upset the Swiss members of the group by mistakenly telling them that they had to be back at the truck an hour too early!*

We got back to the camp just as a thunderstorm was breaking, but we were able to salvage much of our dry washing. I fell asleep before dinner and straight away afterwards.

It turned out that Fred had to leave the trip due to 'domestic problems' and fly back to Australia. There was talk of him re-joining in Guatemala. But for now, we had lost the group barman and one of our best drinkers. We had to set up a new bar tab system which was timely because the previous one run by Fred had made a loss!

24th May 1982: Mexico City - Tehuitzingo

Our departure from Mexico City was delayed whilst I went back into the city to the American Express offices to get money. At the same time one of the drivers, Neil, set off to talk with the Encounter Overland London Office about Fred leaving us. I felt better that I wasn't the only person delaying our departure.

As I expected, I was kept waiting by Amex, even though I arrived when their office opened at 9:30. The delay was a chance to write a few more postcards but I soon ran out of cards to write. After a long wait, they begrudgingly gave permission to re-issue $1000 in U.S. Traveller's Cheques. I cashed $150 to repay the debts I had run up, posted my letters and set off back to the camp. I was running late so took a shared taxi for the final leg back from the Metro station; I wasn't feeling so poor anymore!

After lunch we struck camp and then set off out of the city, stopping briefly on the way to look at the 1968 Olympic stadium. Retracing the route we had entered the city, we once again climbed to the high mountain pass. This time the clouds had lifted and we were treated to good views in all directions. Once out of the Mexico City valley, we branched south onto the road to Oaxaca; and then I fell asleep!

Route from Mexico City to Belize

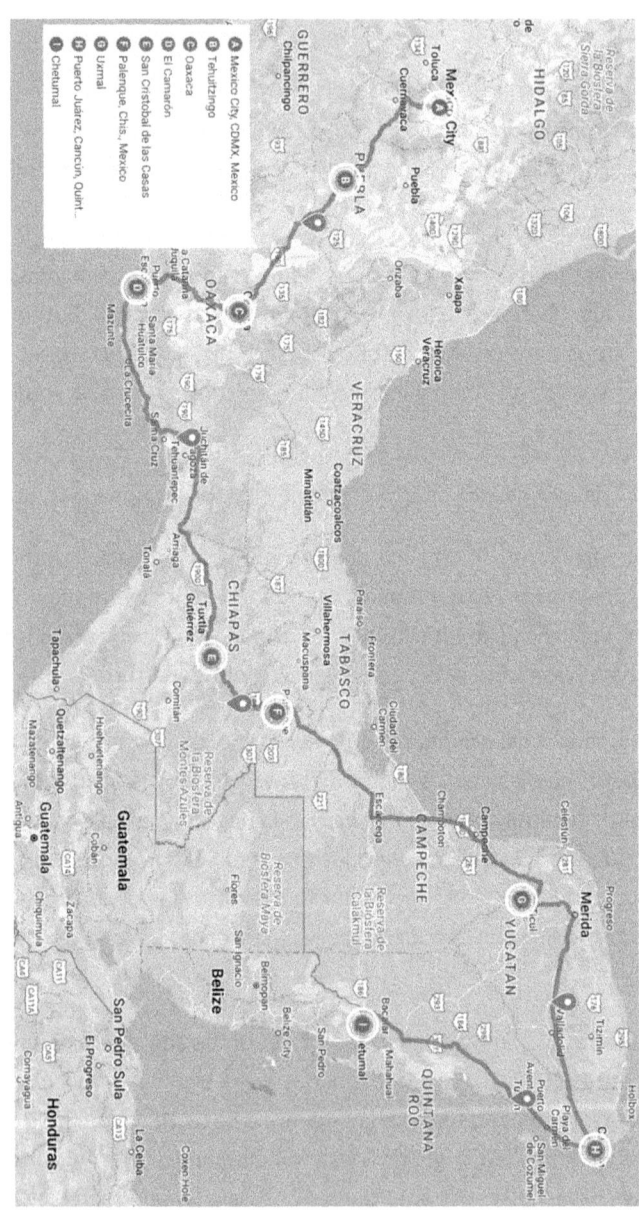

Popocatepetl volcano

We drove through dramatic scenery with glimpses of the snow-capped Popocatepetl volcano (6414m) shrouded in clouds. Gradually the countryside became more arid with cacti reappearing. There were two distinct types of cacti, one with a single spire, and the other that branched out into multiple spires like a tree.

Our overnight camp was close to Tehuitzingo on a patch of common land next to the road. As the sun set, the evening thunderstorms put on a spectacular lighting display in the clouds. A few of us walked to a small village nearby; there was no exercise to be had sitting in the back of the truck.

At dinner, there was much speculation as to whether it would rain overnight. Some people set up their tents, but I didn't. My confidence was justified as there were only a few drops in the night. There might not have been much rain, but there were lots of insects flying around. I was relieved to find out that they didn't bite.

25th May 1982: Tehuitzingo - Oaxaca

It wasn't clear what we had all eaten or drunk the previous day, but a lot of the group now had the trots, including both drivers. I wondered if my recurrent illness on previous trips was finally giving me some sort of resistance or immunity. I dodged the bullet this time.

After many relaxed days in Mexico City, we were now back to hard driving and slow progress as the road wound up and down through mountain ranges. It was tedious but the scenery looked beautiful out the back of the truck.

> The Mexicans enforced their speed limits in towns with aggressive sleeping policemen. The bumps in the road might be OK in an old car if you don't mind losing your shock absorbers, but the truck had to come to a standstill to negotiate them safely.

We only got as far as Huajuapan de Leon before lunch time; stopping there to eat and shop. The truck was parked by the busy local market and a decrepit church. Walking round the market was difficult, as the sheets strung out to provide shade were Indian height and not set up for tall Europeans.

It was later in the afternoon when we arrived at Oaxaca. After failing to find anywhere in town where we could park the truck, we drove out of town down to the campsite. Thunder storms rumbled all around us, but our driver Neil said that the locals thought it would not rain. Nevertheless, we ignored the advice, everyone put up their tent, and after I had enjoyed a nice hot shower the heavens opened. It was a good chance to see in broad daylight where my flysheet leaked!

26th May 1982: Oaxaca – El Camaron

We got up early to visit the classic Olmec/Zapotec/Mixtec settlement at Monte Alban, This was an amazing site on the top of a hill with most of the visible structures dating from the end of the classic Zapotec occupation in about 900 A.D. When I stood on the flat courtyard created by shaving the top off the hill, there was no sensation of being on a mountain top; I was just surrounded by buildings.

Entrance ticket to Monte Alban Archaeological Site

Hiding in the bushes at Monte Alban were boys who furtively tried to sell you 'genuine' antiques; something that would have been illegal if the artefacts were indeed antique. Our group went on a spending spree because the items the boys sold were unique and looked old even if they weren't. I resisted the temptation as the cheap pieces looked crude to my eyes.

351

Monte Alban - A stela on the corner of the southern platform *(by Kipi Turok)*

Monte Alban - Mountain top site *(Figueroa)*

Monte Alban - The Dancers Building – an early Zapotec structure

Monte Alban was a fascinating place to explore, with many ruins only partially excavated and a feeling that so much of its history remained buried. When the mist lifted later in the morning there were great views down to Oaxaca, it was like the view from an aeroplane when landing.

Back down in Oaxaca we persevered and eventually found somewhere near the city centre to park the truck; that gave us a couple of hours free to look around. I had to help with the cooking, so first I had to shop for food in the local market. Then I was free to visit the Santo Domingo church and the attached museum in a colonial building. On my way back to the truck I bought some of the distinctive local black pottery, though I knew getting it back to England in one piece would be a challenge. Our departure was delayed by the late return of Neil who got stuck in the barbers having a haircut.

After driving for a few hours we stopped for the night in the mountains. Our camp was in a wood by a road-side shrine.

27th May 1982: El Camaron – San Cristobal

I slept soundly through the noise of the traffic climbing the steep hill next to our camp and even through the 6:30 wakeup call. It was sticky hot even that early in the morning, especially as it was my turn to dig the rubbish hole.

As we descended about 4,000 feet down to near sea level the conditions in the back of the truck got worse. Sweat poured off every time the truck slowed down or stopped. We dripped our way round Tehuantepec doing the shopping. I was a cook for the day so had a great opportunity to exercise my Spanish in the local market. It was too challenging to buy fresh meat so we decided to cook lentils that night. Soon afterwards we stopped for lunch conveniently close to a fast-flowing brown river where we could all take a much-needed wash.

The next stretch of road down the coast was flat, hot and boring. But after Tuxtla, we climbed again back up into the mountains, clouds and rain. The road passed by many Indian villages where the locals wore traditional red and white ponchos.

At 7 p.m. with the light fading fast, we drove over the final pass and dropped down to San Cristobal de las Casas. It was too late to drive through the town so we camped on the outskirts, on some green grass near a factory. It was another camp near a main road! Once again the storms in the mountains put on a spectacular light show, and I relaxed with a bottle of Vino Tinto from the truck bar.

28th May 1982: San Cristobal - Palenque

Oops! I forgot to tell my cook helper that we could have a lie-in, so Roberta got breakfast ready at 6 and woke everyone up! Our campsite was very public with cars and buses full of workers passing us and having a good look. So we were happy not to hang around!

We drove into town and parked right in the centre by the church of Santo Domingo (1547) and the public market. We were given 1 ½ hours to look around, but for half an hour in the middle, I was on truck guard duty. The town was full of Indians in their local costumes, even at such an early hour.

Chiapas Indians *(by Antonio Turok & Jose Rodriguez)*

On my first break, I visited the Zocalo and bought some postcards. I was able to write a card whilst I was guarding the truck. On gaining my freedom the second time I had a long and unsuccessful search for the Post Office. Pressed for time, I abandoned that quest and instead searched for a craft shop run by a collective of Indian villages. I was on the point of giving up on that quest as well when I ran into two other members of our group who had found the shop around the back of the church. They had an excellent selection at fixed prices; I bought an example of Indian weaving complete with the hand loom.

San Cristobal Las Casas – Market (by Vincente Kramsky)

Weaving from Chiapas Indians

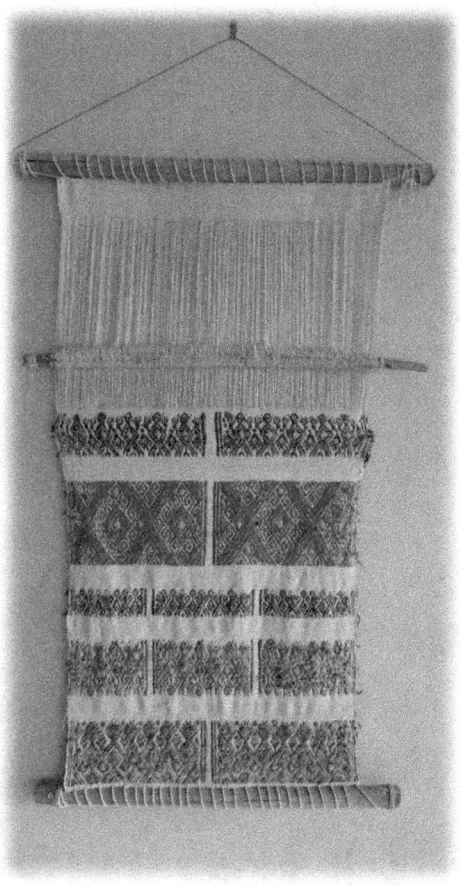

After we had finished our sightseeing and shopping we set off on a minor road towards Palenque. At first, our route took us on a well-surfaced road that passed through Alpine-like pastures and small villages. Once again there were lots of locals dressed in their colourful red and white ponchos.

Then the road degenerated leaving us with about 40 km of dusty dirt track to Ocosingo. We all got filthy, especially because we followed a bus most of the way and got a double dose of dust. When the tarmac surface started again, we stopped for lunch by a mountain stream so we could have a swim and start to feel human again.

Back on the road, it was still dusty, but the scenery was more interesting. We passed through Indian villages and as the road dropped down, the tropical jungle got denser. I spent most of the journey standing looking out over the driver's cab, the view was better and so was the cooling breeze.

Along with the jungle came the sticky heat. When we stopped at Palenque the sweat just poured off us. Luckily our campsite at Balneario Nututun, two miles out of town, had a river for bathing; a chance to get clean and cool down, for a while at least.

Palenque - Nututun bathing hole (by Vincente Kramsky)

Surprisingly, with all that water around, the mosquitos weren't as bad as we expected, but the bar prices in the nearby hotel were pretty painful. Though the humidity was oppressive, it didn't rain; that was lucky in an area with the highest rainfall in Mexico!

29th May 1982: Palenque

The next day we had planned to visit the ruins at Palenque in the morning and then race to Uxmal getting there in time for the evening *Son y Luminaire* show. That was far too ambitious a target given the incredible heat and our slow truck. I had never sweated so much as I did that day, even when sitting still. As a result, everything took a lot longer to do!

We visited Palenque first thing in the morning, but even that early, there wasn't a noticeable reduction in the heat or humidity. I didn't have a guidebook and none were available to purchase, so I resorted to a 'blind man's tour', looking at anything that caught my interest.

Palenque - Tomb under Temple of the Inscriptions (by Vincente Kramsky)

Palenque was fascinating! It even had a tower you could climb to the top of. One high spot was when I descended to the tomb under the Temple of the Inscriptions by the light of my torch; it was a bit spooky on my own! Then they turned on the lights and I was able to get a good look at the carved stone lid before a crowd of tourists arrived.

We had a hot and sticky shopping trip in the town before returning to our previous night's camp for a relaxing afternoon and evening. It was a chance to catch up on washing, and anything else that could be done in the river.

There were a lot of natives around the pool. After our experience in Acapulco, we were more aware of the security risk so we pitched our tents facing inwards towards the truck. I managed to buy a guidebook to the ruins of Palenque in a nearby hotel... better late than never!

Palenque - The Palace (by Vincente Kramsky)

Palenque - Temple of the Sun (by Vincente Kramsky)

Map of Palenque in my diary

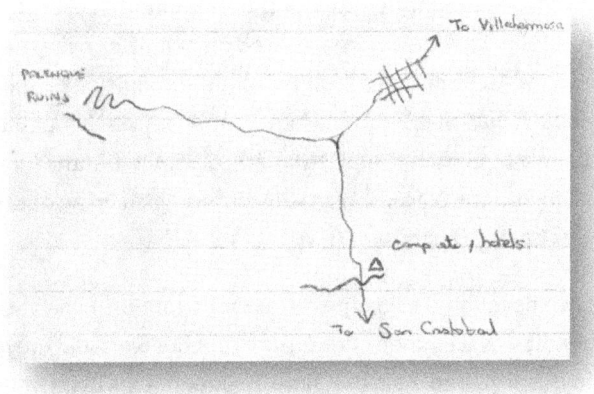

30th May 1982: Palenque - Uxmal

Our modest plan for the day was just to get to Uxmal in time to visit the ruins. Even so, nature and the physical constraints of distance conspired to defeat us. We left our campsite with its refreshing stream and all morning rolled along the flat uninteresting road to Campeche. The Campeche market was quiet on a Sunday and there was nowhere we could buy food to make dinner. The town itself looked interesting, but on a 15-minute shopping stop, there wasn't time to explore much.

From Campeche, the back road to Merida wasn't either flat or straight, so our progress slowed down; there still wasn't anything worth seeing out the back of the truck. The Yucatan was a flat limestone plateau covered with dense scrub but lacking any noteworthy features, natural or man-made. The skies blacked over to match our mood, and thunderstorms were brewing in every direction. It didn't start raining till we were a couple of miles from Uxmal, and then it rained in bucket loads.

We stopped in the site car park where we had intended to camp but it was a river of water six inches deep! Making the best of a bad job we stripped off and washed in the rain; it was also a chance to clean the truck. We then climbed back inside in the dry, brewed tea and coffee and waited for the rain to stop; but it didn't. At 8 p.m., desperate for food, we started to tour the local hotels, looking for a dry bar where we could all sit whilst the cooks prepared dinner. After being turned down by several venues, we were directed to a restaurant a couple of kilometres back on the road to Merida. It was all closed up when we arrived; we thought it was 9 p.m. but there had been a time change and it was an hour later. But the lure of a large order breathed life into the place. Soon the lights were on and an authentic Yucatan meal was being prepared for us.

After the meal, we negotiated using the restaurant's car port / shed as an overnight shelter. It was wet under the leaking roof but we could move our beds around to avoid the drips and we didn't have to put up tents in the mud.

Uxmal - The Pyramid of the Magician (Turistica Peninsular)

31st May 1982: Uxmal – Puerto Juarez

What a joy! We were up nice and early to have a paddle in the quagmire and eat breakfast; at least there were no muddy wet tents to pack up. Twenty-seven days into the holiday I finally succumbed to the trots; I attributed it to the authentic meal the previous night!

Uxmal - The Nunnery Quadrangle - Corbel arch entrance (by Mark Turok)

We finally got to see the ruins at Uxmal, in sapping heat and humidity, but at least it wasn't raining. I was impressed by the Nunnery complex of four buildings. Most of the buildings were in the Puuc style with little decoration except for a frieze on the roof. The Pyramid of the Magician was incredibly steep-sided; I had to hang on hard to the safety chain.

The next stop was Merida, a town that didn't impress me much. It was noisy and dirty, but I spent most of the time we were there looking for a toilet!

From Merida, we made a non-stop dash to Chichen Itza in the hope that we could get there before it closed. We just made it in time, but it had already started to rain. I jumped out of the truck, and with a few others made it through into the "new" city, although by now the site had officially closed. We had a quick free look around in a soaking downpour as lightning flashed overhead. I would have liked to see the ball-court in more detail, but I did get to climb up the Temple of the Jaguars to see the jaguar throne. Needless to say the risk of climbing a pyramid in a thunderstorm didn't occur to us at the time.

Chichen Itza - New City on a sunny day (Turistica Peninsular)

When the 30 minutes we had been allowed was up, we returned to the truck. Neil suggested that as we were already soaked we might just as well have a look around the old city on the other side of the road; no officials were out in the rain looking for trespassers. So I went, along with the hardy ruin freaks amongst us! We explored the Observatory and the Palace complexes, and I got a shock from my umbrella from an overhead flash of lightning! The roads were all lakes and we just waded along. It was great fun; there was no use for a camera or a guidebook!

For the second night in a row, the weather wouldn't let us set up camp. We pressed on to the coast in the hope of finding somewhere dry. It was a long boring drive and most of us were asleep in the back and starvingly hungry before we reached Puerto Juarez. At the first rough campsite we selected the police came and moved us on. We ended up on a cramped sandy track sandwiched between the sea and the road. But at least it wasn't raining!

The mosquitos were bad. The strong wind didn't deter them and there was no room for us to put up tents as protection. The police came to visit us to see what was going on but didn't ask us to move on, so we ate dinner and went to bed in the open.

1st June 1982: Puerto Juarez

With no room for tents, it just had to rain in the night, and it did! I was woken at 5:30. We all knew how it could really rain, so we jumped out of bed and bundled into the back of the truck. As it turned out the storm was short-lived but after it had passed, it was too late to try to go back to sleep. I lay inside my mosquito net killing the bugs that were on the wrong side!

The consensus was that it wasn't going to be a good day to go to Isle Mujeres to sunbake. Instead, we moved further up the road to a proper campsite. I decided to walk the short distance, but in the process got soaked by another passing storm.

The mosquitos at the new campsite were even fiercer if that was possible; they were active even in the pouring rain. During a break in the weather, we got the tents up in record time, with everyone tackling each tent in turn. Even so, most of the morning had gone by the time we had the camp set up.

After lunch, many of the group set off to go into town, but I stayed put. It was a chance to do washing (I didn't have many clothes so everything had to be washed frequently) and a chance to laze about under a mosquito net doing very little. When the others got back there was a big storm that created a lake that flooded one of the tents. Rescue teams set out armed with spades to drain the campsite, whilst I looked on from the dry of my tent.

At the evening meal, when we were all crowded round a lamp, the mosquitos were particularly hungry. It was marginally better to stand eating in the rain in the dark. Then we spruced up and went to a bar in town. The streets were flooded from the heavy rain but that didn't faze our truck; we arrived at the hotel with dry feet. The bar was full of Yanks but the place was mosquito free. A pleasant relaxing time was had by all.

One of our group who should remain nameless stole a sign from the bar. It read

BROKEN ENGLISH

SPOKEN PERFECTLY

We installed it behind our truck windscreen.

2nd June 1982: Puerto Juarez – Chetumal

I woke covered in mosquito bites and collected a few more getting my tent down. We were lucky that it didn't choose to rain that morning. When everything was packed back in the truck we drove down the coast road south to Tulum. It was another flat fast road with no towns or scenery to add interest. After a drink break at a rather smart roadside café, we headed out to the coast and the Mayan ruins of Tulum.

After seeing Uxmal and Chichen Itza, the ruins of Tulum were not particularly impressive, but the setting on a tropical coastline made up for that. The scenery reminded me of the south coast of Bali, except that the sea was calm. My opinion of the place was no doubt coloured by the large number of American tourists who had come down in coach loads from the holiday hotels further up the coast. I bought a few postcards at an inflated tourist price and helped the others prepare a lunch which we ate in the car park.

The drive onwards to Chetumal was equally dull and we arrived there, dry for once, late in the afternoon. The shops were still shut for the siesta, so we set ourselves up in a smart café and drank away our remaining Mexican pesos. The shops in Chetumal were full of expensive imported goods as it was a free port. But everything else was similarly expensive; we had to find our driver Neil to get more cash for food shopping. Neil bought a large drum to fill with cheap Mexican fuel which cluttered up the back of the truck.

3rd June 1982: Puerto Juarez – Benque Viejo

It was a disaster morning. Firstly we were meant to get up before dawn to get across the border into Belize, but when I woke in the dark our campsite was still quiet. When the sun rose I woke everyone up. Breakfast was set, consumed, and cleared away in record time.

Then we discovered that the screw handle we used to hold the stacked tables in place on the trailer was missing. We scoured the campsite in vain looking for it.

Finally, two of the group found that they had lost their Mexican Tourist Cards. Surprisingly, although I had had my luggage stolen, my passport was returned with the Tourist Card. But without a Tourist Card, you couldn't leave Mexico. We drove to the Belize border which was just outside the town in the hope that a kindly official would let us all through, but they refused. So we had to return to the centre of town and find the Immigration Office and then wait for the 'big boss' to come to work. Those of us, myself included, who still had local currency, sat it out in a café. I indulged a growing taste for egg flips after convincing myself that the milk looked safe.

Once the immigration chief arrived, we were quickly issued replacement cards and then returned to the border. The checks leaving Mexico and entering Belize were very relaxed. There was one tense moment when one of our group accidentally declared she had money that she hadn't got!

Route from Belize to Guatemala

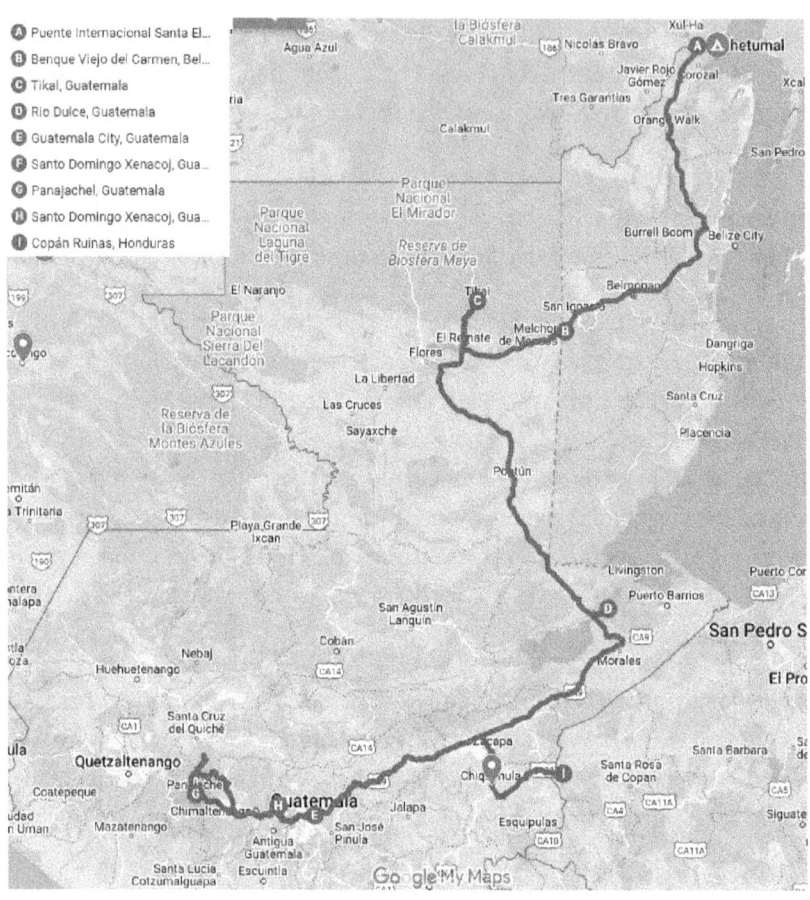

BELIZE

Even though we passed quickly through Belize it was immediately obvious that the country did not belong in mainland Latin America. The inhabitants of this outpost of the British Empire spoke English. The easy-going Creole culture reminded one more of the Pirates of the Caribbean than Catholic Mexico.
We arrived at a rather tense time as Britain was at war with Argentina over the Falkland Islands.

Belize City near the U.S. Consulate (Cubola Postcards)

It was swelteringly hot hanging round at the border. We were all glad when were waved into Belize and the truck started moving again. The road was rough and unsealed and our progress was slow. The north of the country appeared to be mostly swamp and was an ideal breeding ground for mosquitos. Stopping for lunch and being an insect's feast wasn't an attractive option, so we pressed on to Belize City.

Newspaper reporting on the Falklands War 3rd June 1982

Daily Mail

NAPALM: THE PROOF

'Liberty, justice and democracy is what I seek—that is not humiliation'
— Mrs Thatcher, last night

TREACHERY TO YIELD NOW

By ROBERT PORTER and ALAN YOUNG

MRS THATCHER made it absolutely clear last night that Argentina will play no part in the future of the Falklands. To give anything to an aggressor she said, 'would be treachery and betrayal of our own people.'

But she stressed : 'I am not seeking to humiliate anyone. I am just trying to repossess islands which are British sovereign territory. That is not humiliation. That is liberty, justice and democracy.'

Asked about appeals for magnanimity to Argentina, she retorted: 'It is not a word I use in connection with the battle for the Falklands. Magnanimity I think people use today to say "All right, hand something to the Argentines".'

'Under these circumstances to be handed over an aggressor, and a military dictator that would not be magnanimous, it would be treachery or betrayal of our own people, we should not betray our own people.'

'What else did we win protection from Argentina by a small national partisan force, but the U.N. This may not happen again, are...'

The Prime Minister spoke in an interview with the world on major television networks who held the spot for ITN.

'I do not believe for one moment that after what people have understood they would see the Argentine government as stronger, nor gone to their claim, she said firmly. 'Now that they have experienced what it is like to live with the Argentines, so the citizens I doubt very much looking to the Argentines, would be even greater.'

Steadfast

Mrs Thatcher gave the Argentines a tough answer in windows debate what she admitted could be a prolonged and bloody struggle for Port Stanley. She said: 'If they say "Look, we are going to withdraw without the need for us to fight," then there would be no need for a battle,' she added. 'I would be delighted. It would save so many young lives.'

'But she stressed the possibility perhaps, "I do not climb down to anything while I can do" she said: 'Everything, yes everything, has been turned down.'

'On the immediate future of the islands, Mrs Thatcher did not say how Argentina, Mrs Thatcher said talks would be held with the Islanders on whether they could achieve full independence or a kind of self-government.

'The Prime Minister said she had received a sparkling message from Falkland Islanders at Goose Green and Darwin thanking British for being so steadfast and God save the Queen.'

Guns fire on Moody Brook

MAX HASTINGS, in a British position five miles from Port Stanley

The faces of defeat... dejected Argentines captured at Goose Green are guarded by a Royal Marine

Turn to Page 2, Col. 1

The inhabitants of coastal Belize were quite different from the Mexicans we had become accustomed to. They were black and spoke in a sing-song Caribbean English. Within minutes of us stopping in the town, we were surrounded by curious people. It was clear that very few American tourists made it this far.

Once again, shopping was not easy. The market was small and sparsely stocked. Most food had to be imported and was too expensive for us. We managed to buy the essentials and still had a short time left to wander round and soak up the unusual atmosphere.

Belize - Border area with Guatemala (Liberia Progreso)

Late in the afternoon, we set off inland through the swamps heading towards the border with Guatemala. We bypassed the new capital of Belmopan and were soon climbing up into rolling green hills.

When we reached the border town of San Ignacio it was swarming with British troops. We hadn't been following the news and were unaware of how the Falklands War had escalated following an invasion by Argentina. We stopped to chat with the soldiers and found out that the British Army was officially on 'exercises' triggered by the tensions between the U.K. and Latin America. The situation on the border hadn't been helped by Guatamala's recent expressions of support for Argentina.

As we got closer to the border the road got rougher and rougher, almost to the point where I assumed we must have accidently turned off onto a side road. We stopped for the night by the Mopan River near Benque Viejo. The river was good for washing though not particularly refreshing as it was warm. But, unusually for this part of the world, there were surprisingly few mosquitos which made our camp life more relaxing.

We were visited twice by a liaison officer from the British Army who chatted at length with our driver Neil. Apparently, the message was there shouldn't be any problem crossing over into Guatemala. This was a big relief as it would have been a long 1,000km detour to enter directly from Mexico at La Mesilla.

I slept in the back of the truck rigging up my mosquito net to the roof with string.

4th June 1982: Benque Viejo - Tikal

This time we did manage to get up before dawn but it didn't feel so early. Belize was on 'Summer Time', a legacy of being administered from the U.K. We wound down the dirt track to the river crossing and the border. Then we had to wait for Belize to open their side of the border as there was no cooperation between the two countries. We didn't encounter any significant problems getting across, though there was not a lot of love lost between the two sides; it still took about three hours.

Belize dollar (rare)

Mopan River at Benque Viejo (ambergriscaya.com)

The countries of Central America lack natural protection against armed aggression by their neighbours. The only exception is perhaps Panama which is isolated from Columbia by the Darién Gap. So to discourage mechanised incursions, it seemed that they let the roads to their land border crossings degenerate into mere tracks.

GUATEMALA

> Guatemala, recovering from years of civil war and regular earthquakes, was relatively unpackaged, unfiltered and unspoiled. The Guatemalans were a smiling people, embracing a fascinating mix of pagan and catholic beliefs. Once again the mountainous terrain was a challenge for our truck, but after the boredom of Mexico's Yucatan peninsular, the scenic variety was welcome.

We stopped in Flores, 90 km from the border, to shop. The truck parked close to the market on the mainland as it couldn't drive down the narrow causeway onto the island. The lake looked very attractive for a swim as the day was hot, but our schedule didn't permit a long break, nor did it allow us time to look round the island. From Flores up to Tikal the road was surfaced and we made much faster progress.

> *TIKAL*
>
> Six square miles of Mayan buildings and monuments deep in the Guatemalan jungle. Most of the visible remains date from the Classic time (250 to 900 A.D.) after which there was a rapid population decline.

In 1982, the modern settlement of Tikal was just a cluster of buildings close to the airstrip, surrounded by jungle. There was a campsite at the end of the runway which had a toilet block (closed with a broken water pipe) and the shell of an empty visitor centre.

I set off on foot to the Mayan ruins, about a mile away. It was hot and I was disappointed to find that there were no soft drink sellers on the other side of the entrance gate inside the site. In three hours I managed to look round all the main temple groups but then my thirst became unbearable. I had time to walk to the then unrestored Northern group along jungle paths, which gave me a good idea of what Tikal looked like before the archaeologists arrived. There was a lot of work to be done to uncover and stabilise the structures deep in the jungle.

Back at the camp, I had three soft drinks and two cups of coffee to rehydrate. We put our beds up around the toilet block, under the eaves, to avoid putting up tents.

I didn't sleep well because it was hot, the jungle was noisy, and I was being bitten!

Tikal - Temple of the Giant Jaguar viewed from the central acropolis (Liberia Progreso)

Tikal - Temple 2 and the great plaza (Liberia Progreso)

Tikal - Altar 8 with prostrate figures (Liberia Progreso)

5th June 1982: Tikal – Rio Dulce

This was a memorable day for all the wrong reasons! Ten hours were spent driving south along the bumpiest, dustiest road conceivable. At times it was little more than a single dirt track winding through thick jungle. The only break we had was for lunch, at a farm run by an American couple near Poptun. It was interesting to hear an inside perspective on the civil war raging between the military junta and revolutionary guerrillas. The terrorist threat had resulted in a big slump in tourism and their income from tourists. We swam in the farm pool and looked at their pet parrot, but didn't have time to visit the nearby Mayan caves.

We bounced along the 'road' until we reached a high concrete bridge over Lake Izabal. This marked the return to a hard top after 246km of rough track. We celebrated by parking for the night by the remains of the old ferry ramps. We had averaged less than 30 km/hr that day.

6th June 1982: Rio Dulce – Guatemala City

We had a slow start for once, giving the drivers time to do some maintenance on the truck. That was followed by a relaxed stop for shopping in the busy market town of Chiguimula followed by an extended lunch stop by a muddy river. I turned down the opportunity for a swim because I was busy trying to finish a couple of letters to post in Guatemala City the next day.

We soon climbed up from the flat plains into the high mountains. The cooler and drier air was a welcome change after more than a week in the tropical jungle. We even passed through a valley of cacti at one point. There were no interesting Indians to see here and no nice houses; far too much concrete and corrugated iron had been used in their construction.

Surprisingly we encountered very few police along the way, except for one checkpoint in the hills. I wonder if this was because a checkpoint would be an obvious target for the guerrillas active in the area. We couldn't camp in Guatemala City because of the frequent gun fights at night, so we had our first cool climate camp for a long time, on the outskirts of the city.

7th June 1982: Guatemala City

With a day to explore Guatemala City, I did wonder what I would find to do from 7:30 until 4 o'clock. In the end, I had quite an eventful day.

After we were dropped in the city centre, I found the Post Office where I could post the letters and cards that I had hastily written the day before. There were good displays of postcards outside. I was able to stock up on pictures of places we had already visited, and places where we hoped to go in the future.

Guatemala City - National Palace (La Lectura S.A.)

It was early and the banks had not yet opened. I sat in a café passing the time, discussing the trip with a member of our group. When the bank opened there was no problem cashing a traveller's cheque, and the exchange rate of one Quetzal to the dollar made price conversions easy.

As I sat in the main square writing some more postcards, I found myself chatting with friendly Guatemalans. With a civil war frightening away most tourists, a foreigner in Guatemala City was something of a novelty. The National Palace on one side of the square was an elegant building in the colonial style with attractive courtyards and murals on the walls. It was however a mostly modern building as the original was badly damaged in the 1968 earthquake. The Cathedral had also been heavily reconstructed but, as a result, it had a clean look with the primary interior decoration being a series of oil paintings.

I wandered up and down the two main shopping streets, 6a and 7a Avenue, indulging myself in some window shopping. I must even confess to having a Big Mac for lunch. In the afternoon, I headed south towards the Civic Centre, posting the cards I had just written before the ink was even dry.

On the way, I 'ran into' a pleasant man who said he was from Lake Atitlán, the next stop on our trip. He spoke quite good English and he helped by showing me where the National Theatre and Tourist Office were. The latter was eager to help, plying me with lots of information and a free reprint from the National Geographic magazine on The Maya.

National Geographic Articles on The Maya

I had coffee with my 'friend' who then showed me the way by bus to the Parque Minerva where there was a relief map of Guatemala. The map was interesting; it was complete with lakes and flowing rivers. With an exaggerated vertical scale, it helped to make clear the contrast between the flat plains and the volcanic mountains.

Back on the bus, I found my way back to the truck with the help of my 'friend'. On parting, he asked for a $5 loan. Deep down I knew I had little chance of seeing my money again, but felt that it was good value for his help and all the interesting places we had visited.

At the camp, I was a bit annoyed to hear that some of our group had found good blankets in a handicraft market. We drove out of town and stopped in a wood close to St. Domingo Xanco, just as it started to rain. Dinner was a can of stew because our driver Neil had said he would do the shopping but he forgot!

> It didn't occur to me at the time, but in a country torn apart by civil war, where gun fights were common, perhaps rough camping on the outskirts of the city was not a very safe option. But the budget set by Encounter Overland didn't allow us to pay for campsites with security. In this case, saving a night's camping fees probably wasn't so smart.

8th June 1982: Guatemala City – Panajachel

Another unusual day, one when we were not pressed for time. We had the opportunity to take the back (more scenic) route to Lake Atitlán, after dropping our assistant driver Tony on the main road. He had to go back into the city to collect visas. The winding road passed through many villages, and as we travelled further from Guatemala City and closer to Lake Atitlán we encountered more native Indians.

Lake Atitlán is a flooded caldera surrounded by volcanos; it has no surface outlet to the sea. When we reached the rim of the caldera the road descended to Panajachel with good views of the lake and the surrounding volcanos.

After ditching the trailer in the Panajachel campsite, we headed up to the Indian town of Sololá which had a market day. It was a colourful vibrant spectacle with many Indians in their local costume. The handicrafts section of the market wasn't very interesting. There was so much Indian weaving and embroidery being sold in the area, that the bright colours started to tire on the eye, and it left me longing for something pastel!

Lake Atitlán (La Lectura S.A.)

I took a minibus back down to the lake at about midday; the bus was so cramped I couldn't move and it wasn't particularly cheap by local standards. I wandered round Panajachel for a bit till I ran into Neil and another member of the group in a promising-looking restaurant. The strawberry liquidos (milk shakes) and yoghurt with muesli, honey and fruit did a lot to raise my spirits; I had to admit I liked gringo food more than the local fare!

Back at our campsite, the drivers were nowhere to be seen, so I had a bucket wash, put up my tent and then lazed around.

There was a religious festival going on. It seemed to involve dressed-up men chasing the children, and a band touring the streets in front of a procession of religious icons.

Lake Atitián – weaving (La Lectura S.A.)

Something about Panajachel reminded me of Nepal. Was it the chill in the air, the wooden houses, or perhaps the gringo restaurants? I suspected that above all it was the air of relaxation the place seemed to exude. That said, Panajachel was something of a ghost town; guerrilla activity in the previous year had frightened away the foreign tourists.

> I got a letter from Encounter Overland saying that they were offering an extension trip from Columbia down to Peru (flying over the Darién Gap). I wasn't interested.

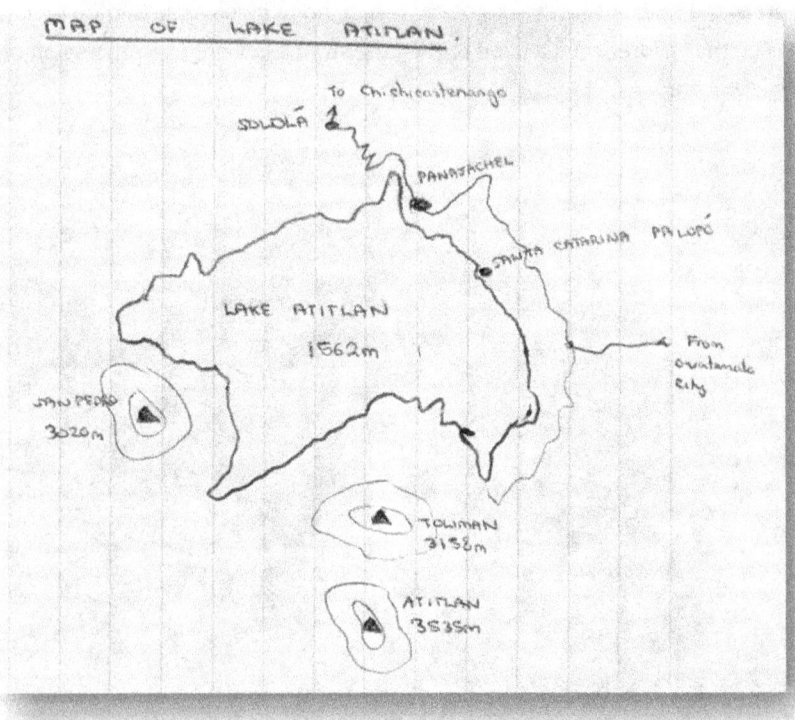

9th June 1982: Panajachel

A lazy start by Lake Atitlan. I woke out of habit before dawn but luckily it was still dark and the campsite was quiet. I had no problem going back to sleep again. I opted out of the camp breakfast and instead walked up the road to have a gringo food fix; a liquido, an omelette and coffee. The best bit was that I could eat my breakfast sitting in the sunshine at a table. Such simple pleasures of life were rare on this overland trip.

When the banks opened, I cashed a bit more money and then helped the on-duty cooks to buy food in the market. I followed my delicious breakfast with an equally tasty restaurant lunch and managed to sit in the dry during the one big thunderstorm of the day. With all that food, I needed to work off the calories. In the afternoon, I took a walk along the coast to Santa Catarina, about 2 ½ miles of scenic track.

During the day I was persuaded to buy a $10 souvenier. I made the purchase just because the desperate man pestering me to buy had lowered his price so much it would have been insane not to say yes.

My health was much better, maybe this was because I tried to avoid drinking water from the truck tank. I suspected at the time that the tank water might not have been chlorinated thoroughly.

10th June 1982: Panajachel – St Domingo Xanco

After two relaxing days, we were all well-rested and looking forward to continuing our travels. We drove up the hill again to Sololá, but this time we carried on to the El Quiché region and the town of Chichicastenango. The truck had been serviced the previous day by our drivers; they had changed the injector pump, but heading up the hill the engine didn't sound too healthy.

Chichicastenango was in the throes of a major religious festival, a two-week celebration at the start of the rainy season merged with Corpus Christi. There were processions of images carried on litters accompanied by massive pipe bomb explosions. The vertical tubes shot smoke up in the air with a deafening roar.

I had to do the food shopping, but then I was free to wander around. There was yet another Indian market with the same goods on sale. But what was more interesting here were the two churches on the square. Here was a unique blend of Christian and Pagan worship; incense was being burnt on the main steps, and the dark interior was illuminated by many flickering candles. The interior walls had been blackened by years of smoke. Looking at the priests in the procession, it was hard to guess what religion predominated; Pagan or Christian. An unforgettable experience!

Chichicastenango - Market scene (La Lectura S.A.)

Chichicastenango - St Thomas Church – interior (La Lectura S.A.)

We drove back to our camp at Panajachel, took down the tents and had lunch. Then we hit the road heading back towards Guatemala City. We made slow progress and the best we could do was to get to the camp we had previously used on the outskirts of the city.

I did the cooking that night, chicken in a wine sauce, carrots in honey, small potatoes fried whole, and banana custard to finish it off. It was a good meal!

Over dinner, I found out that a couple of passengers were going to leave the trip in Guatemala City, and that Fred was not going to come back to rejoin the trip.

11th June 1982: St Domingo Xanco - Copan

We drove through the centre of Guatemala City to drop off the two members of our group who were not continuing, and then we retraced our route to Riohondo. As we descended to the plains, it got uncomfortably hot again. We turned south towards Honduras stopping in the last main town before the border, Chiquimula. It was about midday and most of the town was shut up for the siesta. I had intended to just look around to see what sort of hammock I could buy with my remaining Guatemalan money but ended up buying one. How to ship it to the UK from Panama was a problem for another day!

The road from Chiquimula started as well-graded gravel but had deteriorated to a rutted track by the time we reached the Honduras border at El Florido. Once again, Guatemala was making it difficult for an army to invade across its borders!

Both sides of the border were very relaxed and we got through to Honduras in just over two hours. The Honduras side was very quaint, with a stream flowing across the 'road' and chickens roaming freely.

I saw Indians loading bales of onions onto a local bus. Three people would lift the bale onto the back of one poor loading man, who would then run up the ladder at the back of the bus and sling his load onto the top.

Guatemala - Typical weavings in San Antonio Aguas Calientes (La Lectura S.A.)

Route from Honduras to Panama

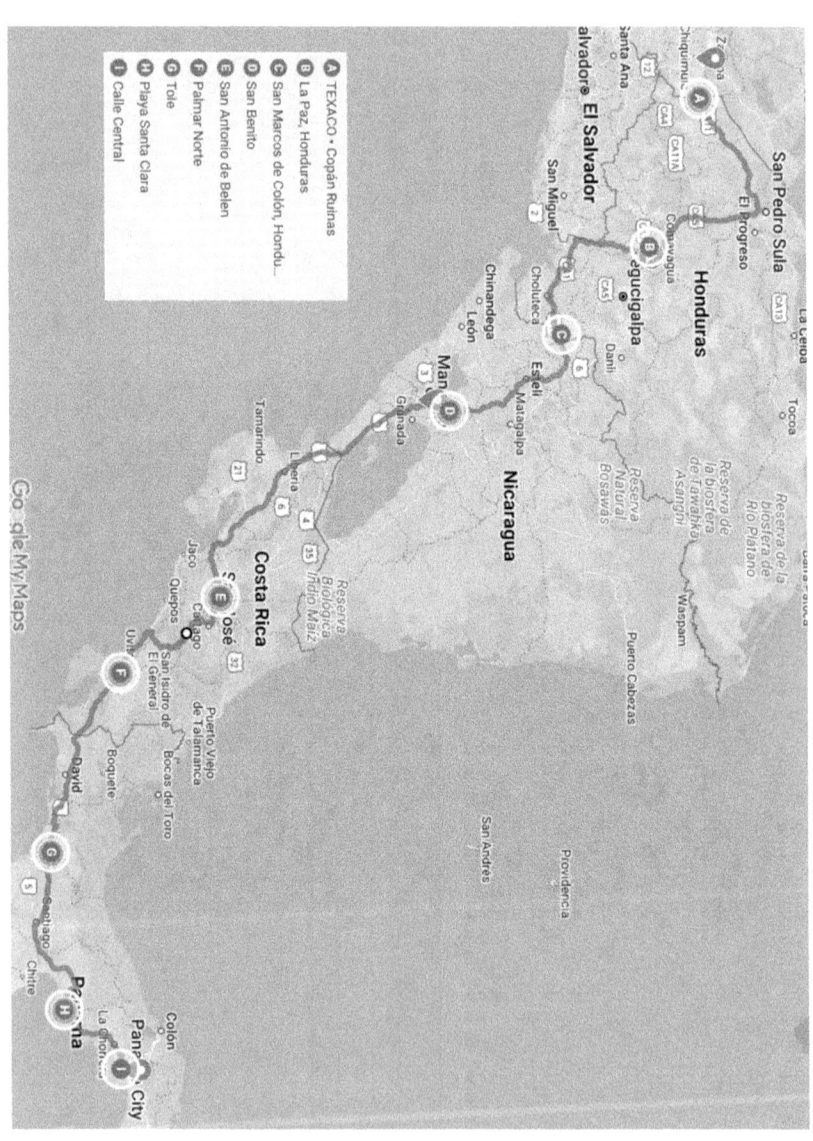

HONDURAS

Our transit through Honduras was necessarily speedy. The country had recently been ravaged by hurricanes leaving roads, farms and buildings destroyed. It was a reminder that Mother Nature could do more damage than civil wars. It hadn't stopped raining and camping was a near impossibility. At last, we were off the gringo trail and it started to feel like a real adventure.

The road on the other side of the border going to Copán was even worse than the approach on the Guatemalan side, a single track winding up over a steep ridge. We camped in a field behind the service station next to the entrance to the Copán archeological site. There was a tap at the garage where I was able finally to have a much-needed wash. As it got dark, there were a lot of fireflies.

COPAN
This Mayan centre flourished from 987 A.D. to 1500 A.D. and had a population of about 200,000 at its peak. In Copán, one finds a large number of stelae and altars with hieroglyphic carvings, all of them belonging to the Classic period. Approximately 10 years elapsed between the erection of each stela.

Copán - Site view (Liberua Evangelica San Pedro)

12th June 1982: Copán – La Paz

We were camped so close to the Copán ruins that we could virtually fall out of our beds and be waiting when the gates opened at 7 a.m. The man selling tickets could not accept Guatemalan Quetzal in payment but that was the only local money we had. In the end, we had to split large denomination U.S. dollar bills to get in. I was able to buy a guide book before looking around which made me happy!

The main features of note at Copán were the stelae which were intricately carved, and the fragrance of the tropical trees. After two hours, we moved to the nearest large town, La Entrada, where we were able to do our food shopping and change money.

Hondurans appeared to be in love with horses. They were grazing by the roadside and being used as a means of transport in the countryside. One of our group caused great amusement by buying a $200 leather saddle to ship home!

Copán - Stela C (Liberia Evangelica San Pedro)

The hills were more rounded in Honduras, which meant that there were fewer mountain ranges to cross. But even so, there were plenty of steep ascents for the truck to grind its way up. The roads were well-surfaced which greatly improved the conditions in the back.

After descending to the tropical lowlands near San Pedro Sula, we climbed back up again into the clouds and the rain, heading south to Tegucigalpa. The rain was unrelenting and heavy; all the camping places we found were waterlogged.

Near the turn-off to La Paz, we saw a building being put up and pulled over to investigate. After much negotiation by the drivers, we were allowed to put up our campbeds in an unglazed and dark room. The place was some sort of orphanage run by a Dutch charity for children from broken marriages. There was a rapidly growing swamp between the truck and the building. So I took an involuntary shower and laid planks across in the rain. Then I washed my hair out of a drum brimming with fresh rainwater.

> *May 1982 Central America floods*
>
> *From Wikipedia*
> In late May 1982, an extended period of heavy rain associated with a long-lived Central America Gyre led to disaster. Particularly hard-hit were Honduras and Nicaragua. Throughout the two countries, at least 308 people were killed and the total damage was $466 million (1982 USD). In the aftermath of the storm, many programs were rolled out to provide relief to the victims.

13th June 1982: La Paz – San Marcos De Colon

The mud had dried out a bit overnight and that made it easier to pack up our dorm and load the truck. The truck however had sunk into the soft ground and wouldn't move. We had to get the 'sand' mats off the side and uncouple the trailer before we could get away.

The road to the capital, Tegucigalpa passed through rolling Alpine meadows. We were even treated to sunshine on arrival, but being Sunday there were not many businesses open and I couldn't post any letters. It wasn't a particularly interesting city either, but it did have a good market. From the main square, I walked up to La Leona Park, a small park with a view over the city. This was the first city view that I had experienced where you could see the slums; wooden shanty towns rising up the surrounding hillsides.

At midday, we left the city to have lunch. We had to stop and eat at a roadside stall because it was raining so heavily. As we descended out of the hills everything was wet, the streams were flooded, the ground waterlogged, and when it wasn't raining heavily, it was drizzling.

There were frequent check-points on the road. We sped through the first ALTO sign (not PARE as is common in other Spanish-speaking countries) and picked up a fine for not stopping. We were more careful in the future. When we reached the Pan American Highway at Jicaro Galan there was water everywhere. The guard at the check-point told us the road ahead was closed at the El Guasaule border crossing; this meant we had to take a slight diversion north to an alternative route into Nicaragua.

We spent our remaining Honduran Lempira drinking in a restaurant, then drove to Choluteca where the river was a raging torrent. As we climbed back up into the hills on the road to San Marcos, we passed through the low cloud and out into welcome blue skies. The sun was shining on us briefly, but then the truck engine died. We restarted it but it failed again a few miles further on, then it ran a bit further before stopping for good. We had fuel, but it had drained to the back of the tank as we climbed up the hill. It was rather a bad design compounded by our running low, having last filled up in Panajachel.

As luck would have it, we broke down right beside a school. So we set up beds under the verandah. There was even a toilet we could use, albeit one without a door. We were camped high above the low clouds and so weren't troubled by rain in the night.

14th June 1982: San Marcos De Colon – San Benito

Although we packed up our camp promptly we weren't going to go anywhere till we could start the truck. There wasn't much traffic going past towards San Marcos, so it took Neil and his jerry can a while to hitch a lift. Whilst we were waiting for him to return, the school children arrived and sat on the road watching us. Neil got a taxi back with a full jerry can which we strapped on the front of the truck as a temporary fuel tank. That was good enough to get us to the first town across the Nicaraguan border. We picked up the three girls who had decided to walk down the road rather than wait for Neil, including one who had decided to take a shower under a waterfall and had to get dressed rather hastlly.

On the Honduran side of the border, we were able to buy Nicaraguan Cordobas at 40 to the US dollar when the official rate was just 8! The fuel failed again, one last time, just over the border, but the truck restarted and we passed through the formalities smoothly. The Nicaraguans were very thorough and inspected all of the luggage.

NICARAGUA

> *Nicaragua was another country where law and order were being challenged by armed groups. At the time, the American-funded Contras were actively trying to get rid of the socialist Sandinista government. It was too dangerous to hang around and too wet to camp.*

We travelled a few miles to the Nicaraguan border town of Somoto where we filled up with diesel (fuel was a lot cheaper than in Honduras). Lunch was taken in a 'motel' a short way up the road. Beef, rice and salad cost just $1; the only issue was the time it took them to prepare 15 meals!

Highway 1 took us to Esteli, a major town that was large enough for us to shop for food. Nearly every building in the town was peppered with bullet marks; a token from the fierce fighting that had recently taken place there during the Sandinista revolution.

> *Esteli was a stronghold for the Sandinista guerrillas in the civil war that had nominally ended in 1979 with the overthrow of the dictator. However, there was still an ongoing civil war in 1982 sponsored by the USA to overthrow the Sandinista government.*

Wandering around, I ran into a 'National Poet' sitting on a wooden seat in front of his damaged house; he was Félix Rubén Espinoza. We chatted away in Spanish and when we parted he gave me a book of his poems as a gift; Poemas Desconicidos (lit. Unknown Poems).

Félix Rubén Espinoza L.

poemas desconocidos

(En saludo al II Aniversario de la Revolución Popular Sandinista).

Estelí.— «AÑO DE LA DEFENSA Y LA PRODUCCION» - 1981

> Al salir del trabajo cansado
> todos los días salgo del trabajo
> con el pelo alborotado
> el bolso me cuelga del pescuezo
> y camino por las calles
> algunas veces
> sintiendo la necesidad
> de escribirte un poema.

> *I leave work tired*
> *Every day I leave work*
> *with messy hair*
> *The bag hangs from my neck*
> *and I walk through the streets*
> *Sometimes*
> *Feeling the need*
> *To write you a poem.*

Poemas desconocidos
Félix Rubén Espinoza 1981

Leaving Esteli the road descended, the air once again became hot and humid and the rain started. We were back in an area that had been hit by the cyclone only a couple of weeks before; it was hard to find any dry land to camp on.

We pulled off the road to stop in front of a farm cottage and greeted the friendly farmer. He had a few cattle but had been heavily impacted by weeks of rough weather and was glad to help us camp in return for a small payment. He let us use his water, and his bath house (which was like an Indonesian mandi). There was the deepest pit toilet I had performed on; you could count the time it took for the shit to hit the bottom! We had a light dinner which was consumed before the gathering thunderstorms started to spit on us.

15th June 1982: San Benito – San Jose

I was woken to the sound of cows complaining about being milked. With bright sunshine, there wasn't any point trying to sleep in. Neil had a long chat with the farmer who complained about the failure of the Sandinista revolution to deliver tangible improvements to the farmers. He presented us with some fresh milk which none of us wanted to risk drinking.

It was probably not safe to pass though the capital, Managua, so instead we cut off the corner and headed directly out to the Masaya Volcano National Park. It was possible to drive right up to the crater rim of the Santiago volcano. It had only erupted twice in the past 1,000 years so they were confident enough to run a surfaced road to the top. Although it wasn't a particularly high or volcano-shaped mountain, it did have a couple of craters, including an impressive one letting off clouds of sulphurous gas.

Nicaragua - Santiago Crater (Wikipedia Commons)

I had time to walk halfway around the more active crater before we drove back down to the colonial city of Granada on the shores of Lake Nicaragua. After years of civil war, the old buildings were looking rather run down. We were allowed a relatively long shopping stop. The local Spanish dialect was hard to understand and the market was not very exciting as it had few goods on sale.

I bought the local paper and, translating the headlines, discovered that Argentina had surrendered to the U.K. in the Falklands. It wasn't clear how this turn of events would affect relations between Encounter Overland (a U.K. company) and the Latin American countries we were to pass through. I also bought a bottle of local rum for less than a dollar!

Newspaper headline - June 15th 1982

ARGENTINA SURRENDERS
San Francisco Chronicle

Guerrillas Dig In
Israeli Tanks Corner PLO In West Beirut

Britain Recaptures The Falkland Islands
Thatcher Says War Is Over

We drove down to the shores of Lake Nicaragua to have lunch. Although the lake looked nice, it was too polluted to swim in and was apparently infested with sharks that had adapted to live in freshwater!

The border with Costa Rica was just a short distance further down the lake shore. After the Nicaraguans had given us a cursory check of our luggage, they waved us through.

COSTA RICA

It was a relief to cross the border and escape the ravages of war and cyclones. Costa Rica was a clean relaxed country. It felt safe walking on the streets. There were well-stocked shops and good food available.

The truck had to be sprayed on the Costa Rican side of the border, but all we had to do was to sit in the café drinking excellent coffee at 10 cents a cup! We were offered a very good exchange rate for dollars. The authorities were interested in verifying that we had no bananas on board, even though we hadn't seen any bananas for sale in Nicaragua!

It was getting late when we finally cleared the formalities. We decided to press on to the capital San Jose and buy dinner on the way. We ate at a pleasant roadside café serving beef steak and beer for $2.50. Then it was back to driving in the dark till we reached a trailer park in San Antonio De Belen at 11 p.m. It had stopped raining but the ground was still wet underfoot. In half an hour we had the tents up and all went off to bed.

16th June 1982: San Jose

Because Tony was fast asleep in the truck, we couldn't prepare breakfast. He was clearly recovering from the hard driving the previous day. Luckily I had taken a bowl from the truck the previous night, so I was able to have a cold shower and do some washing whilst we waited to eat. When we got fed up waiting for breakfast, some of us headed over to a nearby bodega for coffee, hamburger and juice.

Later that morning the truck dropped us in the centre of San Jose which was about 8 km from the camp. My first stop was a market which had excellent leather goods. I bought a folding wallet and a shoulder bag, not cheap but good quality.

The rain started but it wasn't trying hard enough to deter our sightseeing. I chaperoned a few of the girls to a restaurant on the main square that offered a cooked lunch for less than a dollar. Everyone was watching television in the shops because the World Cup was on. That lunchtime we were treated to Spain vs Honduras with the locals strongly supporting the latter.

For the afternoon's sightseeing, the group headed first to the cathedral, which had pleasant painted walls and the usual vaulted panelled roof. Then, stopping at virtually every shop on our route, we made our way to the neo-classical National Theatre. This ornate building was built with funds from a tax on coffee exports. We had to pay for a guided tour but it was worth it to see this sumptuously decorated house of culture in the middle of Central America.

San Jose – National Theatre Facade

San Jose – National Theatre Foyer

San Jose – National Theatre Auditorium

A postcard from Costa Rica (that arrived)

San José, Fuente en los Jardines del Banco Anglo Costarricense y Teatro Nacional con iluminación en noche de gala, Costa Rica, Centro América.

Fountain in the Garden of Banco Anglo Costarricense and National Theater at night.

Hi!

As expected there wasn't much to see after Guatemala. Lake Atitlan was a real gringo hangout - like Kathmandu - with lots to eat & buy. Then the ruins of Copan just inside Honduras were good - but that marks the end of the Indian area - the Indians here were killed by Spanish diseases and so there are no colourful villages. Lots of green countryside with volcanoes. The cyclone had made Nicaragua a bit wet under foot and the drop in tourism because of last years troubles had made Lake Atitlan into a bit of a ghost town. But we have had no real dramas!

Sorry about the printing. I forgot - Coca S.A. I can write properly - lots of love xxx Ashcroft

WOOLLAHRA 2025

AUSTRALIA

I had had my fill of shopping, so I broke away from the group and made my own way to the bus depot. On the way there, I made my usual visit to the Post Office where it cost next to nothing to post a letter to the U.K.; it cost so little that I had my doubts if anything posted would ever arrive. At the bus depot, I had trouble finding the bus that would take me back to the camp. It turned out there were two suburbs called San Antonio so each person I asked would point in a different direction!

Once again I had to treat my ear with drops from the truck's first aid box. It had been hurting when I left Sydney and then flared up again in Guatemala. I was concerned that I was also going a bit deaf in one ear.

17th June 1982: San Jose

The overnight rain cleared to a cloudy morning with the promise of hot sunshine to come. Whilst we were eating breakfast we were entertained by a jazz session from the mobile home next to us, complete with an organ! I caught the local bus back into the city and made another visit to the Post Office to post mail. Then I headed up to the National Museum which was located in an old barracks. This was a well laid out museum with some of the descriptions conveniently in English. The Museum also had a good view over the city.

I wandered through the parks till it was time for lunch which I enjoyed in a Mexican restaurant. Then when the shops opened after the siesta, I bought a souvenir T-shirt. Too soon, the morning's bright sunshine gave way to the unwelcome afternoon rain. I walked back to the bus and somehow managed to stay dry through the worst of the weather.

It was mid-afternoon when I got back to the camp where I had a nice relaxing time doing all the usual chores. Those people who had never left the camp, or who had found their way back, took the truck into the city for a group meal. The service was slow but for about $3, we got a first-rate meal; I'd not been waited upon so much for a long time. The menu was typical of a 1980s Sydney steak house, complete with baked potatoes and sour cream.

Costa Rica - Typcial country town near San Jose (Casa Grafica)

Sketch Map of San Jose, Costa Rica (©Lonely Planet)

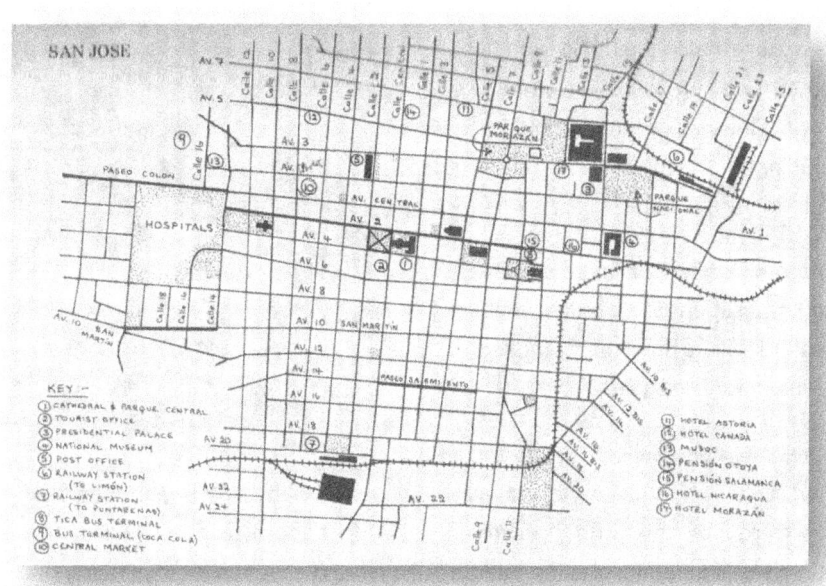

After the meal, people made a move to the disco attached to the restaurant. It was dark and expensive, so we drove up the road is search of a better venue. Unfortunately, I wasn't able to fully enjoy the night, as I was tired, and had an aching ear; the ear drops I was taking didn't have much effect. I stayed in the truck and slept. I can't recall what time we got back to the campsite.

18th June 1982: San Jose – Palmar Norte

Even with earache, I was up early to cook pancakes for breakfast; there was no chance to feel sorry for myself! After driving around the outlying suburbs of San Jose, we passed through the volcanic scenery of the central valley to reach the old capital of Cartago.

Cartago - Basilica of the Angels (Codeca S.A.)

Cartago had a ruined parish church with nice gardens in what was the nave and a more modern basilica that was constructed of wood but finished on the outside to look like it was made of stone. There were no other old buildings in the town as it had suffered from many earthquakes.

Another highlight of the town was finding a supermarket selling yoghurt. I hadn't realised how much I missed having it for breakfast!

Leaving Cartago behind, we started a long climb out of the coastal plain. First, we reached the clouds, and then the rain, as we ground our way up to a summit at 11,000 ft above sea level. We found ourselves in an atmospheric cloud forest. Everything was covered in moss; the scrub looked like heather and the trees were like pine trees, except that they had red flowers and leaf clusters on the boughs.

We were getting a bit cold in the back of the truck in our summer clothes. No one complained when we began the descent and started the search for somewhere flat to pull off and have lunch. When we did stop, it was long past two o'clock and we were all very hungry.

The road onwards to the Panama border was unspectacular but pleasant, with green hills, flat valleys, and fast-flowing rivers. It was now a lot warmer, but that came at the price of continuous rain. Luckily Neil spotted a school where we could sleep in the dry. We were back in the mosquito belt and I was eaten alive when I was outside my mosquito net. I was still tired from the previous night, so headed to my insect-proof bedroom directly after dinner.

Diary illustration of a mosquito-proof bedroom

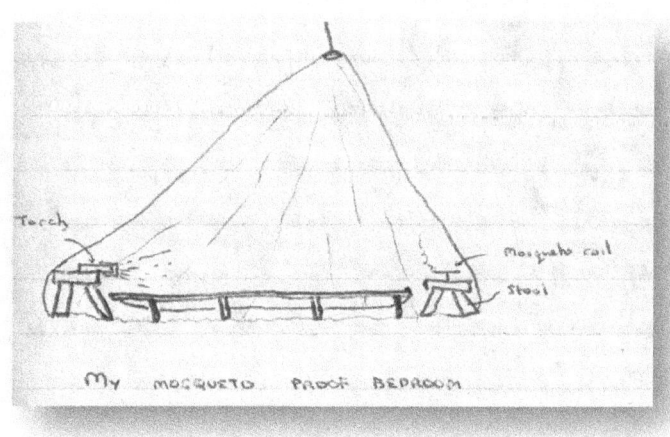

19th June 1982: Palmar Norte – Tole

Once again the early morning mist burned off to give a blue sky and high humidity, weather that was quite tolerable as long as you stayed out of the hot sun. From Palmar Norte, it was only a short drive to the border with Panama where the formalities were very relaxed. It had to be an informal border crossing because the border ran right through the middle of a town, Paso Canoas. We sat in a café on the Costa Rican side enjoying our last Costa Rican coffee.

Costa Rica - Rio Grande de Terrraba at Palmar (Codeca S.A.)

PANAMA

If you like American humburger-cocacola nightmares mixed with colonial buildings, squalid slums and hustlers, here's Nirvana!

The Lonely Planet Guide

To someone fleeing from everything American and looking for adventure, I had low expectations of Panama. And it delivered just that! The pluses were that it was a compact city with an efficient bus system. But it made an uninspiring end to our adventures. It left one questioning why you would travel so far to get to this place.

The Pan-American Highway was a fast road on the Panama side and we sped along to the town of David. Shortly afterwards we passed two "road closed ahead" signs and the trip suddenly became much more of an adventure. A suspension bridge over the fast-flowing Rio Chiriquí had collapsed severing the only main road to Panama City. There was a lot of confusion even though the failure had occurred some three months earlier.

At that stage, it wasn't clear how our truck could get to the other side. However we picked up a guide who showed us how to get a number and a place in the queue. We then backtracked and tried to head south down a dirt track towards the river, but we were stopped by the police. It wasn't our turn to go further as our number was not due till 5 p.m. at the earliest.

I took a walk down the track to the river. It took 15 minutes and the sight when I got there was incredible. Yellow Government bulldozers were towing trucks and trailers separately down the muddy banks and into the river. They then tugged the trucks about a kilometre upstream and out up the muddy bank on the other side.

It was a slow business as the river was flowing swiftly and was three to four feet deep. While I was watching all the activity on the banks of the river, our truck turned up. They had paid $80 for a private tow across and had jumped the government queue.

Diary sketch map of the bridge collapse on the Rio Chiriquí

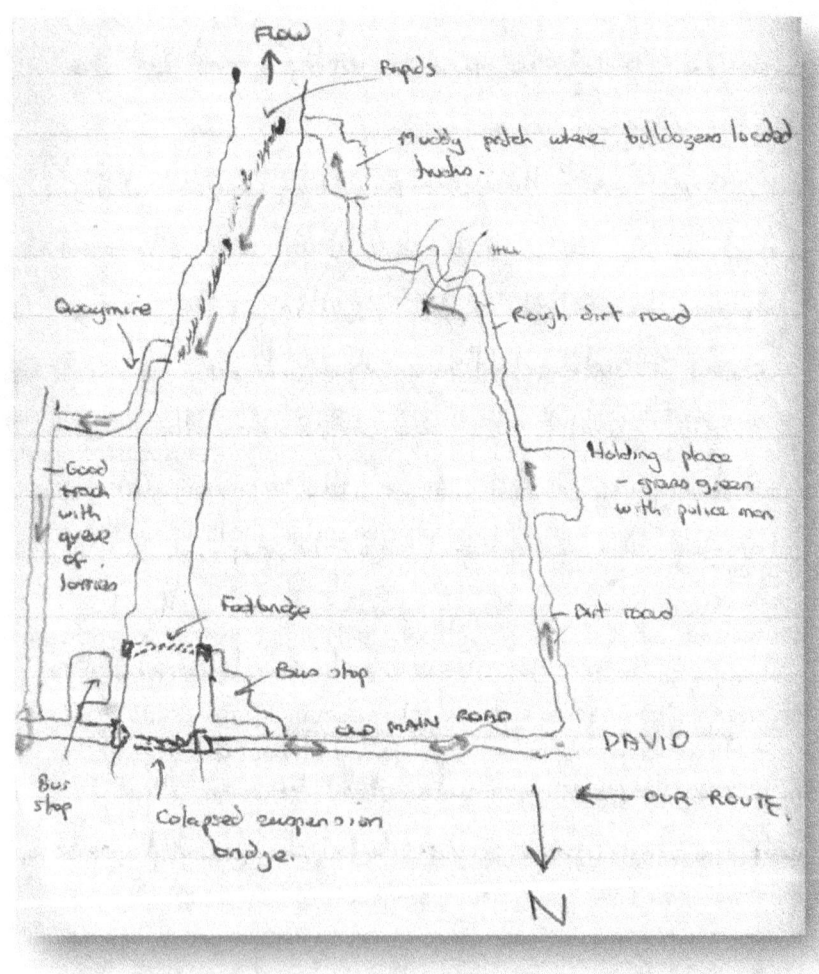

All the luggage was taken out of the trailer and piled up high at the front of the truck. Then a tow-truck hitched up to us and we lurched down into the river. Soon water was over the trailer tow bar and about 9" below the floor of the truck. The cab was flooded, and then we got stuck! We were in the middle of the river but the tow couldn't shift us. There was nothing to do other than to try and start the truck even though the engine and fan were underwater. It is a credit to the rugged Bedford truck that it started and we were able to get moving again.

Soon we were being dragged up the slope on the other side; our nice clean truck caked with mud. It was by now late in the afternoon, so we drove a short way beyond Tole and stopped for the night. Once again, we found a school building next to which we could camp. There were two good streams, one on each side, one was big enough for bathing. The school had nice wide verandahs and a pump for water. There were small bats in the roof but they didn't bother us!

We had lost an hour in the border crossing so we stayed up late.

20th June 1982: Tole – Santa Clara

A consequence of the time change was that most of the group woke up late. But I was one of the first up and, as a reward, had the opportunity to have a full bath in the stream before breakfast.

The road to Panama City passed through rolling hills for a while then dropped down to a flat plain with nothing of interest to see. The morning shopping stop was in Santiago, a large centre which was dead on a Sunday morning. Then we pressed on through heavy rain to a beach camp near Santa Clara, our first beach camp since Acapulco! We arrived in time for a late lunch, but first, we had to put up our tents. It was drizzling when we arrived but just as we were about to eat, the heavens opened in a tropical downpour. A lot of fast spade work was needed to save some tents (including mine) from inundation. By the time we had finished and could go back to eating lunch, the grassy area was riddled with canals.

The rain water drained into a large freshwater lagoon that was held back from the ocean by a sand bar. The storm was so heavy, that after a while, the back pressure was irresistible and water burst through the sand bar spectacularly, flooding over the beach and colouring the sea brown.

The weather put pay to our plans for an afternoon clean out of the truck! It did dry out a bit in the evening, but by then Neil had hit the booze so no work was done.

21st June 1982: Santa Clara - Panama City

I ended my Encounter Overland trip in style with a dose of the "Canal Trots"; an upset tummy was a normal part of life on these camping trips. The tents weren't clean or dry in the morning but we just packed them anyway leaving a camp site crisscrossed with ditches.

We drove fast till we reached the hills that surrounded Panama City; it was funny how I expected the land near a canal to get flatter! Before we hit the city traffic, there was a short mechanical stop to change the oil in the power steering which had been playing up.

The winding road through jungle-clad hills stopped abruptly. We found ourselves crossing the "Bridge of the Americas" over the canal and into Panama City. It was a surprise to see how close the canal was to the city; Balboa, the canal zone port, merged into the old city. There was quite a contrast between the canal zone which was neat and tidy, and the old city next door which was as dirty and tumbledown as any Central American town.

Panama - Bridge of the Americas *(by Foto Flatau)*

Panama Canal - Miraflores Locks *(by Foto Flatau)*

Before lunch, we had a look at the Miraflores locks on the canal. These locks were where the canal descended in two stages to the level of the Pacific Ocean. Unfortunately, at the time when we arrived, there were no ships were passing through the lock; we watched a film show about the process instead.

To fill in time, we visited a bank so we could all settle our debts with Neil and the truck bar, then had a lunch stop overlooking Miraflores Lake by the water treatment works. When we returned to the locks, two large vessels were passing through. Although the observation platform was closed for painting and the sun was hot, we stood and watched the little electric tugs shuffle the boat into the lock with only a couple of feet of clearance on each side. It was a smooth operation but one they had practised many times before!

From the Canal Zone, we headed to the Post Office so we could all pick up our mail. Although we had been able to send letters and cards along the way we hadn't had contact with the outside world since we were in Mexico City, over a month before. I collected a pile of letters that were efficiently stapled together; there was none of the usual rummagings through jumbled boxes of uncollected letters. We then walked up Calle Central to our hotel, the Hotel Colon, where the truck and trailer were waiting for us. After unloading our luggage we were allocated rooms.

I scored a room on the top floor. It was on a corner of the building overlooking Calle Central as it turned to follow the coast. There was a bathroom but no hot water. Even though I was on the top floor, the noise of the traffic was intrusive after so long camping in the countryside.

In the evening, we all met up in the hotel foyer and took a taxi shuttle to the Cascades restaurant on Avenue Balboa. It took the taxi three trips to ferry us all. It wasn't a particularly good spot for a group meal, and the food was uninspiring. Together this made for a rather restrained final meal and a poor celebration of our achievement.

Panama - Central Avenue *(by Foto Flatau)*

We didn't record how far we drove to get from San Diego to Panama City. With all the detours, Google Maps estimates it was about 9600 km.

22nd June 1982: Panama City

I was woken early by buses outside my window and the smell of fresh bread wafting up from the bakery next door. It seemed that every bus in Panama City ran past my room, which was both convenient and inconvenient. There were two types of buses, government and private. The government ones had ROUTE 1, 2, 3 as their destination and had hard seats. The private buses in contrast were gaily painted with loud stereo sound blaring inside to entertain the passengers. The bus fare was the same for both, ridiculously low, but on the private buses, you only paid when you got off.

My first purchase was wrapping paper in which to post my hammock and blanket back to the U.K. The central Post Office wouldn't accept large parcels, so I had to take a taxi across town to the Encomiendas Postal, the parcel office. I shared the taxi with Eliza and Agnes, two Australian girls from my trip who also wanted to post parcels. The taxi fare was only $2 but posting the parcel was not so cheap; it cost $10 for every 5 kg. As always there were a lot of forms to fill in but there were no hassles; they even gave us sticky tape and string!

Panama City - Bus Ticket

By walking a few blocks south, we were able to catch a bus to Via España and avoid another taxi fare. The Tourist Information Office was closed for lunch; lunch in Latin America was an extended affair. We waited! The girls wanted to know how to get to the San Blas islands and I wanted information on buses and airlines. Once the office opened, the lady there was very helpful.

I split up from the others and took a bus to the PanAm airline office. I wanted to rewrite my ticket to avoid an unnecessary dog-leg through Lima but they wouldn't help me. I then walked about ten blocks to the Eastern Airlines office. They would fly me on to Quito at some ungodly hour, but also refused to rewrite my ticket. Feeling quite depressed, I realised that I had been sold a fraud by the travel agent in Sydney as there was nothing 'flexible' about the ticket that I had purchased.

I got a bus back to the hotel and set off to look round the older parts of the city that were nearby. Returning to the hotel, I commiserated with two other girls from the trip, who, like me, were getting nowhere in their fight with the airlines to reticket flights. One problem we all faced was that the airlines would not sell a ticket to a South American country unless you already held a ticket for a flight out, even if you only planned to pass through in transit.

23rd June 1982: Panama City

A cloudy, grey Wednesday morning made one glad to be in a hotel, not a campsite. I had a breakfast of pancakes and coffee in a local café whilst reading in a Spanish newspaper about the birth of Prince William to Prince Charles and Diana.

Then it was straight back into the struggle to sort out my airline tickets. A bus along Avenue Peru took me to the Equatoriana airline office. Once again, they were happy to book me onto the Friday flight to Quito, but not to re-write my ticket.

I took my frustration back to PanAm and told them in no uncertain terms what I felt about the situation. Although I had no doubts in my mind that PanAm was in the wrong, the real fault no doubt lay with the ticketing travel agent back in Sydney. The supervisor was adamant that Equatoriana should change the ticket so I got them to talk to each other on the phone to save my shoe leather. So much for the smart idea of buying a 'cheap' ticket for my adventure in advance! It wasn't so much that they wouldn't do what I wanted, they would also do nothing to help.

Panama - Old Panama Cathedral *(by Foto Flatau)*

Panama - Golden Altar (from the old Panama Cathedral) *(by Foto Flatau)*

In desperation, I even went to the British Embassy in the hope that they might be able to give me some ideas. The nice Scottish lady I talked to was a stumped as I was. I did however find out that I was going to be liable for duty in England on the modest purchases I had made.

There was nothing more I could do in Panama City visiting airlines; I would have to try again in Quito.

A glance at the British newspapers in the reading room showed how selective the news was in the local Spanish papers and how much had gone unreported.

After lunch, I took the Route 1 bus out to Panama Viejo. This was the Spanish capital city till it was thoroughly sacked by Henry Morgan in 1671. Morgan was a Welsh buccaneer who was happy to be paid by the English to disrupt Spanish shipping in the area.

Panama Viejo was situated in the sprawling suburbs of the new Panama City. Because most of the old city was built of wood, little remained except for a collection of stone walls. Making a round trip, the No 2 bus took me back along the sea front to the hotel. I had a short walk around the old pre-canal port and saw the gold altar in the church of St José. This had been hidden from Henry Morgan when Panama Viejo was looted.

I ate that night at a Chinese restaurant close to the hotel, with the eight members of our group who were still staying in the hotel.

24th June 1982: Panama City

My last day in Central America was a quiet one. I enjoyed a budget breakfast in my room; a pot of yoghurt from the supermarket, a glass of orange juice, fresh baked bread from the bakery and a cup of black coffee. There was a lot of letter and postcard writing to do before leaving Panama. With my correspondence up to date, I made a final visit to the Post Office to send the letters on their way. I even found another letter for me waiting there to be picked up!

Panama was a free port and that was supposed to mean a wide range of goods on sale at competitive prices. But I wandered round the shopping area and couldn't find anything I wanted, or could afford, to buy. I consoled myself with an icecream in the Coca-Cola restaurant; a place that had lousy service at the best of times and no service when a good football match was on the TV.

Back in the hotel, I did my packing and said a few goodbyes to people who were leaving before me. I booked a taxi to the airport for 4 a.m. and was pleasantly surprised to find that Eliza and Agnes were also setting out at the same time. They had abandoned plans to go to the San Blas islands and were heading back to El Salvador.

> I managed to dispose of most of my unexposed Ektachrome film to three of the other group members for the bargain price of $2.50 each.

In the evening I had more fried rice for dinner in a café. I dined close by as it had started to rain, the first rain we had had in Panama.

25th June 1982: Panama City – Quito

I had requested a wake-up call at 3:45 a.m. for the taxi. The hotel didn't realise how fast an Encounter Overland adventurer can get going in the morning. I got a rude shock when the hotel woke me up ½ hour earlier; though as a result, I did have time to wash my face and wake up slowly.

The airport was a long way out of town, on the other side of the canal; it took 40 minutes to get there in a taxi driving at breakneck speed on empty roads. The girls' flight was on time, but mine had been delayed. We ran into two other Australian girls from our trip who had saved money by sleeping at the airport; they looked a bit rough! I had time for a few coffees, and then my flight to Quito started boarding. The airport was smart and organised but not my airline. Although the flight was full, and the plane had passengers on board from the previous flight, we weren't issued with seat numbers. This resulted in a chaotic free-for-all as people scrambled for the vacant seats.

ECUADOR

Ecuador was a country I fell in love with.
Firstly there were the mountains. Nothing could have prepared me for how the Andes were both majestic in their grandeur, whilst at the same time being accessible and inhabited.
Then there was music played everywhere, with the haunting sound of the rondador, a simple pan pipe.
As an independent traveller, there was no hassle, no one tried to scam me, and there was no markup of prices for a foreigner.
It was easy and cheap to travel around by bus.

On the downside, the food was uninspiring, but that wasn't enough to dampen my enthusiasm.
I left wanting to come back for more, and indeed I did, over 35 years later!

The flight from Panama to Guayaquil took only 90 minutes. Then there was a 30 minute stop-over whilst the plane emptied. Domestic passengers flying from Guayaquil up to Quito had to fly on a domestic airline, and so the international flight took off largely empty. I was able to move seats to get a good view out the window as we headed up into the Andes. My first impressions were that the mountains were much less folded than the Himalayas. The scenery was dominated by volcanic peaks, flat plateaus, and deep-cut river valleys. The approach to Quito Airport was hair-raising; the plane flew in low over a ridge and, in strong turbulence, dropped down to the runway surrounded by houses. It had to be one of the world's most dangerous city airports.

There wasn't much of a wait for luggage in the airport because I was on such a lightly loaded flight. And there weren't any immigration hassles. After the tropics in Panama, it was cold outside (12° C) but in the clear sunshine, it felt warm.

Outside the airport, there was the usual collection of people touting for taxis. I waited for a while to gather my thoughts and to see if another couple who I knew on the flight wanted to share transport. I couldn't see them in the crowds, so I picked a friendly-looking man and went with him. It turned out that he wasn't an official taxi, just a local making a bit of money on the side. I was able to chat with him (in Spanish). In the process I narrowed my shortlist of hotels from the Lonely Planet Guidebook down to one, the Colonial Hotel.

The Colonial was off the main road, behind the buildings along Maldonado. It was convenient, only a few minutes walk from Santo Domingo square, and it was ultra-quiet because Maldonado was closed for road works. The hotel was a 2-storey building in the typical local whitewashed stone. I asked for a single room with a shower and was shown a pleasant one on the ground floor. It had hot water, a negligible fire risk and only cost about $US 3 a night.

After unpacking my few belongings, I had a rest till it was time for lunch. The city had a frequent and efficient bus system which took me some time to understand. The shops and restaurants were unfamiliar and, as part of my orientation, I wandered around to see what people were selling. Initially, I didn't find many postcards on sale which was a concern to me in my camera-less state.

Before taking a 4-cent bus ride, I had to break some of the large denomination banknotes that I had obtained at the airport. I selected a suitable restaurant and had a hamburger for lunch.

Armed with some small change, I took a bus down Avenue 10 de Agosta towards the new city with El Ejido Park and the airline offices. After picking up a copy of the British Caledonian airline timetable, I found my way to the Tourist Information office which was inconveniently hidden away down a side street. They met my expectations by being singularly unhelpful; they did sell me a map of the country but that was about it.

After visiting a few more airline offices to find out who flew where and when, I went back to the hotel. On the way, I had a coffee at a local café. I had clearly travelled too far from Costa Rica and beyond the borders for good coffee. In Quito, they gave me a cup of hot water into which I could add coffee essence.

Ecuador 5 Sucre note

My first choice for dinner was the Gran Casino (aka The Gringo) Hotel, but they had no food! So I wandered round the old town. It was getting late in the evening and most of the good restaurants were already closed. I ended up eating ravioli in a snack bar.

Having flown in from sea level I found that the altitude (over 9,000 ft) made me lethargic and I had trouble walking up hills. When the sun went in, it got cool quickly; a lot of people were wrapped in blankets or ponchos. I curled up in bed to keep warm and read but was soon fast asleep.

Diary Extract: Hotel Colonial environs

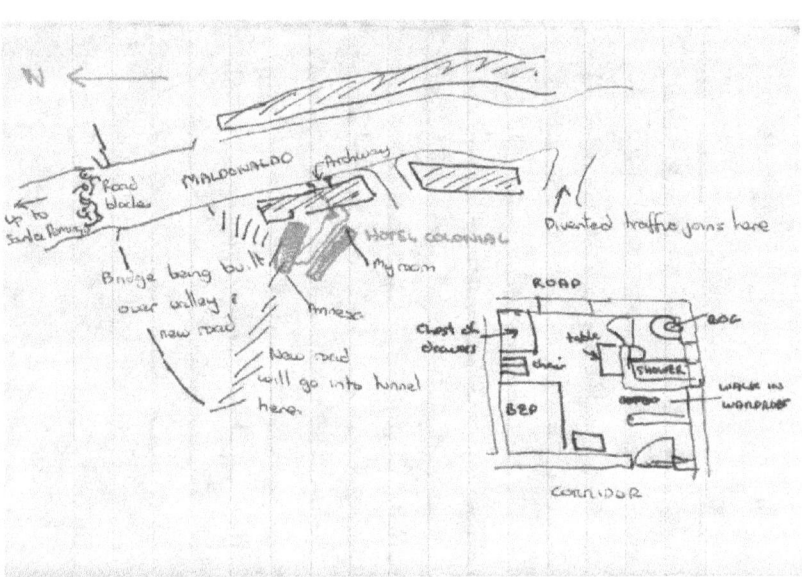

They were showing The Muppets on the TV dubbed into Spanish. It was hard to understand Spanish spoken in silly voices!

26th June 1982: Quito (orientation)

My first morning in Ecuador started quietly, with a short walk into the city to get humidas for breakfast. Humidas are a traditional food of the Andes consisting of a corn filling steamed in a corn husk. Then I visited a supermercardo to top up my food supplies and sat in the sun reading guidebooks.

I was disappointed by the Indian market; there were not many handicrafts on sale. Instead I did a cultural tour of the city churches. The Iglesia de El Sagrario (Church of the Tabernacle) was a fairly typical Baroque church with a heavily decorated gold altar; it also had a magnificent screen at the back of the nave. In contrast, the Cathedral was very plain with an unusual use of glass in the roof for lighting. The altar was more red than golden and there was plenty of bare stonework. The Cathedral appeared to have a grand organ but I didn't get to hear it being played.

Moving away from the central square, La Merced church was far too decorated for my taste; even the plain stonework was painted with a red and white pattern. San Fransisco church, the oldest church in Ecuador dated from 1680. It was in a square surrounded by markets. Inside was more of the same; how much decoration was gold leaf and how much gold paint, I couldn't tell.

That concluded my tour of all the churches that were open. I was also looking for museums, but they were most elusive. I only found one and that was closed. But I inadvertently came across the Post Office and was relieved to find stalls around the outside selling much-needed postcards.

I took a bus out to Alameda Park in the hope of finding a restaurant and a couple of museums but found nothing. Continuing on down Ave Amazonas towards the new city, I kept on looking for any places to eat or souvenir shops that were open. Again no joy!

Having walked a long way with no result, I ended up back in the old city for an uninspiring meal of luke warm chicken which matched my mood at the time. The food situation was looking very unexciting.

Panecillo from the east with the old city

QUITO

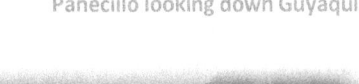
Panecillo looking down Guayaquil

Near Plaza de Santo Domingo

Looking up Rocafuerte

27th June 1982: Quito (Panecillo)

It was so quiet in my hotel on a Sunday that I ended up sleeping in. The hot water service was piping hot, so I had a good long shower before wandering back into the city. It was cloudy, and without the heat of the sun, it felt decidedly chilly. I had intended to have breakfast in a café that I had spotted on Plaza Santo Domingo but, like much of the city, it was closed on a Sunday.

As the sun was starting to win its battle with the clouds, I decided to walk up Cerro Panecillo, a hill that dominates the old city, breaking up the north/south valley into two parts. I took the quick way up, steps (and lots of them) up from Garcia Moreno. It was a hard climb that was made more challenging on an empty stomach and at this altitude. From the viewpoint at the top, 600 ft above the city, there was a 360° panorama. With the sun out, it was tempting to just sit there and enjoy the view. The restaurant at the top, which I had hoped would provide breakfast, was closed. So eventually hunger drove me back down to the city.

On a Sunday there were even fewer places open to eat but I found "Pollo King", a popular, clean restaurant with a good gringo friendly menu. Compared to local options it wasn't cheap. After consuming fruit juice, steak, banana split and coffee I had a happy full stomach and I didn't begrudge paying $4.

Wandering up the hill past El Merced church brought me to the El Tejor market, that I had spotted from the top of Panecillo. This was by far the most authentic and interesting local market that I found in the city.

As all the museums were closed on Sunday, there wasn't much left to do apart from sitting and watching the passing crowds. I did poke my head into several churches and was surprised to see that, with services every hour, the churches were always packed! A guy came up to me in the main square and started practising his English with me (how come I don't get a chance to practice my Spanish?). We had a good chat, finished off over a cup of coffee, and I wasn't asked for money.

It had clouded over and was threatening to rain. So it was time to head back to the hotel.

28th June 1982: Quito

I seemed to be getting into the habit of sleeping in, even when I resolved to get up a bit earlier. Determined not to repeat the mistake of the previous day I made my priority to get some breakfast; it was much easier on a weekday. A restaurant in Plaza Santo Domingo filled my needs with juice, ham omelette, toast and coffee for barely a dollar. When the banks opened at 9 o'clock I was ready outside waiting to cash some travellers' cheques.

Then I was off to the new city, taking the No 2 Comal/Colon bus to Ave Amazonas. I was curious to see what holidays in Ecuador might be within my budget. I popped into a travel agent and found that the airfare alone to the Galapagos Islands was more than I could afford; I'd been misled by seeing lower prices quoted, but they were land-only. Then there were some trips to the Napo River in the Amazon basin that were within my price range, but they didn't look to be the sort of holiday I would enjoy. With that matter settled, I could better estimate when I needed to fly back to England.

To make it simpler to re-write my ticket and skip flying to Peru I decided to fly straight back to London. In the process, I abandoned the idea of stitching together an itinerary from co-operating airlines that would allow me to visit San Juan in Puerto Rico. Off I headed to the British Caledonian airline office and talked to the booking clerk about the direct flight. 'No' she informed me, she couldn't change the ticket. She suggested that I talk to PanAm; so I did. Finally, after many futile visits to airline offices, the sun started to shine on me! The PanAm airline office was just a lady with a telephone performing miracles. She changed the ticket without a word of complaint, whilst I had a coffee downstairs. I returned to British Caledonian with my re-issued ticket and I was finally booked on a flight home, without having to spend an extra cent!

To celebrate, I had a souvenir-buying spree in the government handicrafts shop nearby. The prices were fixed and reasonable with a wide selection of crafts on sale. I resolved to go back there again. They even had more postcards to add to my collection!

Before taking the bus back to the hotel, I explored the nearby bus station where the buses heading north from Quito departed. I had a plan to head north to Otavalo the next day.

After my siesta, I set out to walk around Panecillo to reach the suburbs on the south side. Even though my route circumnavigated the hill, there were still some steep uphill sections to reach the ridge on which the suburb of La Colmena was situated; nowhere was flat in Quito! One of the attractions in heading south was to visit the Southern Shopping Centre, which turned out to be a grand title for a few shops under one roof. Having had enough pavement tramping for one day, I took the bus back to Plaza Santo Domingo.

In the evening, I returned to the "Chicken King" restaurant; at least I knew I could get a good nutritious meal there, albeit at a price.

29th June 1982: Quito (Otavalo)

I woke to a cloudless and promising day. A No. 1 bus from Plaza Santo Domingo took me out to the bus station near El Ejido Park where I had been the previous day. Most of the buses heading out of the city were only minibuses or smaller versions of the Thomas buses used around the city. I bought a ticket with the TACA bus company and got a fast comfortable ride in a Ford minibus out to Otavalo.

After climbing gently through the northern suburbs of Quito, the road abruptly descended into a lower intermont basin. This area, lower than Quito, was dissected by the Pia river flowing in a deep gorge. The rock was a crumbly sandstone modified by volcanic activity. It was very dry; there was dust blowing everywhere. This erosion could also have been exacerbated by overgrazing and the removal of trees.

Diary Extract 1: Ticket to Otavalo

TACA Transportes Andina C. A.

Ibarra Flores 8 - 71 Telef. 950833
Quito 18 de Septiembre N°. 801 Av. Pérez Guerrero Telef. 526279

Camioneta Nro. 92   HORA 9 a a

IBARRA
ATUNTAQUI
OTAVALO
QUITO
STO. DOMINGO

Nombre	BARNES Adrian	
Viaje	IBARRA	Asiento 5
Fecha	29 JUN. 1982	Valor S/. 55

EL EQUIPAJE: Será entregado al conductor. En caso de pérdida la compañía reconocerá hasta el valor de S/. 200,00

NOTA TERMINANTE.- Pasajero que no esté en su Domicilio o en la Oficina, 15 minutos antes de la hora de partida, la Camioneta no volverá por 2da. vez y el pasajero pierde su pasaje.

NOTA: Todo pasajero en estado de embriaguez no puede viajar y pierde su pasaje. Equipaje máximo 10 Libras.

OFFSET "VACA JR." IBARRA

We then climbed up to a level plateau with the snow-covered peak of Cayambe volcano ahead. Cayambe was nearly 19,000 ft high. The permanent snow line at that time of year was about 18,000 ft, so there was just a hint of white on the top. As we neared Otavalo, I saw more and more Indians in traditional costume (a poncho and felt hat) walking by the side of the road. The road twisted down by a blue lake, the Lago de San Pablo, and then we arrived in Otavalo.

Except the bus didn't stop and carried on round the bypass!

Plaza San Fransisco

The facade and tower of the cathedral

QUITO

Church and Monastery of San Fransisco

The cathedral on Plaza Independencia

I had thought that a bus passing Otavalo would stop there, but apparently not. As we shot past the final turnoff to the town, I had to call for a stop, otherwise I would have found myself in Ibarra! This left me with quite a walk into town, but also gave me a chance to look at all the local Indian costumes. Some of the women wore white blouses with embroidery, whilst another group wore a thick cloak-like poncho with a matching felt hat. The men wore pigtails. With the heavy clothing, it was hard to tell the genders apart.

After drinking a coffee, I looked around the town. It was not Saturday so the market was a local affair, not the tourist attraction held at weekends. It wasn't particularly interesting. In fact, were it not for all the Indians in costume, the town would have been rather drab. But the town also had a beautiful setting, surrounded by hills, with the Imbabura volcano towering overhead.

It was after one o'clock and I had had nothing to eat; I was very hungry. The lunchtime queues had subsided and I found a reasonably smart restaurant. Unfortunately, they didn't have any food left! I had to make do with a fruit juice and a toasted cheese sandwich.

After lunch, I went to the upper marketplace where the bus depots were situated and bought a ticket back to Quito on the local bus service. The bus didn't get enough passengers to leave till 45 minutes later. When we got under way I was treated to a much more interesting journey down the back roads. We had a drunk, a lady with chickens and many other colourful people on board.

As we descended to the dusty valley on the way back the wind was visibly eroding the cliffs above us, creating a dust storm and throwing pebbles and small boulders down onto the road. It appeared that we were lucky not to be hit.

Otavalo

Equatorial Monument with Cayambe Mountain

Otavalo Indians

Back in Quito, the trip by the local bus turned out to have taken barely longer than the fast minibus. I wandered through the markets looking for a travelling bag but ended up going back to the government-run souvenir shop and buying a local woven bag for $5.

That evening I ate at a Chinese 'Fuente se Soda' near the main square. It was the most un-Chinese Chop Suey I had ever tasted; I didn't believe the chef was Chinese!

I had intended to leave Quito the next day. But I decided that I was too tired to spend the evening packing up, so I treated myself to an extra rest day.

Steps near the Plaza de Santo Domingo

La Rhonda at night

The trip to Otavalo was also a journey to the Northern Hemisphere. We passed over the Equator a few kilometres south of Cayambe.

30th June 1982: Quito (Rest Day)

A bonus rest day!

For breakfast, I went to the Chifa Chang restaurant on Chile. I didn't have a guidebook with a list of gringo restaurants, so choosing where to eat was somewhat of a gamble. That morning I was in luck, the Chifa Chang served me a tasty breakfast of scrambled eggs, fruit juice and coffee.

I found the telegram office in the Post Office building and sent a short 'expect me on this date' message home. Whilst I was there I had another look through the postcard racks in the tiny shops under the Post Office. There were lots of shops to look at; each one seemed to stock a different subset of the available *tarjeta postal*.

The La Campania church was open so I peeked inside. It was impressive with all the solid gold decoration and no gold paint. Despite myself, and my rejection of what the Spanish did to the native Indians, I quite liked the place!

After my siesta, I stitched up the back pocket of the trousers I had bought in Mexico so that I could keep my passport there; the passport was too heavy to hang round my neck all the time and would make an obvious bulge in the front of my shirt. Besides, my one remaining money belt, that had come with me all the way from England, was on its last legs.

My major outing in the afternoon was to look at the Anthropology Museum located over the Central Bank. The museum was well laid out. It was interesting to compare it with similar museums in Mexico and San Jose. There were scant references to the Incas, just a bit of Inca gold on display.

I checked with my hotel that I could leave a bag with them when I left Quito, then spent the evening sorting out what I would take with me heading south, and what I would leave to pick up when I got back to Quito.

1st July 1982: Quito - Baños

I was up bright and early, almost at sunrise, for the first time since arriving in Ecuador. I left my rucksack with the hotel, paid my bill and set off on a mini-adventure with just my day pack and a shoulder bag.

> When I arrived in Quito I asked the Tourist Office if the new bus depot at El Recreo was in use and was told "No". But after days of searching the central city looking for buses to Riobamba, I concluded that southbound buses didn't enter the old city. I asked at my hotel and they confirmed that it was better to go to El Recreo, a new interchange on the southern fringe of the city.

I jumped on a bus out to the El Recreo interchange and had no difficulty finding buses to Ambato. The trick was not to buy a ticket in the bus company offices but instead to wait for a bus to leave going where you wanted to go. Competition was so stiff the buses were rarely full when they left. The fare for a two-hour journey to Ambato was ridiculously cheap, less than $1.

Latacunga Market

Indian women in the fields

After leaving the narrow valley cradling Quito City, there was heavy cloud. I couldn't see the volcanos that we passed on our way south. The scenery that I could see wasn't very spectacular.

Cotopaxi from the road to Ambato on a cloudless day

At Ambato I had to repeat the same sequence, standing at the bus depot until a moving bus came past crying out "Baños". The hour trip down into the Amazon basin was an even better bargain, barely 30 cents! As soon as we passed Patate the road became very scenic, dropping down into the Rio Pastaza as the river cut its way out through the Eastern Sierra. The scale of the valley and mountains here was far more reminiscent of the scenery in the Himalayas.

> *The pass going out of Quito, after Machachi, was 11,400 ft above sea level on the railway line, and the road was even higher. We passed over it in the clouds.*

It was cloudy but not actually raining when the bus arrived in Baños. I set off with my *South America on a Shoestring* map to find the recommended hotel, Hotel Sangay; recommended no doubt because it had an English owner. It was right up on the edge of the town, by the thermal baths from which Baños got its name. It was a bit posh by my backpacker standards at about $7 a night. But I was shown a nice room on the ground floor (low fire/earthquake risk) which I decided to take. This was the closest that I had ever stayed to an active volcano. Tungurahua towered above Baños and I saw evidence of past lava flows beside the road as we entered the town.

I arrived at the hotel an hour before lunchtime, so had time to get settled in before walking the streets in search of food. Round the main square, shops were selling a local sweet, Melcocha. Making it involved repeatedly throwing a rope of sugar cane paste onto hooks till it hardened, resulting in a delicacy not unlike English Edinburgh Rock. Another interesting innovation was the egg shop which housed the chickens as well as the eggs being sold.

It was obvious that Baños was not set up as a gringo food hang-out despite it being on a popular backpacker route down to the Amazon. There were plenty of restaurants but most items on the menu were local fare. I had the *'meriendo'* (afternoon snack) at a place close to my hotel. The deal was a *'seco'*(Ecuadorian stew) and coffee for $1, not particularly cheap but it was nourishing and tasty.

Lunch needed walking off. After checking out departures at the bus depot, I walked down to the River Pastaza which flowed in a deep narrow gorge beneath the town. Baños was built on a triangular plateau with cliffs on two sides and the river gorge on the remaining side. Water cascaded from the cliffs around the town and then on the other side, spilled over in falls down to the river.

Although it was cloudy all day and it was the rainy season, there was not much more than a few minutes of fine drizzle. Baños, being 3000 ft lower than Quito, should have been warmer, but without the sun and with a cool wind it didn't seem that way. However it was excellent walking weather. It would have been nice to see the volcanos which were hiding in the clouds. In that regard, it brought back memories of past holidays in Scotland!

Back at the hotel, I had a warm shower and put on another layer of clothing before going out to find dinner. I headed for a restaurant that I had seen at lunchtime. It was so popular then it was full; I figured it must have something going for it. I ordered *'churrasco'* which was a grand name for a fried egg on a steak. The side salad included avocado, which I had last seen in Australia, and for the first time, beetroot. It was dark outside, far too dark, when I ventured back to the hotel.

Diary Extract: My Plan of Baños

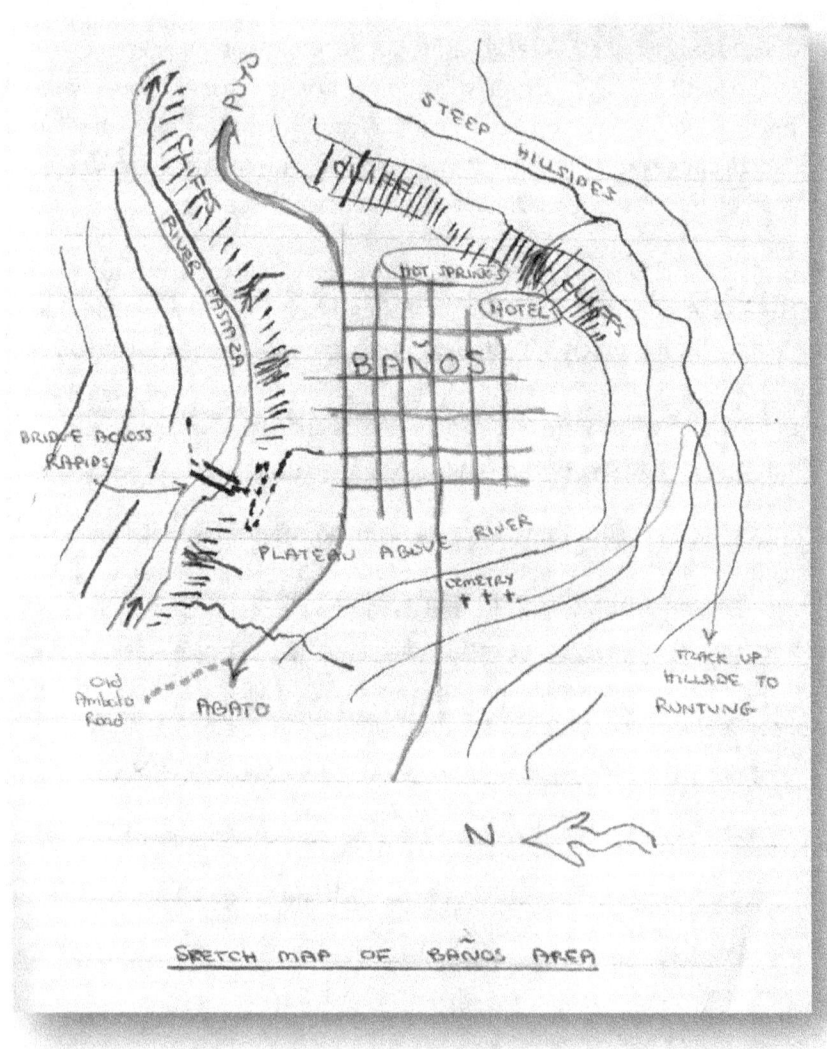

2nd July 1982: Baños (Orientation)

Someone up there wanted to prove it was the rainy season. The clouds came down the hillside, and then it started to rain. I was in a café having my breakfast when the clouds opened. Fortuitously I had my umbrella with me and was able to splash back to the hotel keeping relatively dry. The Indians didn't seem to believe in plastic raincoats. They just wandered about in the rain, getting their ponchos wet and looking increasingly bedraggled.

There wasn't much to do in the hotel apart from watching the clouds swirling up the valley from the east, and catching up on my letter writing. The weather didn't imporove till midday when the clouds started to lift. I had a makeshift lunch in my room from my supplies, then ventured out, even though it was still spitting occasionally.

Baños -Town View

Baños - Central Park

Taking the road out of town west to Ambato, I turned right down onto the old main road by the police post. The old road was just a dirt track that crossed over the river to the north side, passing over a deep rocky canyon. The river valley had been blocked in the past by a lava flow and the river had tried several possible routes before finally cutting a deep canyon through the lava obstruction.

There were spectacular views from the lava dam with the obstructed river far higher on one side than the other. At one point where the river had cut into the valley walls, you could see the bedrock overlaid by a thick coat of lava. The track continued high above the river to the village of Lligua, where I turned back. The cloud was descending and it had started raining again before I got back to the town.

Dodging the rain, I did a bit of shopping and was particularly relieved to find a shop selling postcards. The Basilica in the main square was modern (1920's) and uninspiring. It was a place of pilgrimage because of the supposed apparitions of the Blessed Virgin Mary, who was said to have appeared in a 200-foot waterfall nearby. The Señora de Santa Agua was also responsible for some other miracles which were depicted on the walls of the church. I observed that the town and its restaurants were always full of schoolchildren during the day; perhaps it might have been the school holidays.

3rd July 1982: Baños (Riobamba)

I woke up nice and early. As it wasn't raining, I decided to take a trip to Riobamba. Breakfast was taken in the same café as the previous day; the attraction being that they baked their own fresh bread. By 8 o'clock I was at the bus depot and didn't have to wait long till a bus left going in the right direction.

The bus took the new direct route up to Riobamba following the Chambo River; it cost just 50 cents for the hour trip. With the bus falling apart (not all of them were as bad), the driver getting a pittance, and dirt cheap petrol from the Amazon it was easy to see why public transport was so inexpensive.

Riobamba Market

The clouds were well down on the mountains, so once again there was little to see out of the bus windows. The route was interesting in a different way. There were several landslides across the road and a bridge had been washed away. The road climbed up into increasingly desolate scenery; a steady ascent all the way to the town of Riobamba.

After having become used to the scale of Baños, Riobamba was a large town. It was brimming with people who had come into town for the Saturday markets. Although the town was close to 9,000 ft, it felt warm as the sun shining.

Frightened by the impending bill from my 'luxury' hotel, I changed a $US20 bill. Then I visited the tourist office to get a photocopied map of the town. I also asked them where I should catch the bus back to Baños; but the answer they gave me was wrong.

My main reason for visiting Riobamba was to see the Saturday markets that were held in plazas around the town. I was only able to find two of the eight market areas, one was selling food and the other clothing. In between the plazas, the streets were packed with pop-up pavement stores and people. There weren't many tourist souvenirs on offer, but there were plenty of gringos, like me, looking around.

> *I saw a lot of the local delicacy being prepared, roast guinea pig. It looked disgusting when raw, speared on a stake, and distinctly unappetizing when cooked.*

Railway stations are always a good place to pick up a cheap meal, and Riobamba Station was no exception. A '*churrasco*' in a small restaurant near the station cost me just over $1. Whilst I was there, I saw the converted Thomas bus that passed for a fast train between Quito and Guayaquil; it wasn't a real train in my books. Near to the station was Park 21 de Abril which was on a slight rise, so had a panoramic view over the plains surrounding the town.

I didn't want to go back from the markets empty handed, so I returned to the clothing market prepared to haggle. After some deliberation, I bought another wool poncho for about $5. Then it was time to find a bus back to Baños.

I walked out of town on the road I had come in on and soon found a bus going to Baños. The weather had improve, it was good to see the mountains on the way back. Baños was bathed in sunshine when I arrived, a somewhat unusual event at that time of year.

Before returning to the hotel, I had a coffee and finished my food shopping. I wasn't going to be fooled by the weather. I paid my hotel bill and sat inside. Sure enough, it soon started to pour with rain!

I enjoyed tea in my room from my supplies; yoghurt with granola, buns with strawberry jam and honey. I washed it down with the local mineral water that apparently was good for the health.

4th July 1982: Baños - Misahualli

Another early start; I was greeted by the sun coming up over the valley, with the clouds still high up in the hills. After a breakfast sourced from my supplies, I set off for the bus depot. When the bus to Tena arrived it was already full so those taking short local journeys were kicked off to make room for more lucrative long-distance passengers like myself. I ended up standing at the back, wedged between two seats and an Indian lady. I wasn't able to see much out of the window but what I did see was spectacular.

The single-track road clung to the side of the river valley high above the water but with a sheer drop down. The road was unsurfaced all the way but well graded, except where streams or roadworks had made a mess. At one point we were so high up that there were clouds below us in the valley. Waterfalls tumbled everywhere, sometimes over the road. After two hours, when we rolled into Mera, my limbs were aching from standing. Luckily, for no apparent reason, the bus emptied allowing me space to move. But just as I had secured a window seat I was required to get out and fill in a form at the army post. It was the usual "who are you" to keep track of foreigners. But the bottom section was "Who to inform in case you disappear?"; I was not planning to disappear so I left it blank!

The road just after Mera hit an all-time low; major roadworks had churned up the surface. We made very slow progress taking another 30 minutes to get to Puyo, a large town on an important road junction. Our driver had an argument as to whether he had to go on. In the end, it was decided that he could go to Tena, However we then had the usual delay as he wandered around town looking for some more passengers.

I saw my first llama. But it wasn't in the highlands ... it was in the town of Puyo!

We had left the mountains behind and the terrain was much easier to drive through. The road onwards to Tena was in much better condition. It just wound around gentle undulations, with occasional views of black mountains stretching into the cloud on one side and endless jungle on the other.

As we gradually descended, the vegetation became more and more like rain forest. By the time we reached Puerto Napo and crossed over the Napo river, the transformation to tropical Amazon vegetation was complete.

After 5½ hours travelling from Baños, we reached Tena, a trip that cost me just $1.50. I lept out of the bus and into a restaurant to have lunch. All that was on offer was the usual soup and '*seco*', but the place was clean. I felt the heat and had trouble adapting to the humidity with such a sudden change in climate. I wandered slowly around the town looking to see where the various buses departed from. Tena was a disappointing place, Puyo had been much more attractive. There was little there to detain me, so I resolved to press on to Puerto Misahualli as soon as I could.

The most frequent transport between Tena and Puerto Misahualli were converted pick-up trucks with seats in the back. I took one of these for the 25 km ride into the Amazon down the Rio Napo. It was a reminder of being in the back of a truck again, dusty and bumpy. The canopy was designed for locals; it was far too low for Europeans. But the Indian lady sitting opposite me had her boobs dangling out, so I couldn't politely duck and lean forward!

> *The Indians in the Oriente have different features from the natives of the highlands. They have long noses, not the rounded stubby ones found in the highlands. Also they have a less rounded face; an attractive look particularly in the young children.*

When the 'taxi' pulled into the village at Purto Misahualli, I realised that I had made a good choice of where I could experience the Amazon. The sun was shining brightly with few clouds; there was thick jungle all around. It was just what I imagined the Amazon whould be like, minus the topless natives with spears!

My guidebook only had a short paragraph on Purto Misahualli which indicated that there was a choice of two budget hotels. In fact, there were only two hotels in town. I opted for the rather grand-sounding Residencia La Posada, a wooden two-story building on a corner of the main square. It had a café downstairs and rooms upstairs, rooms with running water, a shower and the promise of electricity; pretty good value for $1 a night. For that price, you couldn't complain that you didn't get soap, towels or toilet paper!

From the balcony, I had a view of everything going on in the main square and enjoyed a pleasant cooling breeze. After an hour's siesta in a deck chair, I had started to acclimatise to the heat.

Later in the afternoon, I wandered down to the beach to watch the river boats. The port was the the end of the road for cargos heading east down the Rio Napo deeper into the Amazon. It was situated where the Rio Misahualli flowing down from Tena met up with the Rio Napo. They were both fast-flowing rivers, but at the junction where they met there was still calm water and a beach, a landing point for dugout canoes powered by outboard motors. The beach was a hive of activity. I put my foot in the water to sample its swimming potential but quickly decided that a cold shower at the hotel would be warmer.

When I decided it was time to eat dinner, I couldn't see anywhere actually serving food; people were drinking but no one was eating. Maybe I was a bit early. It was easier to go back to my room and have another meal out of my rucksack. I toyed with the idea of booking on an organised trip into the jungle the next day, but decided that as I was neither equipped for hot sun nor heavy rain, it would be wise not to go.

As soon as it got dark the electricity failed! I went downstairs to the café for a beer and sat in the candlelight. A group of three Americans (Dad who worked in the village and two kids) invited me to join them playing cards, which happily filled the rest of the evening. There were a lot of cockerels on the streets that night; there must have been a Sunday cock fight. At least they didn't hang around long enough to join in the dawn chorus!

Diary Extract 2: My plan of Misahualli

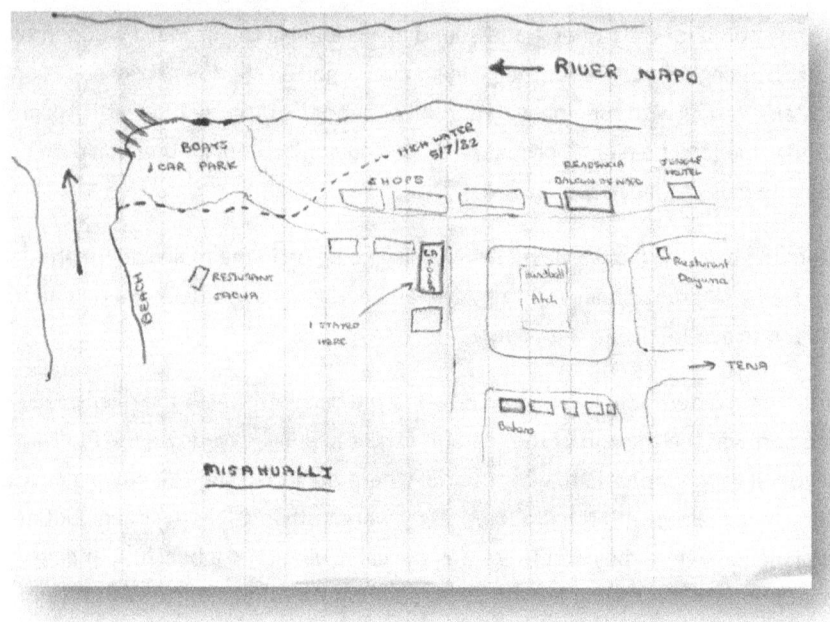

My guidebook described the Residencia La Posada as 'interesting'; it certainly was! The partition walls were only rough wooden slabs; noise from within and outside the hotel continued well into the night. During the night it started raining and I feared there might be a lot of mosquitos in the jungle. I lit a mosquito coil just in case but didn't see any.

5th July 1982: Misahualli

When I was awakened by the hotel coming alive at 6:30, I was glad that I didn't have plans to go anywhere that morning. There was a steady drizzle with no sign of the previous day's sunshine. I went to the village bakery to get some hot fresh rolls, ate one, and then visited the other Residencia to have the rest of my breakfast. A meal of omelette, bread, cheese and coffee was the cheapest so far. A backpacker could live in Misahualli for $4 a day!

As I sat on the hotel balcony writing , the day started to dry out. By mid-day, the weather was looking decidedly hopeful, so I went down to the beach. The Rio Napo was flowing faster than on the previous day and was now very brown; the mountains must have had some heavy rain in the night. The water level had risen, and the beach was much smaller. In contrast, the Rio Misahualli coming down from the foothills was still running clear.

The Residencia La Posada served lunch in the café/bar downstairs. It was just the standard fare of soup, juice, meat and rice. Eating there passed the time whilst the weather improved even more.

In the afternoon, I set out with my umbrella, and walked along the beach then down a path on the other side. This path followed the Rio Misahualli upriver untill it reached a loop track going back to the village. The rainforest close to the town was wet but not a patch on what I had seen in the Yukatan. By the time I reached the track back to the village, it had started to rain quite hard. Nevertheless, I pushed on up the track for ¾ mile or so till I got to a small village with an interesting suspension bridge over the river. At that point, the heavens opened and I had to rush for shelter. When the rain appeared to be set in, I decided to head back to the hotel, getting quite wet in the process.

The rain eased later in the afternoon. When I looked out, the beach had entirely disappeared and the Napo was just about lapping at the doors of the first houses. Once again I couldn't find any restaurants open in the evening, so had a snack in my room instead. The power went off even earlier. I had stolen a candle and now cut it in two to make an acceptable light in my room.

That evening I watched the full moon rising over the dark town and its reflection in the water. It was beautiful.

Luckily the bar downstairs closed early on a weekday, so the jukebox didn't disturb me. There appeared to be an outdoor cinema going full blast on the other side of the square. Even with that noise and a few other distractions, I had no problem getting a good night's sleep.

6th July 1982: Misahualli - Baños

The hotel with its flimsy walls wasn't the place to be able to sleep in. I was woken when the family started work in the morning, soon after six o'clock. After breakfast, taken out of my supplies, I paid my bill and waited for a truck or a taxi to appear. The river level had dropped considerably overnight, exposing a muddy beach again.

I got a lift back to Tena in a specialised pick-up conversion; it had transverse bench seats in the back and seemed to be specially designed to transmit each bump in the road directly to your spinal vertebrae. There weren't any buses in the bus depot when I arrived. I filled in time by walking round town which did nothing to dispel my previous negative impressions of the place. After a coffee, I returned to the depot when a Co-op de Baños bus was scheduled to depart, but there was still no activity. I asked what had happened to the bus and was told that they weren't expecting a bus till 1 p.m. They gave me a long story about the delay, in Spanish that I couldn't understand.

However, there was a battered old bus in the depot; San Fransisco was its adopted saint and it was probably Santo Fransisco who was responsible for the miracle of keeping it on the road. I asked the driver where he was going, and he said Puyo. In a moment of desperation, I bought a ticket and sat down inside. The bus was ½ full so I figured that he would go soon. But no, he didn't move for another hour by which time the bus was packed. It was the same story all the way to Puyo, a trip that was extended to nearly three hours by the need to wait for passengers on the way. At one point, the passengers who were standing had to get out, their luggage was put on the roof, and they were then repacked in order to get a few more people in. There must have been about 25 passengers in a bus with only 20 seats! I came off quite well having a seat, but didn't get much of a view because of the people standing all around me.

When we reached Puyo it was unusually quiet. I walked between one depot and another looking for a bus to Baños; I couldn't understand it- there weren't any. There should have been several buses each hour. In the hour I was waiting, no buses arrived and none departed. I was starting to become suspicious. Two people told me to take a taxi, but a taxi to where and why? I couldn't understand what they were saying.

As a last resort, I tried the San Fransisco depot asking for a bus to Baños. To my surprise, the lady said "Yes, it leaves for Baños at 3:30" whilst pointing to the wreck outside. So I boarded the bus, not without some misgivings; why was this bus different from the others? My question was answered when we drove past a sign saying that the road to Baños was closed from Tuesday to Friday; it was Tuesday!

Sure enough, when we got to the roadworks about halfway to Baños, there was no passable road. Bulldozers were trying to widen a ledge high above the river; the old road just stopped in a mound of grit. The bus driver took his half of the fare and pointed in the direction of another bus, on the far side of the roadworks. Along with the other passengers, I had to scramble up to the level where the bulldozers were working, then make my way through the mess to reach the old road on the other side. I made a big mistake; I trod on what I thought was sand, but it turned out to be a quagmire. I sank in the mud up to my knees and then fell over! I had no choice but to press on; I couldn't get any dirtier!

Conveniently there was a stream on the other side where I could wash off the worst of the mud; it was the same stream that was flowing onto the ledge and turning it to mud. As had been pointed out, there was a bus waiting on the other side to take us to Baños. I was lucky to get a window seat with a good view of the waterfalls we passed. The clouds were not too low, so I finally was able to enjoy the mountain scenery.

On my return, I chose a different hotel in Baños that was more accomodating to my budget. The Residencia Olguita was in a nice modern building overlooking one of the plazas. Better still it was only $1 a night. I must have looked a pathetic sight as I turned up at reception, wet, bedraggled and covered in mud but they gave me a room!

Needless to say, my first task was to wash my trousers, shoes and socks. Then I chatted to a German backpacker who was staying in the hotel. As I had missed out on lunch, I compensated by having a good dinner at one of the better restaurants.

Agoyan Falls on the road to Baños

7th July 1982: Baños - Quito

After the ordeal of the previous day, it was no surprise that I slept very well. I woke to another dismal day in the mountains; a day with low clouds and no imminent chance of seeing the sun. I decided to head back to Quito, rather than get wet again attempting a walk. At the bus depot, there was no problem finding a bus to take me back to Ambato. It was also easy to change onto a bus going to Quito. Such a contrast to the previous day!

After a fast trip in a lightly loaded bus, I found myself back at Quito's El Recreo interchange with a slight problem; I had no idea which bus route would take me back to the old city and my hotel. After walking a short way down the main road I jumped on a bus that was at least heading in roughly the right direction. Then I saw a No. 1 bus which I knew passed close to the hotel, so I switched buses.

At the hotel, they gave me my old room back. It was easy to get my rucksack unpacked. My next priority was to give my jeans a good soak to remove the last of the mud. For lunch, I headed back to a familiar haunt in Plaza Santo Domingo for a hamburger and coffee.

I wanted to visit the British embassy to catch up on the news. It was in the north-east corner of the city. This meant that I had to catch one bus out to The Almeda, and then switch to another bus that went up Avenue 12 de Octubre. The bus I was on got close to the embassy, but turned off the wrong way in La Floresta and I had to jump off! At this point the heavens opened, it started tipping down and the drains were overflowing. I walked nearly a kilometre to the Embassy, by which time it had stopped raining and I was soaked. After all that effort, the Embassy was shut and it didn't appear to have a reading room.

There was a lookout behind the Intercontinental Hotel that had a view over the deep valley of the Rio Manchángara. Halfway down the valley side, perched on a ledge was the monastery of Guapulo. It was a very scenic location with a drop of about 500 ft down to the monastery and then a similar drop down to the river.

I finished off my somewhat disastrous expedition by messing up the buses on the way back. The first bus I jumped on just went a few blocks, then terminated in La Floresta, it took me three buses to get back to the old city. The only positive thing about the afternoon was that I wasn't too affected by the altitude this time, probably because my ascent from the Amazon had been quite gradual.

Monastery of Guapulo

8th July 1982: Quito (Crux Loma)

What a contrast the day was! There wasn't a cloud in the sky when I looked outside at 7 a.m. I changed my plans for the day, deciding to climb Crux Loma. This was the more southerly of the two antenna-topped peaks to the west of Quito. My guidebook said that I should allow four to five hours for the ascent and another two to get back down.

The first part of the walk was across the old city to Plaza San Fransisco, to the El Tejar market and then up the steps through El Tejar. El Tejar was not a particularly salubrious suburb. As I walked further up Velasco Fernándes above the village the road became rough and more pigs and cattle were grazing by the roadside. The track took me to the base of a waterfall used for the city water supply, then degenerated into a mule track that climbed up beside the waterfall.

(next page) Diary Extract 3: Climbing Cruz Loma

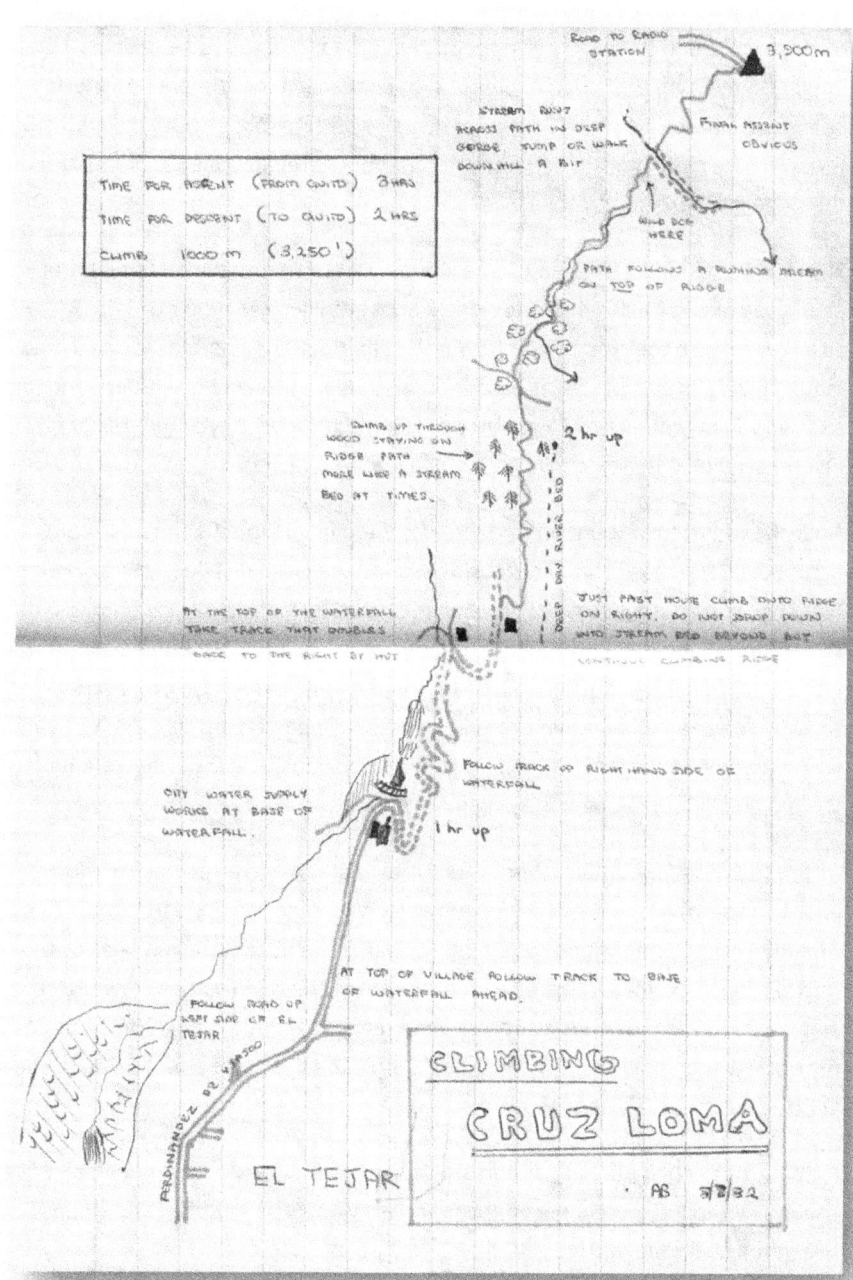

After the first hour, I estimated that I had climbed up 1,300 ft to reach an altitude of close to 11,000 ft. It was at this point that I made a big mistake because I was no longer on the map that I had of Quito. When I reached the top of the waterfall, I headed too far to the right. Soon there was no path to follow, but I did get to walk through a field of llamas! I had a rough scramble to rejoin the path on the top of the ridge, at the 2-hour mark.

The day was clouding over and some clouds started to turn dark. I felt a lot of pressure to keep on climbing the ridge. I kept a small stream on my right. It was strange because the stream was flowing on the ridge top; perhaps it was a man-made culvert as part of the city water supply. I was getting out of breath and had to abandon my routine of 25 minutes of climbing followed by 5 minutes of rest. I just pressed on whenever my body would let me.

Near the top of the mountain, the streams were even more perverse. I came across one stream that was contouring around the ridge in a deep chasm. I didn't want to jump across because I was being hassled by a wild dog, so I followed the stream for a bit till I found a safer crossing point. The final few hundred meters were an ordeal. I had pushed myself too hard at a high altitude; my head started to swirl and I had to sit down and rest. I must have passed out or slept for a while whilst my body recovered. When I regained consciousness, my heart rate had slowed and I was no longer gasping for breath.

At the top of the mountain, there was a radio station and a spectacular view to the east and south. It was like being on a plane, even Panecillo appeared to be flat. Ahead of me, the moorland rose gently towards the distant rugged peak of the Rucu Pichincha volcano. I asked the technician at the radio station how high I was and he said 12,900 ft. That was an all-time record for me, so it was no wonder that my body was complaining. By my calculations, the peak was about 2,700 ft above Quito City.

I sat on the triangulation pillar and ate the lunch that I had brought with me. Even though I wrapped myself in a pullover and poncho, I still felt cold. The clouds had brought a chill wind with them.

At 1:30 I set off down the hill. This time I kept to the path and had a stick and stones to discourage the wild dogs. I tried to dam the stream to get enough water to wash, but the exercise made my head swim again. So I just kept on walking to get down to a lower altitude.

Two and a half hours later, I was safely back at the hotel. It was strangely quiet. All the Germans had gone out to watch the World Cup semi-final. The locals had lost interest now that Ecuador was out of the competition (along with Brazil). Even after I returned from having a meal out at the Polo King my heart was still racing and protesting about what I had subjected it to that day.

9th July 1982: Quito (Rest Day)

My final weekday in Quito was reserved for finishing off my souvenir shopping. After my usual breakfast, I set out under a bright blue sky to get my last batch of postcards from the stalls next to the Post Office. At the bank, I found that the exchange rate for $US had risen 3% in the two weeks that I had been in Ecuador. I later learned that the Ecuadorian Sucre was floating and that it had devalued nearly 40% in the past year. That went some way to explain why life in Quito was so inexpensive for me.

The *South America Handbook* recommended a handicrafts collective in Colon. I took a bus out there but found their display disappointing; so much for the guidebook! Instead, I headed for the Government craft shop that I had found a few days earlier, but they had just closed for lunch.

Back in the old city, I had lunch at a self-service restaurant indulging in strawberries and cream! That was followed by a siesta followed by a few more trips to handicraft stores.

Ecuadorian Handicrafts - Wooden Box (lid)

10th July 1982: Quito (Pululagua)

For my last day in Ecuador, Quito turned on its best weather so far. The sun shone all day and it didn't cloud over. I dedicated the day to visiting the Equator and the Pululagua volcano.

The minibuses to Mitad del Mundo (The Equator) departed from a plaza one block away from Plaza San Fransisco. I had no trouble catching one. The first part of the journey was tediously slow, as we pushed our way through the El Tejem market. Soon we were speeding out of the city, past the airport and heading north. The route taken was to the west of the main road to Otavalo; it followed a gentle valley downhill for about 20km.

Diary Extract 4 Plan of Quito and Roads North

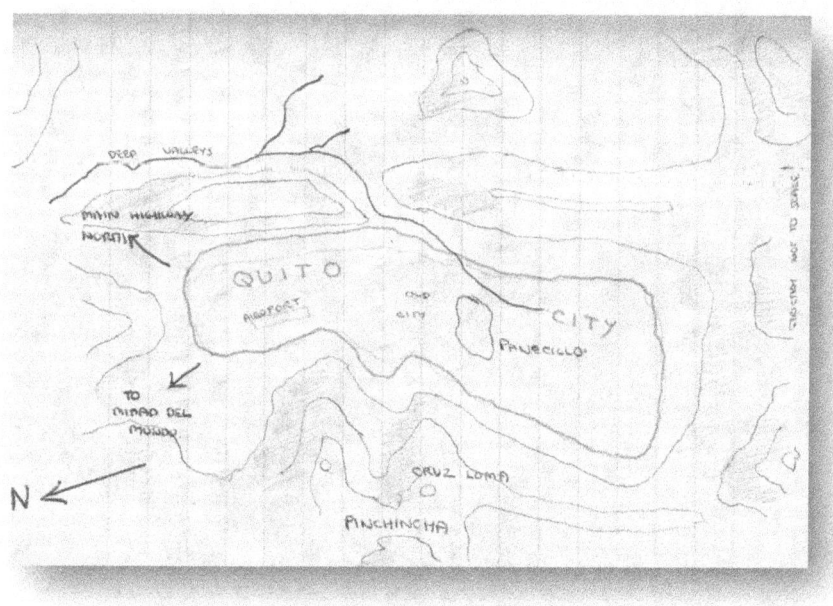

The Equatorial monument, *Mitad del Mundo*, was on a flat open space to the west of the town of San Antonio. It was surrounded by building works. I agreed with the guidebook that there was nothing special about the place, particularly as the Equator doesn't pass through the monument at all!

My main reason for the trip was not to see a misplaced monument but to walk to the nearby Pululagua crater. It was hot walking in the sun, particularly as I had to stay on the road going up so as not to miss the turnoff to the crater. It was all uphill for an hour and a half, but I was rewarded with a great view looking back. On the way, I collected some unusual flowers which I pressed in my diary.

Flowers collected on Pululagua

The Pululagua crater was spectacular and well worth the exertion to get there. The floor of the crater was flat land used for agriculture. On the way back, I was able to leave the road to follow the tracks used by locals. By cutting off the corners, I reduced the walking time to about an hour.

I had intended to eat at a restaurant by the Mitad del Mundo monument but it was a smart place with prices to match. I was dusty and bedraggled, so opted just for a cool drink before getting on a bus back to Quito.

After a snack of coffee and empanadas (a bit like fried Cornish pasties), I had one final unsuccessful look for a cassette of local music and then returned to the hotel. Doing a trial pack showed me that everything easily fitted into my rucksack and that it wasn't too heavy. Then I treated myself to a T-bone steak for dinner; I didn't know when I'd be able to afford to eat like that again!

11th July 1982: Quito -

I was woken at 2 a.m. by a noise in the room. When I traced the source of the disturbance to a mouse, I ignored it and went back to sleep. I was pretty sure it wasn't a rat.

It was another cloudy Sunday morning in Quito, with few restaurants open for breakfast. I had to eat once again in the café next to the hotel. The food wasn't bad there, but it was expensive.

After finishing my packing, I checked out of the hotel and walked to Plaza Santo Domingo where I could pick up a taxi to the airport. I paid the local fare, which was a fraction of the rate charged to incoming tourists at the airport. It was still a lot more expensive than the slow crowded city bus.

When I got to the airport late in the morning, I found that the check-in wasn't going to open for another hour. I was able to change my remaining Ecuadorian Soles into pounds and dollars, and then I waited. When I saw people boarding my plane, I knew that I had missed an announcement. I raced through the formalities with no other passengers in sight, and with no one to search my hand luggage!

The plane was a nice new DC10 which instilled some confidence. It was a short hop to Caracas with a good meal served, but sadly there were no complimentary drinks. British Caledonian had English newspapers on board. I was disturbed to find The Times was reporting that there would be a major rail strike in the U.K.

Although the flight to Caracas had been quite empty, the plane filled up for the next leg to San Juan in Puerto Rico. We had longer on the ground there but weren't let off the plane. On the final leg to Gatwick, I scored two seats to myself and so was able to get a bit of rest.

England welcomed me home, after nearly two years away, with low clouds and mist. There was some duty to pay on my souvenir purchases. Then I took a coach trip to Heathrow to meet my parents.

And then what next?

That was the big question that I had to answer. In the meantime, I had a comfortable bed and plenty of time to relax and reflect on my memorable journeys around the world.

> *Mark Twain extolled the mind-expanding benefits of travel in "The Innocents Abroad", his account of an 1867 tour of Europe and the Holy Land. "Travel", he wrote, "is fatal to prejudice, bigotry, and narrow-mindedness, and many of our people need it sorely on these accounts. Broad, wholesome, charitable views of men and things cannot be acquired by vegetating in one little corner of the earth all one's lifetime."*

Epilogue

In just over two years, I had visited 26 countries and queued to cross 19 land borders.

Travelling overland brought me face-to-face with the rich diversity of race, religion and lifestyle that somehow coalesce to make up our world. It introduced me to the history of places and people that had not been mentioned in my schooling. It was an experience that challenged the attitudes and assumptions that had previously defined my childhood and early adult life.

The adventure changed me in so many ways:

- I had developed a deep inner confidence that helped me conquer the unknown.
- I had found an unshakable determination that let me carry on through illness and physical hardship.
- I had learned to see the good in so many people from all walks of life.

My vision and understanding of the world had changed, and sadly I wasn't going to be able to slot back into the old, comfortable lifestyle I had left behind.

In so many ways the adventure of my life had only just started…

The Author

Adrian is a trans-woman living in Sydney.

Adrian was born in the UK and studied engineering at the University of Surrey. She emigrated to Australia in 1982 after travelling overland around the world. In the same year, she married Megan, an Australian.

Together they have enjoyed many more adventures overseas. They have a daughter who also lives in Sydney with her husband and two children.

Also by this author:

My Knight's Quest
Imprint: Cammeraygal Press
ISBN 978-1-7636362-1-7

www.ingramcontent.com/pod-product-compliance
Lightning Source LLC
Chambersburg PA
CBHW051622230426
43669CB00013B/2149